BECKETT'S ART OF SALVAGE

This innovative exploration of the recurring use of particular objects in Samuel Beckett's work is the first study of the material imagination of any single modern author. Across five decades of aesthetic and formal experimentation in fiction, drama, poetry and film, Beckett made substantial use of only fourteen objects – well-worn not only where they appear within his works but also in terms of their recurrence throughout his creative corpus. In this volume, Bates offers a striking reappraisal of Beckett's writing, with a focus on the changing functions and impact of this set of objects, and charts, chronologically and across media, the pattern of Beckett's distinctive authorial procedure. The volume's identification of the creative praxis that emerges as an 'art of salvage' offers an integrated way of understanding Beckett's writing, opens up new approaches to his work and offers a fresh assessment of his importance and relevance today.

JULIE BATES is an Assistant Professor in the School of English at Trinity College Dublin. Her research focuses on modern and contemporary literature and visual art, with a particular interest in experimental forms and material culture. She is a contributor to the *Oxford Handbook of Modern Irish Theatre* (2016). Her current research project, *Pockets of Time*, explores the use of worn materials to chart the passage of time on a personal scale in contemporary literature and visual art.

BECKETT'S ART OF SALVAGE

Writing and Material Imagination, 1932–1987

JULIE BATES
Trinity College Dublin

CAMBRIDGE
UNIVERSITY PRESS

University Printing House, Cambridge CB2 8BS, United Kingdom

One Liberty Plaza, 20th Floor, New York, NY 10006, USA

477 Williamstown Road, Port Melbourne, VIC 3207, Australia

314-321, 3rd Floor, Plot 3, Splendor Forum, Jasola District Centre, New Delhi - 110025, India

79 Anson Road, #06-04/06, Singapore 079906

Cambridge University Press is part of the University of Cambridge.

It furthers the University's mission by disseminating knowledge in the pursuit of education, learning and research at the highest international levels of excellence.

www.cambridge.org
Information on this title: www.cambridge.org/9781108792554
DOI: 10.1017/9781316711521

© Julie Bates 2017

This publication is in copyright. Subject to statutory exception and to the provisions of relevant collective licensing agreements, no reproduction of any part may take place without the written permission of Cambridge University Press.

First published 2017
First paperback edition 2020

A catalogue record for this publication is available from the British Library

ISBN 978-1-107-16704-9 Hardback
ISBN 978-1-108-79255-4 Paperback

Cambridge University Press has no responsibility for the persistence or accuracy of URLs for external or third-party internet websites referred to in this publication, and does not guarantee that any content on such websites is, or will remain, accurate or appropriate.

Contents

List of Illustrations		*page* vi
Acknowledgements		vii
List of Abbreviations		ix
	Introduction: Miscellaneous Rubbish	1
1	Relics	22
2	Heirlooms	68
3	Props	115
4	Treasure	162
	Conclusion: Beckett's Art of Salvage	206
Bibliography		221
Index		235

Illustrations

1. John Haynes, 'Breath' (1999) — *page* 5
2. Steve Schapiro, 'René Magritte at MOMA, 1965' — 38
3. Vincent van Gogh, *Shoes* (1886) — 56
4. Vincent van Gogh, *Three Pairs of Shoes* (1886) — 57
5. Independent Newspapers, 'Dublin character PJ Marlow also known as Johnny Forty Coats' (1943) — 80
6. Dorothy Kay, 'May and Samuel Beckett' (*c.* 1908) — 99
7. Independent Collection, 'Crowds on College Green, cyclists and tram' (*c.* 1940–50) — 122
8. Eason Photographic Collection, 'Ranelagh Road from Canal Bridge, Dublin' (*c.* 1900–39) — 134
9. Seanie Barron, 'Blackthorn stick with a blackthorn root as handle' (2014) — 152
10. John Haynes, 'Rosaleen Linehan, *Happy Days*' (1999) — 177

Acknowledgements

I gratefully acknowledge the following scholarships and grants that provided substantial assistance to the publication of this book: a post-graduate research studentship at Trinity College Dublin in 2010, an Irish Research Council post-graduate scholarship in 2011, travel grants awarded by Graduate Studies / Trinity Trust in 2010 and 2011 and a grant in 2016 from the Trinity Arts, Humanities and Social Sciences Benefaction Fund. I had the great pleasure of writing the PhD thesis out of which this book arose with Professor Nicholas Grene as my supervisor: a more knowledgeable, scrupulous and generous reader would not have been possible. I also want to thank, for their encouragement and guidance, Professors Gerald Dawe, Steven Connor and Sam Slote; for their editorial care, Vicki Cooper and Kate Brett; and the anonymous readers at Cambridge for their perceptive responses. Many thanks to the individuals and institutions that granted permission to use the images in this book, all of whom were a pleasure to deal with. For their support and advice, I want to thank in particular my mother Ann and sister Maeve, Triona Kirby, Rosie Lavan, Nathan O'Donnell and Alex Runchman. Thanks finally, and most emphatically, to Guy Woodward.

Abbreviations

BR *Beckett Remembering / Remembering Beckett: Uncollected Interviews with Samuel Beckett and Memories of Those Who Knew Him*, ed. James and Elizabeth Knowlson (London: Bloomsbury, 2007)
DF James Knowlson, *Damned to Fame: The Life of Samuel Beckett* (London: Bloomsbury, 1997)
GI–IV *Samuel Beckett: The Grove Centenary Edition*, 4 vols., ed. Paul Auster (New York: Grove Press, 2006)
GC C.J. Ackerley and S.E. Gontarski, *The Grove Companion to Samuel Beckett: A Reader's Guide to His Works, Life, and Thought* (New York: Grove, 2004)
JMC *Journal of Material Culture*
JOBS *Journal of Beckett Studies*
LI–IV *The Letters of Samuel Beckett*, 4 vols., ed. George Craig, Martha Dow Fehsenfeld, Dan Gunn and Lois More Overbeck (Cambridge: Cambridge University Press, 2009; 2011; 2014; 2016)
LM Anthony Cronin, *Samuel Beckett: The Last Modernist* (London: Flamingo, 1997)
LRB *London Review of Books*
OED *Oxford English Dictionary*

Introduction: Miscellaneous Rubbish

Bags, Beds, Bicycles, Bowler Hats, Crutches, Feminine Hats, Greatcoats, Old Boots, Pockets, Rocking Chairs, Sticks, Stones, Wheelchairs, Widow's Weeds

Over a fifty-year period, from 1938 when he first established a life in Paris until he moved to a nursing home in 1988, a year before his death, Samuel Beckett worked in only three different studies. He did most of his writing in these rooms, all of which have been described as austere and utilitarian, containing no more objects than were strictly necessary: a bare desk and basic chair, shelves with dictionaries and reference books and the all-important wastepaper bin.[1] In the main, the critical assessment of Beckett's writing sits comfortably with this impression of a series of sparse writing rooms, unfurnished as monastic cells, in which Beckett might escape all physical and material distractions and devote himself to a purely cerebral process of composition in order to create intellectually charged and largely abstract or conceptual works of art. In recent decades, however, there has been a turn in Beckett scholarship towards readings that are attuned to Beckett's place in the world and its impact on his writing.[2] These readings are engaged in dismantling the forbiddingly intellectual aura around Beckett and seek to present his work in less rarefied and more accessible ways.

In this book, I want to add my voice to these readings, as I examine Beckett's dependence upon a small group of material elements during fifty-five years of creative experimentation across a wide range of media. Beckett's attachment to objects is evident even in his writing studies that

---

[1] Beckett's biographer, James Knowlson, describes Beckett's studies in this manner. See descriptions in *DF* of Rue des Favorites, to which Beckett moved in 1938: pp. 289, 340, Ussy-sur-Marne, where Beckett wrote from 1953: p. 388, and Boulevard Saint-Jacques, to which he moved in 1960: p. 472.

[2] Such studies include production histories of Beckett's plays by Dougald McMillan, Martha Fehsenfeld and S.E. Gontarski; historicist studies by Seán Kennedy and others; and most importantly for my purposes, studies of Beckett's material imagination by Steven Connor.

have been described as 'monk-like' (*DF*, 472). Knowlson's description of a photograph by John Minihan of Beckett's Boulevard Saint-Jacques study in Paris indicates, however, that Beckett surrounded himself with small but telling decorative embellishments, from shells and pebbles collected on beaches to masks and sculptures:

> Behind him, as he sat at his dark green desk, was a row of shelves holding a few mementoes: on one shelf there was a sandstone mask of a face with its tongue sticking out (sent to him by the poet, Nick Rawson) and a small, square, brass-framed clock; on another there was a small sculpted figure with its head bent down between its knees like Dante's Belacqua; below that again was a very large watch, standing upright on a stand … Outside, on a narrow balcony protected by a double metal rail, stood a sculpture sent to him as a gift by the Russian sculptor, Vadim Sidur (1924–86).[3]

Beckett drew on his own fondness for collecting small objects when he gave the following tender lines to the protagonist of *Malone Dies*, the middle novel in his so-called trilogy, written from 1947 to 1948.[4]

> Perhaps I thought it pretty, or felt for it that foul feeling of pity I have so often felt in the presence of things, especially little portable things in wood and stone, and which made me wish to have them about me and keep them always, so that I stooped and picked them up and put them in my pocket, often with tears, for I wept up to a great age, never having really evolved in the fields of affection and passion, in spite of my experiences. (*GII*, 240–41)

Further indication of the intimate relationship between Beckett's play with small objects and his creative process is given in Knowlson's account of how in 1960, during the composition of *Happy Days* in the Boulevard Saint-Jacques apartment, Beckett 'acted out' Winnie's movements, 'using his own spectacles and toothbrush and borrowing one of Suzanne's bags, her lipstick and make-up mirror' (*DF*, 476). This image of Beckett emptying the contents of his partner's handbag onto his desk and lifting up the various objects in turn, miming different ways of brushing his hair, putting on lipstick or handling a mirror, stands in rather stark contrast to his austere stereotype. This serious and methodical play with the handbag, hairbrush, lipstick and mirror was necessary, of course, so that he could

---

[3] James Knowlson, 'A Writer's Homes – A Writer's Life', in *A Companion to Samuel Beckett*, ed. S.E. Gontarski (Oxford: Wiley-Blackwell, 2010), pp. 13–22, pp. 14–15.
[4] Because this book is concerned with tracing Beckett's evolving creative practice, the most germane date is that of a work's composition, and not its publication in either French or English. Where the date of a play's first production is relevant, I have noted it.

choreograph Winnie's gestures to his satisfaction, but it also indicates how much attention Beckett brought to bear on the material elements of his writing, and how those material elements were, for him, intimately involved in the act of imagining. In this respect, Beckett's creative process echoes that of many philosophers who, as Simon Glendinning has noted, when they conjure the external world, tend to 'populate it with small-to-medium-sized dry goods: chairs, pens, desks, sticks and so on'.[5]

In this book, I am concerned with the nature of Beckett's creativity, and with how his imagination is, in Steven Connor's words, 'matter-riddled'.[6] Beckett himself noted how his writing was engaged in a radical exploration of the relationship between form and imagination: 'We don't write novels any more, I don't like to talk about it, but it is an imaginative work, a work of imagination … it is a question of imagination.'[7] Having been struck by the seeming anomaly of his severe restriction of the number and type of material elements in fifty-five years of work, characterised by unceasing aesthetic and formal experimentation, I decided to pay closer attention to these objects. Over four chapters, I explore how Beckett restricted himself to fourteen key objects throughout his writing, turning to this imaginary prop-box and wardrobe for the costumes, props and possessions of his characters. These objects are crucial elements in Beckett's evolving creative praxis. I propose that by tracing their use in Beckett's work, it will be clear that his writing can best be described as an art of salvage. I had originally intended to examine over thirty objects, but in the course of thinking about their function, impact and pattern of repetition in Beckett's writing, found myself whittling their number down to a final tally of fourteen, when I was pleased to discover that I had echoed Malone's description of his hoard of treasure in *Malone Dies*: 'all that is left to me of all I ever had, a good dozen objects at least' (*GII*, 241–42).[8]

---

[5] Simon Glendinning, *On Being with Others: Heidegger, Derrida, Wittgenstein* (London: Routledge & Kegan Paul, 1998), p. 8. Unlike those objects seized upon by the philosophers as markers for the external world, the poor materials with which Beckett's imagination was engaged for half a century is not arbitrary, nor are the objects gratuitous, something that distinguishes Beckett from other modern writers. See Janell Watson, *Literature and Material Culture from Balzac to Proust: The Collection and Consumption of Curiosities* (Cambridge: Cambridge University Press, 1999), p. 1.
[6] Steven Connor, 'Beckett's Atmospheres', in *Beckett after Beckett*, eds. Anthony Uhlmann and S.E. Gontarski (Gainesville: University Press of Florida, 2006), pp. 52–65.
[7] Michael Mundhenk, 'Samuel Beckett: The Dialectics of Hope and Despair', *College Literature*, 8.3, Samuel Beckett (Fall, 1981), 227–48, p. 227.
[8] Amongst those objects jettisoned in successive drafts of the book were buttons, dressing gowns, glasses and spectacles, handkerchiefs, jars and urns, laces, pieces of string and elastic, trousers, books, keys, knives, lamps, locks, medicines and painkillers, mirrors, mysterious objects, pots, ropes, rubber balls, tins, travelling outfits, trays, umbrellas, parasols and watches.

By charting the functions and effects of these objects, chronologically, across generic boundaries and from fourteen different starting points, this book maps the pattern of Beckett's distinct authorial procedure. This aspect of the project, where Beckett's creative oeuvre is considered in its entirety, provides an integrated overview of a body of work that has often appeared daunting in its formal and generic range. Such an approach also avoids attributing to Beckett an overarching creative plan, a pre-defined and unchanging creative vision. This, to my mind, is the most serious weakness of responses to Beckett that derive from *a priori* theories, since they fail to allow for the central elements in every creative process of trial and error, experimentation and recycling: elements that are particularly in evidence in Beckett's prolific and extraordinarily varied oeuvre.

In the opening pages of *Molloy*, the first novel in the trilogy, written in 1947, the narrator speaks openly of the loneliness and desire for company that prompts him first to create a character and then to resolve to visit his mother. He does so by linking this narrative urge with the shabby raw materials used in these conjuring acts: 'Smoke, sticks, flesh, hair, at evening, afar, flung about the craving for a fellow. I know how to summon these rags to cover my shame' (*GII*, 11). This book explores the connections between Beckett's poor materials and his creative imagination. I have categorised these objects as 'miscellaneous rubbish', a phrase that recurs several times in Beckett's writing. Famously, the set for *Breath* – his play that premiered in 1969 and scandalously condenses life into half a minute, punctuated at its beginning and end by symmetrical cries – is described as a 'stage littered with miscellaneous rubbish'. The Gate production of *Breath* at the Barbican theatre in London in 1999 was directed by Robin Lefèvre and designed by Giles Cadie. John Haynes photographed the set (Figure 1) in which can be seen broken machines, a water bottle and a sombrero, among other assorted items.

Composition of the set for *Breath* has varied widely. Kenneth Tynan included writhing naked bodies in the premiere, something referenced by the artist Amanda Coogan in 2006 when she incorporated mannequin limbs in her production. Damien Hirst directed *Breath* for the Beckett on Film project in 2001 and filled the stage with the medical waste that had been a feature of his previous artworks. These various responses to Beckett's cue of 'miscellaneous rubbish' indicates, first of all, the enduring receptivity of artists and designers to Beckett's writing, but it also gestures to one of the arguments of this book: that through his use of the selected poor materials of his writing, Beckett was commenting on his

Introduction: Miscellaneous Rubbish 5

Figure 1 John Haynes, 'Breath' (1999).
Courtesy of John Haynes and Lebrecht Music & Arts.

own contemporary period – the modern Ireland and Europe that vanished during his lifetime.[9]

The analogy in *Breath* between a rubbish dump and the world also features in *The Unnamable*, the final novel in the trilogy, written between 1949 and 1950: 'don't let us go just yet, not yet say goodbye once more for ever, to this heap of rubbish' (*GII*, 334), as it does in the late prose work *Ill Seen Ill Said* (1980–81): 'Sigh upon sigh till all sighed quite away. All the fond trash' (*GIV*, 469). Human and animal behaviour are equated in a further recurrence of the phrase in *Molloy*. Molloy discovers love in a rubbish dump and, several pages later, finds himself in a blind alley 'littered with miscellaneous rubbish and with excrements, of dogs and masters, some dry and odourless, others still moist' (*GII*, 55). In the 1956 radio play *All That Fall*, it is unclear whether Maddy Rooney is describing her life or mind as a dump: 'Then you might fall on your wound and I would

---

[9] In this, Beckett may be aligned with other modernist writers who employed the rubbish heap as a metaphor for both the world and their creative practice during the inter-war period, including T.S. Eliot, W.B. Yeats and Evelyn Waugh. However, Beckett's creative treatment and use of this trope is distinctly idiosyncratic. Where these other writers employ the metaphor in discrete works, Beckett restricts himself to his chosen poor materials for the entirety of his writing career.

have that on my manure-heap on top of everything else' (*GIII*, 177), while Molloy imagines that he must physically resemble discarded material thrown up on a beach:

> It was a wild part of the coast. I don't remember having been seriously molested. The black speck I was, in the great pale stretch of sand, who could wish it harm? Some came near, to see what it was, whether it wasn't something of value from a wreck, washed up by the storm. But when they saw the old jetsam was alive, decently if wretchedly clothed, they turned away. (*GII*, 69)

Beckett's identification of miscellaneous rubbish with the world, minds and bodies of his characters indicates its importance in his writing. His characters treat their few shabby material possessions with a reverent attention uncommon in literature. Another writer whose characters are besotted by everyday things is the early-twentieth-century Swiss author Robert Walser. W.G. Sebald has identified in Walser's work an obsessive interest in objects, describing Walser's characters as those who, 'out of fear and poverty, cannot afford emotions' and who therefore 'have to try out their seemingly atrophied ability to love on inanimate substances and objects unheeded by anyone else – such as ash, a needle, a pencil, or a matchstick'.[10]

My comparison of Beckett with Walser is an associative strategy employed throughout the book. I have tried wherever possible to discover apt points of comparison between Beckett's use of objects and that of other writers and, occasionally, painters. My extensive use of such comparisons identifies points where Beckett's work approaches or diverges from that of other writers and visual artists, and helps to define more precisely the nature of his distinct creative practice. The very singularity of Beckett's work and the increasingly specialist nature of scholarship devoted to him has tended to isolate him from the wider world of creativity which he shares. Anthony Cronin's 1996 biographical study of Beckett is subtitled 'The Last Modernist', a formulation that has found wide acceptance in analysis of Beckett's legacy.[11] However, one of the consequences

---

[10] W.G. Sebald, 'Le Promeneur Solitaire: A Remembrance of Robert Walser', in *A Place in the Country*, trans. Jo Catling (London: Hamish Hamilton, 2013), p. 19.

[11] Peter Boxall has challenged the scholarly enthusiasm for this formulation, given the number of contemporary writers, dramatists, artists, film-makers and theorists (not to mention academics) who have discovered in Beckett's writing a 'fertile breeding ground' of new ideas. Boxall is certainly right to make this point, but I am concerned here with the ways in which Beckett's work draws upon and is engaged with a certain European intellectual and cultural tradition, something not necessarily true of those inspired by Beckett. See Boxall, ' "There's No Lack of Void": Waste

of viewing Beckett's writing as a cultural endpoint has been the scholarly identification of Beckett as a unique case, and his isolation from the literature and wider European culture out of which his writing arose. The associative correspondences in this book reorient Beckett's writing within an expanded field of writers and artists. The comparisons made in the book span works of fiction, drama, poetry, painting and philosophy from the seventeenth, eighteenth, nineteenth, twentieth and twenty-first centuries; from Austria and the Austro-Hungarian empire, Belgium, Britain, Bulgaria, France, Germany, Ireland, Italy, the Netherlands, Norway, Romania, Sweden and Switzerland. The book also features brief reference to works of literature from Ancient Rome, the Soviet Union and North and South America.

Beckett's miscellaneous objects are of various types and sizes, from large examples of domestic furniture to more portable aids to movement, small pocket-held objects and items of clothing. This latter category has a particularly intimate resonance and imaginative potential, as scholars within material studies including the anthropologist Daniel Miller have established: 'The sensual and aesthetic – what cloth feels and looks like – is the source of its capacity to objectify myth, cosmology and also morality, power and values.'[12] These qualities were exploited in eighteenth-century it-narratives, popular fictional accounts by everyday objects of their journeys and adventures. Objects were chosen according to their ability to pass regularly and unobtrusively from house to house, or person to person, and because the tendency at that time was to throw very little away, such objects could conceivably migrate from one owner to several others, and thereby relate many different experiences.[13] An it-narrative logic applies to the clothes and small objects that feature in Beckett's writing, which circulate between texts and media over a cycle of many years, their material condition declining as they pass from one character to another, participating in the intimate experiences of those characters and assisting the production of a range of narratives. It is notable that Beckett made a point of registering, in each appearance of items of clothing, the deterioration

---

and Abundance in Beckett and DeLillo', *SubStance*, 37.2 (2008), 56–70, p. 63 and *Since Beckett: Contemporary Writing in the Wake of Modernism* (London: Continuum, 2009).

[12] Daniel Miller, 'Introduction', in *Clothing as Material Culture*, ed. Susanne Küchler and Daniel Miller (Oxford, New York: Berg, 2005), pp. 1–20, p. 1. See also *Cloth and Human Experience*, eds. Annette B. Weiner and Jane Schneider (Washington: Smithsonian Books, 1989).

[13] See, for example, the 1760 text *The Adventures of a Black Coat*, in *British It-Narratives, 1750–1830*, 4 vols., general ed. Mark Blackwell, volume eds. Mark Blackwell, Liz Bellamy, Christina Lupton and Heather Keenleyside (London: Pickering and Chatto, 2012), Volume 3: *Clothes and Transportation*, ed. Christina Lupton.

caused by wear and tear by previous characters. In this way, Beckett draws a line of material continuity through many of his works, but also applies an odd, doll-like logic to the dress of his characters.

This book is concerned with 'rubbish', a category of material that has long proved inspirational, from the eighteenth-century German poet Friedrich Schiller who stored rotten apples in a drawer of his writing desk and 'opened the drawer when he needed inspiration, so that he could look on their brownness, inhale the breath of over-ripeness', to the recent interest in material studies and philosophy in waste as a material that is good to think with.[14] In *Culture and Waste* (2003), Gay Hawkins and Stephen Muecke describe waste as having 'a complex role in formations of value'.[15] Similarly, in *Making Waste* (2010), Sophie Gee proposes that the waste she examines in eighteenth-century texts 'are signs of the peculiar transformations that take place in literary texts; perversely, they show us that meaning has been made'.[16] William Viney, similarly, examines in *Waste* (2014), 'how philosophical ideas can be formed in relation to how matter acts', and argues for a 'philosophy *of* things' focused on 'thought as it emerges from life in a material world'.[17] Such attentiveness to the ontology of waste has informed this study, but the 'miscellaneous rubbish' of Beckett's writing cannot be contained within the larger category of waste, for it is neither undifferentiated matter nor used up beyond further utility. Most importantly, Beckett's rubbish has acquired familiarity from the personal or familial use it has served, which sees it hoarded and granted a pivotal role by Beckett's characters and narratives alike. In *Rubbish Theory* (1979), the social scientist Michael Thompson notes that 'Apart from tramps, most people choose not to carry all their possessions around with them and really rich people would be physically incapable of doing so even if they wanted to.'[18] Beckett's decision to make tramps of many of his characters means that, of necessity, they must hold on their person

---

[14] On Schiller's rotten apples, see Rebecca West, *Black Lamb and Grey Falcon* (London: Canongate, 2006), p. 484. For the discovery of meaning in waste within recent material studies, see: Michael Shanks, David Platt and William L. Rathje, 'The Perfume of Garbage: Modernity and the Archaeological', *Modernism/Modernity*, 11.1 (2004), 61–83; Dylan Trigg, *The Aesthetics of Decay: Nothingness, Nostalgia, and the Absence of Reason* (New York: Peter Lang, 2006); *Trash*, ed. John Knechtel (Massachusetts: MIT Press, 2006).

[15] Gay Hawkins and Stephen Muecke (eds.), 'Introduction: Cultural Economies of Waste', in *Culture and Waste: The Creation and Destruction of Value* (Lanham: Rowman & Littlefield, 2003), p. x.

[16] Sophie Gee, *Making Waste: Leftovers and the Eighteenth-Century Imagination* (Princeton: Princeton University Press, 2010), p. 17.

[17] William Viney, *Waste: A Philosophy of Things* (London: Bloomsbury, 2014), p. 1.

[18] Michael Thompson, *Rubbish Theory: The Creation and Destruction of Value* (Oxford: Oxford University Press, 1979), p. 1.

those things of most value to them. Without homes, jobs, families or other social connections, the imaginative turning out of their pockets and inventorying of their shabby possessions therefore establishes the world of these characters. This 'rubbish' of hand-me-downs, cast-offs and detritus had already been discarded and fallen out of circulation before being salvaged by Beckett's characters. This has profound implications for the agency of these objects.

Within material studies, it is generally presumed that once an object has been discarded or become rubbish, it no longer has any agency.[19] So it is with Beckett's poor materials: the objects under study seep agency along with their other defining characteristics from their first appearance to their last. These items of costumes, accessories and furniture were already worn-out when Beckett first introduced them and become ever more so in their subsequent use by a series of characters. Each chapter in this book follows the progress of a group of objects through Beckett's writing. This approach reveals a pattern where most of the differentiating and ludic aspects of the objects have been lost by the time they appear in the latest works. In their final appearances, their colours faded and bleached and the descriptive passages attenuated, these objects that were once so vivid seem strangely to have lost their distinguishing features, as though they had been submerged in water. Beckett's fidelity to his poor materials, their consistent presence from one genre or medium to another throughout ongoing and radical formal experimentation, indicates their importance in his creative process and their unique position in his writing. These objects serve a distinct function in Beckett's writing that they do not in the work of other writers. As a result, the existing critical models for an

---

[19] Cornelius Holtorf draws on studies by archaeologists and anthropologists including Schiffer, Kopytoff, Strathern, Latour, Tilley and Thomas, and identifies their shared focus: '[these] life history studies ... share the assumption that the life of a thing started at the time of its manufacture and ended at the time of its deposition in the ground. Discarded things are of course subjected to all sorts of natural processes, but their lives are over: they become rubbish, ruins, mummies.' See Holtorf, 'Notes on the Life History of a Pot Sherd,' *JMC* (March 2002), 7.1, 49–71, p. 54. See Michael Schiffer 'Archaeological Context and Systemic Context', *American Antiquity* 37 (1972), 156–65; Vincent LaMotta and Michael Schiffer, 'Behavioural Archaeology: Toward a New Synthesis', in *Archaeological Theory Today*, ed. Ian Hodder (Cambridge: Polity, 2001), pp. 14–64; Igor Kopytoff, 'The Cultural Biography of Things: Commoditization as Process', in *The Social Life of Things: Commodities in Cultural Perspective*, ed. Arjun Appadurai (Cambridge: Cambridge University Press, 1986), pp. 64–91; Marilyn Strathern, *The Gender of the Gift* (Berkeley: University of California Press, 1988); Bruno Latour, *Science in Action. How to Follow Scientists and Engineers Through Society* (Milton Keynes: Open University Press, 1987); Christopher Tilley, *An Ethnography of the Neolithic: Early Prehistoric Societies in Southern Scandinavia* (Cambridge: Cambridge University Press, 1996); Julian Thomas, *Time, Culture and Identity: An Interpretive Archaeology* (London and New York: Routledge, 1996).

analysis of the material elements of literature are not always applicable in Beckett's case.[20]

This book adopts a broadly phenomenological approach. The philosopher Edward Casey has defined this method of inquiry as 'an enterprise devoted to discerning and thematising that which is indistinct or overlooked in everyday experience'.[21] The form of attention paid to material elements of everyday experience in phenomenology is frequently complicated by the distinction drawn by the philosopher Martin Heidegger between objects and things, a distinction that has been clearly defined by the literary critic Steven Connor: 'objects are what we know, objects are things that know their place, and whose place we know. Things arise when objects down tools and refuse to cooperate with us, break down, or have their functions mysteriously interrupted'.[22] If Beckett's miscellaneous rubbish is well-worn and lacking in agency to begin with, and further diminished by a series of characters, it cannot accurately be classified as a 'thing,' in the sense in which Heidegger uses this term.[23] Indeed, the distinct form of Beckett's material imagination prevents these objects from ever becoming imbued with the semiotic potential of things. I have described the material elements under study as objects to emphasise their brute, inert quality. Although Beckett's lonely characters lavish many of these objects with affectionate attention, none of them acquire the valorized status of a symbol with which they might transcend their material condition. They are made of matter and subject to decay, a condition that Beckett is at pains to illustrate for his material canon as much as for his characters. In *Vibrant Matter* (2010), Jane Bennett describes things as 'vivid entities not entirely reducible to the contexts in which (human) subjects set them, never entirely exhausted by their semiotics'.[24] Beckett's objects, by contrast, never disassociate themselves entirely from the human subjectivity

---

[20] The literary and cultural critic Bill Brown has undertaken extremely interesting studies of things in literature, but his focus is on the ways in which literature can provide access to social history, and literary analysis can approach the status of a historiographical operation. The divergence in our respective approaches means that I do not draw in this book on the influential ideas elaborated in his 'Thing Theory.' See *Critical Inquiry*, 28. 1 (Autumn, 2001), 1–22 and *A Sense of Things: The Object Matter of American Literature* (Chicago and London: University of Chicago Press, 2003).

[21] Edward Casey, *Remembering: A Phenomenological Study*, 2nd edn (Bloomington: Indiana University Press, 2000), xxi.

[22] Steven Connor, 'Thinking Things', *Essays at Cultural Phenomenology* (2009), www.stevenconnor.com/thinkingthings/thinkingthings.pdf [accessed 3 April 2012].

[23] Martin Heidegger, *Being and Time: A Translation of Sein Und Zeit*, trans. Joan Stambaugh (New York: State University of New York Press, 1996) and 'The Thing', in *Poetry, Language, Thought*, trans. Albert Hofstadter (New York: Harper & Row, 1971).

[24] Jane Bennett, *Vibrant Matter: A Political Ecology of Things* (Durham: Duke University Press, 2010), p. 5.

that projects meanings onto them, as is apparent in the paternal heirloom of the greatcoat, the functional crutch or stick, and most acutely in the case of the desperately needed contents of the pocket and bag.

The fourteen objects under study are interesting precisely because they are utterly reducible to their context, which is to prop up the narratives and characters that have been left with precious little fictional or dramatic support by Beckett – and in so doing, they give us a new and fuller perspective on the operation of Beckett's creativity. Beckett's canon of material elements more closely resembles the objects Bruno Latour identifies as existing only for archaeologists before they are unearthed, analysed, displayed and recovered once again for society and culture: for Latour, an object is only such when 'it is still under the ground, unknown, thrown away, subjected, covered, ignored, invisible, in itself. In other words there are no visible objects and there never have been. The only objects are invisible and fossilised ones'.[25] Elsewhere, Latour has described an object as a 'matter of concern'.[26] Both definitions are helpful in seeking to classify the materials that Beckett selected to serve as items of furniture, costume and props in his writing. These objects are emphatically not symbols, and neither are they part of a project in which Beckett deliberately seeks to comment upon his personal life or social history, although I will argue in the first two chapters of the book that this is the cumulative effect of the repeated appearance of certain objects in his work. Instead, what these objects evoke is the strangeness of Beckett's decision to restrict himself to their limited resources throughout his writing.

In *The Social Life of Things* (1986), a collection of essays by anthropologists and historians that examines the role of material culture in social life, the anthropologist Igor Kopytoff suggests that 'biographies of things' might be written and that such an approach could 'make salient what might otherwise remain obscure'.[27] For Kopytoff, the questions to be asked of a thing in such a study are the same as those one would ask in undertaking the biography of a person:

> Where does the thing come from and who made it? What has been its career so far, and what do people consider to be an ideal career for such things? What are the recognised 'ages' or periods in the thing's 'life', and what are

---

[25] Bruno Latour, 'The Berlin Key or How to Do Words with Things,' in *Matter, Materiality and Modern Culture*, ed. P.M. Graves-Brown (London: Routledge, 2000), pp. 10–21, p.11.
[26] Bruno Latour, *Reassembling the Social: An Introduction to Actor-Network-Theory* (Oxford: Oxford University Press, 2005), p. 70.
[27] Kopytoff, 'The Cultural Biography of Things,' p. 67.

the cultural markers for them? How does the thing's use change with its age, and what happens to it when it reaches the end of its usefulness?[28]

These questions have certainly informed my approach to the four objects in the canon that have notable social histories: bowler hats, greatcoats, widow's weeds and bicycles. Kopytoff's approach, however, has strong Marxist implications, and his particular focus is on the social processes involved in the circulation of goods, rather than on the objects themselves. This emphasis on commodification and exchange is evidently not relevant for the cast-offs and hand-me-downs, the overlooked and abandoned objects that make up Beckett's canon, non-commodities all for which Kopytoff provides an interesting gloss: 'To be a non-commodity is to be "priceless" in the full possible sense of the term, ranging from the uniquely valuable to the uniquely worthless.'[29] The poor materials hoarded by Beckett's characters are priceless in both senses of the term. This goes some way toward explaining the appeal for the reader or audience of the obsessive relationship Beckett's characters have with such objects.

To date, few existing studies have been completed of a group of objects in the work of a single artist or writer.[30] The most pertinent literary analysis of material elements thus far is Francesco Orlando's *Obsolete Objects in the Literary Imagination: Ruins, Relics, Rarities, Rubbish, Uninhabited Places, and Hidden Treasures* (2006). Orlando's lengthy title reflects one of his suggestions about the relationship between writers and physical decay: that such material prompts the form of the list. While Beckett's miscellaneous rubbish does not fit into any of the twelve complex categories of decrepit objects identified by Orlando, his conception of the relationship between time, decay and value is central to my own approach.

> Time uses up and destroys things, breaks them and reduces them to uselessness, renders them unfashionable and makes people abandon

---

[28] Kopytoff, 'The Cultural Biography of Things,' pp. 66–67. Kopytoff's concept has been influential in material studies and refined by Karin Dannehl as requiring 'a tightly defined, definite time frame, the focus on the subject against a context, and the express purpose of highlighting exceptional or unusual features'. See 'Object Biographies: From Production to Consumption,' in *History and Material Culture*, ed. Karen Harvey (London: Routledge, 2009), pp. 123–38, p. 124.

[29] Kopytoff, 'The Cultural Biography of Things', p. 75. Similarly, Neil Cummings suggests that 'an object's real life begins' when it is moved from person to person, bought, thrown out, collected, displayed, broken, sold, recollected and re-displayed. Something closer to the flea-market economy.' See Neil Cummings, 'Reading Things: The Alibi of Use', in *Reading Things*, ed. Neil Cummings (London: Chance Books, 1993), pp. 12–29, p. 19.

[30] See Thomas Baldwin, *The Material Object in the Work of Marcel Proust* (Bern, Oxford: Peter Lang, 2005), and the unpublished doctoral dissertation by Margaret Quinn, *Objects in the Theatre of Samuel Beckett: Their Function and Significance as Components of his Theatrical Language*, McMaster University, 1975.

them; time makes things become cherished by force of habit and ease of handling, endows them with tenderness as memories and with authority as models, marks them with the virtue of rarity and the prestige of age. The scale that weighs a positive quality here and a negative one there is unstable and unpredictable, and it also shifts according to what one might call quantitative doses. Time wears things out *or* lends them dignity; it wears things out *and* lends them dignity. And in fact a thing may be either *too* worn-out, or *not* worn-out *enough* by time, to be dignified by it.[31]

In this passage, Orlando articulates the ambiguous and formative relationship between things and time that makes worn-out objects so attractive for literary exploration. The process by which we identify both physically and psychologically with the passage of time registered by the patina of age of well-worn, loyally serving objects is evident in the elevation of banal objects to the status of relics, or of worn functional materials to that of antiques, as it is for the tenderness of Beckett's characters for their few possessions. Uniquely, however, the recurring material elements of Beckett's writing are not merely a source of fascination, as are the many categories of object studied by Orlando in other literary works, but contribute profoundly to Beckett's distinctive aesthetic. Salvage implies familiarity with the myriad ways in which time devours matter and reduces everything to poor materials. This idea informs Beckett's writing on many levels. It is notable, in this respect, that Beckett made use of cheap, common notebooks and paper for the composition of his works, including school copybooks the pages of which are already poorly deteriorated, long after he could afford writing materials of better quality. This decision is oddly characteristic: a manifestation of his asceticism, but also perhaps an acknowledgement of the material contingency of the words on which he laboured.[32]

A number of studies have already examined objects in Beckett's work. In a 2013 article in the *Journal of Beckett Studies*, Georgina Nugent-Folan compares the indeterminacy of certain of Beckett's descriptions of objects with the distinctive approach of Gertrude Stein, while in a 2014 article in the same journal, Alexander Price applies a reading through the lens

---

[31] Francesco Orlando, *Obsolete Objects in the Literary Imagination: Ruins, Relics, Rarities, Rubbish, Uninhabited Places, and Hidden Treasures*, trans. Gabriel Pihas, Daniel Seidel and Alessandra Grego (London: Yale University Press, 2006), pp. 11–12.

[32] I am indebted for this observation about the poor quality of Beckett's writing materials to an exchange with Jane Maxwell, the Principal Curator at the Manuscripts and Archives Research Library in Trinity College, while viewing some of Beckett's manuscripts in January 2016.

of 'thing theory', concentrating on Beckett's depictions of bedrooms.[33] In 'An Umbrella, a Pair of Boots, and a "Spacious Nothing": McGahern and Beckett', a 2014 article in the *Irish University Review*, Richard Robinson compares the function of the comic umbrella and tragic boots in the works of Beckett and John McGahern, concluding that they act as surrogates or extensions of character's bodies, with 'the adjacency of the object to the body' offering only 'cold comfort'.[34] These readings are necessarily limited to the scope of a journal article. More extended analyses include Paul Davies's chapter in *The Ideal Real* (1994), when he proposes that 'In the pretrilogy prose, things or objects are an attribute of habit, in the sense in which it is outlined in Beckett's *Proust*: objects are mediums of constancy in the environment, and a change in them, their appearance or arrangement, brings about suffering in the self or subject.'[35] Liesl Olson concludes *Modernism and the Ordinary* (2009) by contrasting Beckett with Proust. Like Davies, Olson does not explore the function or impact of any particular object in Beckett's writing. Instead, Olson identifies in Beckett's work an overall 'disdain for the everyday' but suggests that, like Proust, he seeks to 'embody the everyday, especially its temporal dimension' through distinct 'stylistic practices'.[36] In his introduction to *Paraphernalia* (2011), Steven Connor suggests that 'as the use of any object becomes habitual, it starts to approach the condition of something we wear, or have about our persons (a habit is, after all, an item of clothing, as well as a form of behaviour)'.[37] This well summarises the attitude of Beckett's narrators and characters to these recurring material elements. The magical things of Connor's study, however, all exceed their inanimate condition. Beckett's objects, by contrast, are useful and important for him precisely because they lack any inherent quality that might be considered magical. The resonance of objects in Beckett's work is, paradoxically, due to their abject material condition. It is their very ordinariness

---

[33] Georgina Nugent-Folan, 'Ill buttoned': Comparing the Representation of Objects in Samuel Beckett's *Ill Seen Ill Said* and Gertrude Stein's *Tender Buttons,*' *JOBS*, 22.1 (2013), 54–82; Alexander Price, 'Beckett's Bedrooms: On Dirty Things and Thing Theory', *JOBS*, 23.2 (2014), 155–77.

[34] Richard Robinson, 'An Umbrella, a Pair of Boots, and a 'Spacious Nothing': McGahern and Beckett,' *Irish University Review*, 44.2 (2014), 323–340, p. 332.

[35] Paul Davies, *The Ideal Real: Beckett's Fiction and Imagination* (Rutherford: Fairleigh Dickinson University Press, 1994), pp. 27–42, p. 30. See also Naho Washizuka, 'Pity and Objects: Samuel Beckett's "Dante and the Lobster"', *Journal of Irish Studies*, 24 (2009), 75–83, which aligns itself with Davies's approach.

[36] Liesl Olson, *Modernism and the Ordinary* (Oxford: Oxford University Press, 2009), pp. 10–11.

[37] Steven Connor, *Paraphernalia: The Curious Lives of Magical Things* (London: Profile Books, 2011), p. 11.

and banal utility which gives them such potential in Beckett's and his characters' hands.

One of the most crucial secondary resources for this book has been *The Grove Companion to Samuel Beckett* (2004) by C.J. Ackerley and S.E. Gontarski. Ackerley and Gontarski call Beckett's imaginary world the 'Beckett Country', in a nod to Eoin O'Brien's influential 1986 study of the features of the Irish landscape in Beckett's work. In their introduction, Ackerley and Gontarski identify what they consider the typical features of this singular imaginative space:

> It is a premodern world where bicycles out-number motorcars, where theatres are lit by footlights, where clothes are fastened by buttonhooks, where parents still pass on family greatcoats and bowler hats to their offspring, hats tethered to coats – a world of chamber pots, which put humanity in greater proximity to evacuation, and oil lamps. Beckett's roots reside firmly in turn-of-the-century turf, amid the Anglo-Irish bourgeoisie. It is a propertied world, where possession assured not only propriety but existence as well, a world whose dictum may have been, 'I own, therefore I am.' The residue of that tradition remains traceable in Beckett's work, the Ascendancy Big House having become Gothic in *Watt* and *Footfalls*. Beckett's creatures retain a curious, antibourgeois relationship to possessions or property, of course. They simultaneously seem obsessed by and strangely negligent of them or it. (*GC*, x–xi)

This passage well identifies how certain recurring objects establish within Beckett's writing an evocative past, a dynamic that is explored more fully in the first chapter, 'Relics'.

'Relics' focuses on the objects used to cap and shoe most of Beckett's characters: bowler hats and old boots. As early as 1984, J.C.C. Mays made the comprehensive observation that 'Beckett understands his career, in an important sense, as an escape from what he inherited'. Ireland, in Mays's evaluation, 'is most important to Beckett as an inheritance to deny, or a set of appearances to go behind, or a range of authorities to disagree with'.[38] While Beckett's writing may at times seem to be the product of an isolated interiority, it is not in fact rootless, but rather uprooted. Vestigial traces of Beckett's rejected roots linger on, and bowler hats and old boots are two such traces. It will be seen that the pattern of Beckett's use of bowler hats satisfies Mays's identification of an antagonistic relation between Beckett's upbringing and his writing.

---

[38] J.C.C. Mays, 'Young Beckett's Irish Roots', *Irish University Review*, 14.1 (Spring, 1984), 18–33, pp. 26, 21.

In the case of old boots, however, Beckett extends the possibilities and implications of uprooting oneself to come up with a form of writing that seeks to rid itself of such ties to a far greater degree, encompassing the disorientation and homelessness that followed the violent upheavals of twentieth-century Europe. In Chapter 1, I examine Beckett's creation of fugitive writing, a literary form that evacuated certainty and stability from itself to become disoriented, ephemeral, impotent, vagabond and centrally preoccupied with exile. The relics of bowler hats and old boots are salvaged objects that conjure up the vanished worlds of middle-class Protestant Ireland and the larger world of Europe before it was shattered in the twentieth century.

'Heirlooms' (Chapter 2) explores Beckett's use of personal memory, a matter that has been much analysed by his biographers and critics.[39] The most compelling and influential studies of Beckett's use of auto-biographical material to date have been S.E. Gontarski's *The Intent of Undoing in Samuel Beckett's Dramatic Texts* (1985) and H. Porter Abbott's *Beckett Writing Beckett* (1996). Gontarski's argument centres on his examination of the process of 'vaguening' by which Beckett transforms life into art, while Abbott finds in this art an 'autograph,' or signature of self.[40] 'Heirlooms' proposes a new way of reading the personal origins of recurring objects in Beckett's work and is organised around a group of objects with strong biographical resonances: greatcoats, ladies' hats, widow's weeds, maternal beds and rocking chairs. The type of salvage here is the process by which traces of parental memory are embedded and preserved in this set of objects. By examining this process, it is possible to evaluate the impact exerted on the form of Beckett's writing by these memories. 'Heirlooms' demonstrates that the parental memories at the heart of many of Beckett's works are not vestiges of a deep autobiographical or autographical project that he built up and then sought to erase, as Gontarski has suggested, but are established piecemeal in his writing by an obsessive use of objects with parental associations. By tracing Beckett's use of a set of recurring objects that draw upon the wardrobes and personalities of his own parents, I suggest that these parental

---

[39] As Peter Boxall has observed, 'The autobiographical status of Beckett's fiction, at least from *Watt* onwards, is always subject to narrative uncertainty, but that the remembered selves and objects that people the majority of his landscapes have some autobiographical content is beyond serious doubt.' See 'The Existence I Ascribe: Memory, Invention and Autobiography in Beckett's Fiction,' *The Yearbook of English Studies*, 30 (2000), 137–52, p. 138.

[40] S.E. Gontarski, *Beckett's Happy Days: A Manuscript Study* (Ohio: Ohio State University Libraries, 1977), pp. 33–46.

heirlooms create 'sites of memory' in his writing that greatly alter its register and form.[41]

In order to limit the extent to which the argument of this book is contingent on drawing a correlation between Beckett's life and his writing, Chapters 3 and 4 are not concerned with the means by which Beckett may have been inspired by social or personal matters external to his work, and instead explore the echoes and patterns he developed across many media and decades of writing. 'Props' (Chapter 3) focuses on those objects that help Beckett's characters to get around: bicycles, wheelchairs, sticks and crutches. The host of limping, maimed characters in Beckett's work have most often been assimilated into philosophical or psychological symbolism, and I hope to challenge this critical tendency.[42] This chapter also asserts the pivotal importance of movement in Beckett's writing, which has often been described as a fictional and dramatic space characterised by paralysis, inertia or stasis. This chapter provides attentive consideration to the weak, sick and deteriorating bodies in Beckett in order to establish the implications of his emphasis on the need to keep moving, no matter the impediment. In 'Props', I consider how bicycles, wheelchairs, sticks and crutches serve Beckett as literary prosthetics. Embodying his creative imperative in a host of crippled characters who desperately struggle on despite their wish for rest, Beckett dramatises the imperfect but irresistible nature of his own impulse to write and salvages from this cruel and ungainly authorial need the singular dynamic of his characters' frustrated but determined movement in his novels, stories, poems and plays.

'Treasure', the book's final chapter, explores the contents of Winnie's bag in the 1960 play *Happy Days* and of Malone's pocket in *Malone Dies*.

---

[41] The 'sites of memory' in Beckett's writing are not intended to recall Pierre Nora's *lieux de mémoire*, which are concerned with manifestations of the past on a national, rather than a personal level, and with the conscious shaping of national identity through symbolic history. Beckett, by contrast, depicts the chance possession or retention by his characters of objects evocative of a personal and social past that has vanished and will neither be recovered, nor used to create or stabilise the identities of those characters possessed of 'heirlooms'. See Pierre Nora, 'Between Memory and History: Les Lieux de Mémoire,' *Representations* No. 26, Special Issue: Memory and Counter-Memory (Spring, 1989), 7–24.

[42] There have been many studies of the fragmented body in Beckett's theatre and fiction, most of which use a philosophical or psychoanalytic approach. See Linda Ben-Zvi, '*Not I*: Through a Tube Starkly', in *Samuel Beckett*, ed. Jennifer Birkett and Kate Ince (London: Longman, 2000), pp. 259–65; Anna McMullan, *Theatre on Trial: Samuel Beckett's Later Drama* (London: Routledge, 1993); Katherine Weiss, 'Bits and Pieces: The Fragmented Body in *Not I* and *That Time*', in *Other Becketts*, ed. Daniela Caselli, Steven Connor and Laura Salisbury (Tallahassee: JOBS Books, 2002), pp. 187–95; and '… Humanity in Ruins …': The Historical Body in Samuel Beckett's Fiction', in *Samuel Beckett: History, Memory, Archive*, ed. Seán Kennedy and Katherine Weiss (New York: Palgrave Macmillan, 2009), pp. 151–68.

While other chapters acknowledge Beckett's critically neglected polyvocal status as novelist, playwright and poet, the scope of this chapter is deliberately reduced in order to identify how the central situation of *Happy Days* constitutes a variation on Malone's predicament in the earlier novel. This chapter also considers how each work stands as a turning point in Beckett's body of work, in terms of the way objects are used to support, and indeed to create, his fictional and dramatic narratives. While the objects that feature in earlier chapters are resonant, useful or ludic, it is no exaggeration to describe the last remaining possessions of Malone and Winnie as treasure: a store, stock or accumulation of anything valuable. 'Treasure' explores the salvage involved in the grapple to hold onto these last objects, which provide the means for isolated characters to continue telling themselves stories about their worlds and themselves. There has been surprisingly little analysis to date of the extreme privation and isolation of Beckett's characters, and this chapter proposes that these facets of Beckett's writing reveal much about his singular formulation of the ethics of literary invention.

Beckett conveys the central place of objects in his writing in a pair of single, dismissive, but enormously telling lines in the trilogy. In *Molloy*, Moran declares: 'There are men and there are things, to hell with animals. And with God,' while the narrator of *The Unnamable* insists: 'People with things, people without things, things without people, what does it matter' (*GII*, 159, 286). His unease with objects attaining the status of symbols is indicated by a comment about Yeats's 1926 poem 'Sailing to Byzantium':

> An aged man is but a paltry thing,
> A tattered coat upon a stick, unless
> Soul clap its hands and sing, and louder sing
> For every tatter in its mortal dress[43]

Beckett praised the first lines that equate an old man with a scarecrow and convey the fragility of all living things, the inevitability and inherent grotesqueness of age and decay, but rather drily expressed his disapproval of the miraculous transformation in the subsequent couplet. The comment was recalled by his friend, the playwright Israel Horovitz, who visited Beckett in the nursing home where he spent his last months a fortnight

---

[43] W.B. Yeats, *W.B. Yeats: The Major Works*, ed. Edward Larrissy (Oxford: Oxford University Press, 1997), p. 95.

before his death. Horovitz described seeing Beckett 'dressed in a tattered old robe, working with pen and ink at a bridge table.'

> I stopped and stared a while, for some reason remembering Beckett's shock, twenty-two years before, at discovering that I didn't know Yeats's 'Sailing to Byzantium.' Before I left the table that night, Yeats's poem had passed from Mr Beckett's memory to my memory, along with Sam's small scholarly note of caution: 'I don't totally approve of that "Soul clap its hands" part!'[44]

This brings us to the question, did Beckett consciously decide to rely on the fourteen objects examined in this book as the primary material elements in his writing? From the very beginning, Beckett's characters were anachronistic. I believe that they may have first been introduced to signal the social alienation and contemptuous attitude of his early fictional characters by dressing and 'arming' them with outmoded and odd clothes and props. These material elements were then transposed to later works, Beckett having come to accept them as the markers of the imaginative world he had established, by which means this material canon became his wardrobe and prop-box for fifty-five years of experimental writing. When Beckett died, John Banville published an astute tribute in the *Observer* in which he identified several of my concerns in this book:

> A large part of Beckett's inspiration was a certain set of technical problems, one of which was how to get the maximum effect from a minimum of means. This is not as simple an ambition as it may appear ... This is Beckett's greatness as an artist, that out of a search for solutions to Modernist, or post-Modernist, dilemmas he could produce work so moving, funny and vividly real. Real, yes, for he *was* a realist. Now that the Fifties murk has lifted, and the labels – Absurdist, Existentialist, whatnot – have fallen into disuse, we can see how firmly his writings are rooted in the solid, the commonplace. He tried to rid his fiction and drama of nineteenth-century clutter not out of contempt for the world but, on the contrary, out of regard, out of, one might even say, reverence. In his work the thing shines. All is immanence, thereness. The *moment* in Beckett, carries an extraordinary weight ... And as always, it is the humble things that attract the greatest attention: a knife-rest, the belly-band of a horse, pencil stubs, ear-wax, odds and ends. I picture an old one, a stravager of the roads, clutching a little hoard of valuables polished by age and use: so Beckett with his wordhoard. 'I love the word, words have been my only love / not many.'[45]

---

[44] Israel Horovitz, 'A Remembrance of Samuel Beckett', *Paris Review*, 142 (Spring 1997), 189–193, p. 192.
[45] John Banville, 'Waiting for the Last Word', *The Observer*, 31 December, 1989, p. 36.

I want to propose that the 'little hoard of valuables polished by age and use' identified in this passage by Banville served Beckett as a creative lumber room. This type of room, put aside for the storage of useless or disused odds and ends, features as a setting in a range of literary works, from Jane Austen's *Mansfield Park* (1814) to Saki's 'The Lumber Room' (1914) and Thomas Pynchon's *The Crying of Lot 49* (1965). Most pertinent for a comparison with Beckett, however, is the lumber room that Gregor Samsa inhabits in Franz Kafka's *Metamorphosis* (1915).

> His family had gotten into the habit of putting in this room things for which they could not find any other place ... many things had become superfluous, and though they certainly weren't salable, on the other hand they could not just be thrown out. All these things migrated into Gregor's room.[46]

The banishment of a son rejected by his family to a room full of clutter that could neither be sold nor discarded may have been a powerful literary premise to Kafka, whose parents kept a small shop selling umbrellas and other 'fancy goods'.[47] In an indication of Beckett's material anachronism, the contents of his imaginative lumber room are directly comparable to the clothes and objects that feature in the work of Kafka, who was acutely interested in current fashions.[48] Mark Blackwell concludes his survey of literary lumber rooms by suggesting that 'overlooked things sometimes have a crucial place in literary history'.[49] This astute comment applies even more so to Beckett, whose oeuvre of half a century in diverse media constitutes the creation of an imaginative world using 'overlooked' objects and uncertain states of consciousness. One of the most important features of a lumber room is that its contents have been removed from circulation and are no longer either in trade or use. This state of gathering dust, caught in some form of shabby perpetuity, might equally describe the ontological quality of Beckett's narratives, as well as the material belongings of his characters. By paying close attention to those material elements, this book will provide a new perspective on the evolving yet consistent creative

---

[46] Franz Kafka, *Metamorphosis*, trans. and ed. S. Corngold (New York: Norton, 1996), p. 33. See also Kafka's designation of a pigeonhole on his writing-desk as a lumber room, in a mediation on the 'wretched' disorder of his desk that recalls George Perec: 24 and 26 December 1910, *The Diaries of Franz Kafka 1910–1923*, ed. Max Brod (Minerva, 1992), p. 33.
[47] Ritchie Robertson, *Kafka: A Very Short Introduction* (Oxford: Oxford University Press, 2004), p. 1.
[48] See Mark M. Anderson, *Kafka's Clothes: Ornament and Aestheticism in the Habsburg Fin de Siècle* (Oxford: Clarendon Press, 1994).
[49] *British It-Narratives, 1750–1830*, gen. ed. Mark Blackwell, 4 vols, *Volume 4: Toys, Trifles and Portable Furniture*, vol. ed., Mark Blackwell (London: Pickering and Chatto, 2012), xvii.

practice that finds expression in Beckett's works. His material imagination is a lumber room in which the remnants of European culture have been dumped, and by limiting his imagined world to these scraps, Beckett creates a stark, uncompromising literary realisation of the end of this culture. In Beckett's writing, we see six hundred years of Europe boiled down to the odds and ends of a bourgeois household and music-hall wardrobe. I believe that Cronin was correct in identifying Beckett as 'The Last Modernist', as it is unlikely that Europe will again produce a writer as immersed in its heritage as Beckett, whose cultural inheritance spanned its intellectual and creative achievements. The fourteen recurring objects in Beckett's writing are hoarded by his characters, together with their anachronistically refined turns of phrase, because they constitute the remaining scraps of a shattered world.

CHAPTER I

Relics

Bowler Hats, Old Boots

Fugitive Writing

This chapter examines the degree to which Beckett's work constitutes a reflection on the social collapse, chaos and destruction that characterised the European twentieth-century. The mass slaughter of the First and Second World Wars, together with the deportation, emigration and profound loss of orientation felt by survivors of both wars; the collapse of empires; the establishment of repressive regimes; the disruption of national boundaries and identities – all conspired to mark the twentieth century with a dismantling of *Heimat*. The literal meaning of this German term is 'homeland', but the word carries with it a host of associated meanings, including natural habitat, security and identity.[1] Loss of *Heimat* means social alienation and exile, and the extent to which this disorientation was a symptom of the age is suggested by a line written by the Bulgarian-born British writer Elias Canetti in 1943: 'It is only in exile that one realises to what an important degree the world has always been a world of exiles.'[2]

The objects under study in this chapter are relics: as the material remains of a shattered world, they offer a vivid commentary upon the social identity and certainty that was lost in this period. Bowler hats and old boots in this way serve a similar function in Beckett's writing as the objects in Sergei Dovlatov's *The Suitcase* (1986).[3] The narrator is permitted to bring only a single suitcase with him when he leaves the Soviet

---

[1] See the range of definitions offered by the *Oxford Language Dictionaries*: '(Heimatort) home; home town/village; (Heimatland) home; homeland'; 'natural habitat.'
[2] Elias Canetti, *The Human Province*, trans. Joachim Neugroschel (London, 1985), p. 29.
[3] *The Suitcase* was first published in 1986 in Russian, and in English translation in 1990 by Grove Weidenfeld.

Union for America, as Dovlatov did in 1978. Upon his arrival, the suitcase is placed in a wardrobe where it sits forgotten for years until he rediscovers it and its contents in wonder, prompting the stories that make up the novel. These stories include 'The Winter Hat' and 'The Nomenklatura Half-boots,' for Dovlatov, like Beckett, was alert to the symbolic and practical value of headgear and footwear. At the end of the novel, the narrator steps back from the memories that have overwhelmed him to cast a cold eye on the suitcase:

> The suitcase is on the kitchen table: a rectangular plywood box, covered with green fabric, with rusted reinforcements on the corners.
> My Soviet rags lie around it. The old-fashioned double-breasted suit with wide trouser cuffs. A poplin shirt the colour of a faded nasturtium. Low shoes shaped like a boat. A corduroy jacket still redolent of someone else's tobacco. A winter hat of sealskin. Crêpe socks with an electric sheen. Gloves that are good if you need to cut a hungry Newfoundland hound's hair. A belt with a heavy buckle, slightly bigger than the scar on my forehead …
> So what had I acquired in all those years in my homeland? What had I earned? This pile of rubbish? A suitcase of memories?[4]

The narrator's caustic tone notwithstanding, the contents of this suitcase allow Dovlatov to sketch the vanished world his narrator has left behind, and I suggest that Beckett's relics have a similarly resonant potential. The material elements that recur throughout Beckett's writing are directly comparable to those described in *The Suitcase*: a medley of objects, some purely functional, others loaded with evocative cultural associations, gathered together initially in the arbitrary, practical gesture through which Dovlatov's narrator packed his suitcase for exile and Beckett assembled the wardrobe and prop-box of his earliest characters, but both sets of objects subsequently offer fertile creative potential as relics of the lost world from which they have been brought.

Beckett infamously insisted that he preferred 'France at war to Ireland at peace'.[5] Comments such as this point to Beckett's rejection of Ireland as home, a refusal of affiliation that had caused his permanent move to France and was then confirmed by the war. Letters written in Paris after the war, however, reveal how changed Beckett felt his adopted city to have become and describe his growing sense of estrangement from

---

[4] Sergei Dovlatov, *The Suitcase*, trans. Antonina W. Bouis, ed. Katherine Dovlatov (London: Alma Classics, 2013), p. 129.
[5] Israel Shenker, 'Moody Man of Letters,' *The New York Times*, 6 May 1956. Quoted by Eoin O'Brien in *The Beckett Country: Samuel Beckett's Ireland* (Dublin: Black Cat Press, 1986), p. 384, n. 4.

France. In January 1948, he wrote to Thomas MacGreevy: 'The news of France is very depressing, depresses me anyhow. All the wrong things, all the wrong way. It is hard sometimes to feel the France that one clung to, that I still cling to.'[6] It is clear that the sense of cultural belonging Beckett had experienced in Paris in the late 1930s was now threatened. I suggest that this double exile sharpened his sensitivity to the widespread contemporary experience of displacement and inspired one of the defining features of Beckett's mature writing: its thematic and formal identification with homelessness. On a personal level, Beckett was an emigrant rather than an exile: his return home was not prevented by an antagonistic regime; rather, home had become untenable for him. That he did not feel banished once and for all from Ireland is evident in his return trips. For as long as his mother and brother lived, Beckett made infrequent journeys back to Ireland to see them. After their deaths, however, there was no longer great cause for Beckett to visit Ireland. While he may not have been banished from his country of origin, he imaginatively claimed the condition of homelessness rather than mere dislocation. Absent in Beckett's writing are social and domestic relations, the progress of the protagonist through the period of youth and up the social ranks to maturity, the establishment of new relationships, or, indeed, any other indication of a prospective future for his characters. Instead, they are all in decline, fondling their memories and the objects that they have managed to save from the annihilation that surely awaits them all.

I want to describe the literary form created by Beckett as fugitive writing to draw attention to its elusive, ephemeral and vagabond qualities. Fugitive writing is centrally preoccupied with exile, be it literal or metaphysical. One of the most striking features of a type of writing that takes exile as its starting point is that it thus evacuates certainty and stability from itself. This is the mark of fugitive writing: characterised by impotence, uncertainty and a disavowal of authority, the dispossessed, restless and powerless perspective of its wandering, wondering narrators endows such writing with a singular and utterly compelling quality. Robert Kiely has noted this quality of 'homelessness' in Beckett's fiction, and relates Beckett's literary strategy to György Lukács's observation of the 'transcendental homelessness' in all fiction:

---

[6] George Craig et al., ed., *The Letters of Samuel Beckett*, vol. 2 (Cambridge, 2011), p. 72. From 1893–1943, Thomas McGreevy favoured the 'Mc' spelling of his name, but adopted 'MacGreevy' after 1943. I have followed the chronology of this preference in my spelling of his name.

If the novel, as Lukács has said, originates in the 'homelessness' of the human creature in the universe, the young Beckett – struggling to distance himself from Ireland and Joyce and eventually from the dominance of the English language – carries this condition into every linguistic crevice until the inherited images of the most familiar literary tradition seem like the empty shells of ruined and abandoned shanties.[7]

The potential of such a form has also been considered by Gabriel Josipovici, who concludes his 2011 study *What Ever Happened to Modernism?* by asking if the displacement he identifies as a distinctly modernist experience leads, in art, to pathological distortion or a fresh perspective:

> Modernism may not be a consequence of the crisis of the bourgeoisie but it may be the product of a general European rootlessness in the wake of the French and Industrial revolutions. All will then depend on whether we see such rootlessness as pathological or as giving those who are imbued with it a certain vantage point, allowing them to see things which might otherwise have remained hidden.[8]

Beckett's organisation of his work around exile, isolation and confusion answers Josipovici's question and demonstrates how rootlessness in literature may be simultaneously pathological and liberating.

Relics

The manner in which literary characters are capped and shod signals their place in the world. The headgear and footwear of Beckett's characters tell the story of his responses, as a writer, to personal and local matters, and to the wider, cataclysmic events of the twentieth century. Beckett's deployment of bowler hats and old boots over the years allows us to chart the ways in which his singular, inimitable voice issued in defiance of, and in opposition to, a number of social and artistic conventions: the battered and ill-fitting bowler hats of Beckett's characters gesture to the social decline of those characters, while their gaping and deteriorating boots speak of the many journeys these figures have made.

---

[7] Robert Kiely, 'Samuel Beckett Harping: No Place to Go, No Place to Go', *Harvard Review*, 5 (Fall, 1993), 76–94, p. 82. Lukács suggested that the novel form is itself inherently 'an expression of transcendental homelessness', an observation that was later modified by Mikhail Bakhtin to a 'linguistic homelessness'. See John Neubauer, 'Bakhtin versus Lukács: Inscriptions of Homelessness in Theories of the Novel' *Poetics Today*, 17.4 (Winter, 1996), 531–546.
[8] Gabriel Josipovici, *What Ever Happened to Modernism?* (New Haven and London: Yale University Press, 2011), p. 187.

Bowler Hats

The London hatters James and George Lock designed the first bowler hat in 1850 in response to a commission for a close-fitting hard hat to protect gamekeepers' heads from overhanging branches and stay in place during their pursuit of poachers. The design was sent to hat makers called Bowler to make the prototype, whose name suited the hat's round shape so well that it stuck. Few objects are as symbolically modern as the bowler hat. In *The Man in the Bowler Hat* (1993), Fred Miller Robinson conducts 'a cultural study of modern life as seen through a sign of its times', observing that the bowler was 'ubiquitous headgear in the late nineteenth and early twentieth century' and the quintessential icon of modern times.[9] Once it had migrated from the country to the city, the bowler exerted a bewilderingly democratic appeal: 'The middle-class citizen in the bowler could be a prosperous merchant, or a less prosperous member of the new administrative and professional classes, or a dandy, or a gent – each concerned, in various ways, with gentility.'[10]

In an *Irish Times* article in 2010, Mark Hennessy enumerated the bowler's many past wearers, from Churchill to the City gent to 'street-traders, omnibus drivers, fish-sellers, shipyard workers, knife-grinders and countless other trades', women in Bolivia and Peru and Monty Python's 'Ministry of Silly Walks'.[11] Practically, the only wearers Hennessy omitted were Unionist marchers and female cabaret performers, two groups that are not often subject to comparison, yet their adoption of the bowler as an integral part of their costumes testifies to its adaptability. Together with white gloves and sash, the bowler imparts authority and a sense of venerable tradition to the Unionist parade, but when combined with the revealing costume of the cabaret performer, this same respectability is inverted in a playfully erotic act of misappropriation. As Hennessy's list indicates, the bowler was a costume staple for a bewilderingly diverse array of people throughout the first half of the twentieth-century, the same period in which Beckett drew upon it for his poetry, fiction and drama. Surprisingly, perhaps, Beckett's use of the bowler follows the cabaret

---

[9] Fred Miller Robinson, *The Man in the Bowler Hat: His History and Iconography* (Chapel Hill and London: The University of North Carolina Press, 1993), pp. xi, 31, 7. Robinson discusses the popularity of the bowler hat or 'derby' in America at some length, but I am predominantly concerned with its European cultural context.
[10] Robinson, *The Man in the Bowler Hat*, p. 27.
[11] Mark Hennessy, 'The Hat that Never Went Away – It Just Took Long Vacations', *Irish Times*, 14 October 2010, p. 14.

pattern of incongruence. During more than twenty years of writing, he used the bowler to emphatically register his unease with certain social conventions of the society into which he had been born. The two conventions inscribed by Beckett in the bowler are middle-class work and habits of thought. It is because bowlers are identified as part of the bourgeois working uniform and as literal thinking caps that they are such effective comic props. Robinson remarks of *Waiting for Godot* that:

> What Beckett's bowler-hat props signal to us is that – however abstract the play's landscape, metaphysical its range, and theological its implications – the experience it describes has a social history, rooted in how mostly ordinary people thought about and presented themselves in very specific and resonant circumstances.[12]

In this chapter, I want to show that the bowler hat was as helpful an object to Beckett as a magician's top hat, serving as a bourgeois prop, comic accessory and thinking cap in his poetry, fiction and drama from the 1930s to 1950s. Each use has its corresponding emotional register: the former derisive, the latter two largely playful. All bowlers, however, are subjected to distinctly rough treatment. Initially the object of satire, bowlers must be abused in Beckett's work before they can be reclaimed for the no-man's-land of clowning non-conformism.[13]

Bourgeois Bowlers

In *The Grove Companion to Samuel Beckett* (2004), Ackerley and Gontarski describe the combination of boots, greatcoat and hat as the 'essential accessories' of Beckett's protagonists, but the implications of Beckett's decision to create a uniform for his characters remain unexplored (*GC*, 70). Capped and shod in a bowler and old boots, I propose that his creatures have no choice but to walk the same roads and grapple with the same round of thoughts. While they may be vaunted in middle-class society, the values and practices embodied in the bowler are identified by Beckett's narrators or characters as insidious, largely because they are habitual, as all social norms must be. Habit, according to Beckett in his 1930 study

---

[12] Robinson, *The Man in the Bowler Hat*, p. xi.
[13] Beckett's use of the bowler hat has already received some critical attention. Seán Kennedy considers the bowler hat within a Catholic / Protestant binary of identity politics and in terms of Pierre Bourdieu's *habitus*. I am more interested, however, in the staggeringly broad range of associations of the bowler hat, and its correspondingly great potential for Beckett as a prop and item of costume. See *The Beckett Circle*, 33.2 (Fall 2010), 1–24, p. 13.

of Proust, 'is the ballast that chains the dog to his vomit' (*GIV*, 515). This is well illustrated by the last two appearances of bowler hats in Beckett's work, in *Texts for Nothing 8*, part of a fictional series written from 1950 to 1952 and published in 1967, and the mime *Act Without Words II*, written in 1958 and performed in 1960. Within both texts, the drudgery of work and thought are seen to be united through material objects: the characters are confronted with a set of clothes including a bowler that is identified as their uniform. This pile of clothes and their engagement with it reveals Beckett's vision of the clothes making the man. Towards the end of *Texts for Nothing 8*, the narrator notices 'with a final effort of will, a bowler hat which seems to my sorrow a sardonic synthesis of all those that never fitted me'. The bowler appears beside 'a complete pair of brown boots lacerated and gaping'. The ghostly narrator identifies them as 'insignia' that offer him a final opportunity of embodiment, or, as he puts it, to 'enthrone my infirmities' (*GIV*, 322, 323). In *Act Without Words II*, Beckett again places a bowler hat beside a pair of boots. The mime opens with two players, named only A and B, encased in sacks. Beside the more industrious and worldly B is 'a little pile of clothes' that is 'neatly folded (coat and trousers surmounted by boots and hat)' (*GIII*, 215). The routine begins and ends with the pile of clothes positioned ahead of the players' direction of movement, so it appears as though it is leading the way off-stage and determining the action of the piece. In *Act Without Words II*, the uniform shared by both players marks them as creatures of habit, trapped and defined by the social conventions embedded in it and incapable, it seems, of breaking out from these limitations.

In these last appearances of the bowler, its function and impact in Beckett's writing is distilled: through it, bourgeois work and thought are presented as functions of habit that reinforce and reify each other. Both are associated with at best a loss of agency and worst a surrender to the herd mentality, typical of background characters in Beckett's work. As he swings on his crutches along an empty road outside a town just before dawn, Molloy considers the dangers of being abroad during the working day:

> Morning is the time to hide. They wake up, hale and hearty, their tongues hanging out for order, beauty and justice, baying for their due. Yes, from eight or nine till noon is the most dangerous time. But towards noon things quiet down, the most implacable are sated, they go home, it might have been better but they've done a good job, there have been a few survivors but they'll give no more trouble, each man counts his rats. It may begin again in the early afternoon ... but it's nothing compared to the

morning ... Day is the time for lynching, for sleep is sacred, and especially the morning, between breakfast and lunch. (*GII*, 61–62)

Unless he wishes to be 'purged', the safest recourse for an old man who is not a local is to spend the day in hiding, which is what Molloy determines to do, hoping that if he is discovered sleeping he will be shown mercy by the society in which he reluctantly finds himself, a community whose work is caricatured as rat-catching and lynching.

Many other characters in Beckett's fiction and drama are also alienated from, and fearful of, the claims and comforts of society, and are similarly vulnerable when they come into contact with representatives of the social order. The policemen of Beckett's fiction are particularly odious in this regard, as are figures of authority throughout his dramatic writing, from Pozzo in *Waiting for Godot* (1948–49) to Hamm in *Endgame* (1953–57), the Director in *Catastrophe* (1982), or Bam in *What Where* (1983). One of the most obvious thematic characteristics of all Beckett's writing is a skewed realism that rejects the socially valorized categories of family, work, love, sex and health, and focuses instead on indigent, sick and alienated characters. This defining feature of his writing is present even in Beckett's first texts, but becomes increasingly prominent over time, as his focus shifts exclusively to characters on the margins of society with profoundly contingent lives whose time and energies are entirely occupied by their physical and mental ailments. These vagrant central characters are haunted by obsessive preoccupations that set them apart, making communication with others difficult, all the more so when background characters are as noxious, bullying and antagonistic as those in Beckett's work.

Examples of this are legion in Beckett. Even before we get to characters crawling in the mud, assailing each other in the buttocks with tin-openers in the prose work *How It Is* (1958–60), we have the breathlessly melancholic and elderly Maddy Rooney who gets stuck halfway up the steps of the train station modelled on Foxrock in the radio play *All that Fall*, and is openly, loudly mocked by the largely genteel crowd waiting on the platform. In the novel *Molloy*, the elderly and lame titular character runs over a dog on the bicycle he is attempting to cycle while on crutches, and is quickly surrounded by 'a bloodthirsty mob' that seems to encompass the entire town, for he describes seeing in it 'white beards and little almost angel-faces' (*GII*, 28). Other people, as imagined by Beckett, are the sinister 'they' referred to in the opening moments of *Waiting for Godot*, when Estragon replies testily to his friend Vladimir's enquiries about where and how he spent the night: 'Beat me? Certainly they beat me' (*GIII*, 4).

This aspect of Beckett's work – its manifestation of mistrust and fear of a social order founded on nothing more substantial than communal self-interest, propriety and maintenance of the status quo – is comparable to many other twentieth-century writers and artists who identified a distinctly malign potential in unquestioning adherence to social norms. As a middle-class Protestant Dubliner in modern Ireland, however, Beckett inherited a distinct aversion to politics and social revolt. In his exploration of the difficulty of assimilating Beckett within the field of Irish studies, Rónán McDonald has described Beckett's class background as 'professional Protestant bourgeoisie', and notes the paucity to date of academic analysis of this particular set.

> Though hardly a politically or socially disenfranchised group, it is not one whose story is told loudly in narratives of modern Ireland – be they nationalist or revisionist. Not least, perhaps, because … it is a rather insulated class that tended not to conceive of itself in political terms. So it tended to slip through the net of orthodox stories of Ireland, landed Anglo-Irish ascendancy yielding power to a burgeoning Catholic middle class, and, at the same time, to be overlooked by the politically motivated efforts to hear marginal, submerged or politically disenfranchised voices.[14]

Elsewhere, McDonald is at pains to distinguish Beckett from the 'Ascendancy', the 'land-owning Protestant class to which J.M. Synge and Lady Gregory belonged and to which Yeats aspired.' McDonald identifies distinct cultural differences between this set and the Beckett family, not least their cultural and intellectual insularity.

> Beckett's was not a family that would have been comfortable in the literary salon. Though comfortably off and respectable, the family were not cultured or bookish, belonging rather to a high-bourgeois professional class. Hence, they were perplexed and worried when Beckett threw over a promising and respectable academic career for the insecurity of the Bohemian lifestyle and his mother kept the scandalously titled *More Pricks Than Kicks* well out of sight of household visitors.[15]

Drawing on the suggestion by Andrew Kennedy that Beckett experienced 'the orderliness and the sheltered "old style" gentility of a pre-First

---

[14] Rónán McDonald, 'The Ghost at the Feast: 'Beckett and Irish Studies', in *Beckett and Ireland*, ed. Seán Kennedy (Cambridge: Cambridge University Press, 2010), pp. 16–30, p. 27.

[15] Rónán McDonald, *The Cambridge Introduction to Beckett* (Cambridge: Cambridge University Press: 2006), p. 8. Steven Connor, similarly, has argued for the need to more critically examine the role of Beckett's Protestant cultural inheritance in his writing than that offered by Declan Kiberd or Sinéad Mooney. See Connor, 'Beckett's Low Church', *Beckett, Modernism and the Material Imagination* (Cambridge: Cambridge University Press, 2014), pp. 133–51.

World War childhood, at the relatively quiet edge of the Western world', McDonald concludes that because 'there was no need for someone of his background to think politically', it was natural for Beckett as a writer 'to subscribe to that strand of cosmopolitan modernism which tended to disdain politically motivated art or cultural nationalism'. McDonald suggests, moreover, that Beckett's 'scornful attitude to the aims and ambitions of the Irish cultural revivalists, though presented as anti-provincialism, might also partly derive from the political immunity of his middle-class family background.'[16] In this chapter, I want to build on these suggestions by McDonald, and to propose that the political and cultural insularity Beckett experienced in his childhood and youth had a dramatic bearing upon Beckett's imagination, one that we can trace by examining his use of the bowler hat, which is treated in his work as a material remnant of that culture.

Beckett's parents were estranged from both the political and cultural developments of their time, and neither politics nor art were discussed in Cooldrinagh, their rather staid home in the affluent Dublin suburb of Foxrock. The writer Georges Belmont and publisher John Calder, both friends of Beckett's, have described his family and background. According to Belmont, May Beckett had 'great taste, she had a great taste for flowers and colours. She had a beautiful house, lovely old carpets – I mean, in a way but in a good way, she was very *bourgeoisie*'.[17] Calder responded to this observation by noting that Beckett's was a 'middle-class family that really was very respectable in Dublin terms', and that his parents 'couldn't understand why he wasted his time, not going into the family business, not earning a decent living, always without money, wandering around,' and 'letting down' the family name.[18]

Beckett was born in the first decade of the twentieth-century, a very formal period when, according to *Esquire*, 'Only a man very low on the social ladder would appear in public hatless.'[19] In a letter to the writer Aidan Higgins in 1952, Beckett described himself as 'deficient in the professional outlook', and this does indeed seem to have been the case (*LII*, 319). Having spent from 1928 to 1930 working as an English language assistant

---

[16] McDonald, *The Cambridge Introduction to Beckett*, pp. 8–9. See also Andrew Kennedy, *Samuel Beckett* (Cambridge: Cambridge University Press, 1989), p. 4.
[17] Georges Belmont and John Calder, 'Remembering Sam', in *Beckett in Dublin*, ed. S.E. Wilmer (Dublin: Lilliput Press, 1992), pp. 111–28, p. 120.
[18] Calder, 'Remembering Sam', pp. 120–21.
[19] O.E. Schoeffler and William Gale, *Esquire's Encyclopaedia of Twentieth Century Men's Fashions* (New York: McGraw-Hill, 1973), pp. 322–23.

at the École Normale Supérieure, Beckett returned from the creatively and intellectually heady atmosphere of Paris to live with his parents in Cooldrinagh. In the words of one of Beckett's biographers, the poet Anthony Cronin, Beckett came home 'affecting a French beret', just as the young Joyce had done in a Latin quarter hat before him – the shared gesture indicating the importance of costume to both young writers when their identity was still a matter of performance, particularly as far as their parents and home city were concerned. Cronin describes the reaction of Beckett's parents to his choice of headwear when he was preparing to lecture in Trinity: 'His mother and father suggested that when going out he should at least wear a bowler hat, then considered essential to respectability and the normal garb of the males of his class' (*LM*, 128). Several heated arguments with his mother followed this, but Beckett was intransigent.

> When Beckett did venture forth the state of his clothes and general appearance caused comment – in college, in Cooldrinagh and among his acquaintance generally. His usual garb was a grey shirt, grey Aran sweater and a pair of grey flannel pants. Both the sweater and trousers showed plentiful traces of food, drink and other matter. On top of these he wore a belted trenchcoat which was also in need of cleaning and sometimes his black beret. His shoes too were permanently dirty and in need of repair. It was all a far cry from the bowler-hatted young man his mother would have liked to have seen. (*LM*, 139)

According to Belmont, Beckett's father had hoped very much that his youngest son would succeed him in his quantity surveying business, in the Beckett and Medcalf offices on Clare Street, but when Beckett 'said he wouldn't, he wasn't interested at all', his father and he together wrote to Beckett's older brother Frank, who was in the Indian Civil Service, 'feeling quite happy there', to ask him to take Beckett's place. Frank did so.[20]

The 1930s were marked by uncertainty for Beckett. He could not decide upon a career, certainly not one that was agreeable to his parents.[21] Throughout all his abrupt changes of plan in the 1930s, Beckett was grimly aware of the expectation that he would follow Frank's reluctant footsteps and make the daily journey to the office on Clare Street. In letters

---

[20] Belmont, 'Remembering Sam', pp. 121–22.
[21] Beckett considered or tried out many careers in the 1930s: he worked as a lecturer and applied to be a trainee 'cinéaste' with the film director Sergei Eisenstein, sought work in the British National Gallery and an advertising firm, justified a six-month trip around the galleries of various cities in Germany, funded by his mother, as training for his potential future career as an art critic, and, despite his poor eyesight, even considered putting himself forward for pilot training (see *DF*, 224–26; *LM*, 165, 198, 233–34; *LI*, 166, 171).

to McGreevy, he voiced his anxiety and frustration with the prospect of being forced in this direction.

> I was not serious when I said about going into the office. There is no room for another clerk in the office, and even if there were I simply could not do the work. It will have to be private school or training college or else unhandy Andy in the garage and back garden at home. If I could even mend a puncture. (*LI*, 119)

At one point, when Beckett received yet another rejection from a publisher, Frank asked in exasperation, 'Why can't you write the way people want', and responded to his younger brother's plea that he could 'only write the one way, i.e. as best [he] could' by remarking that 'it was a good thing for him he did not feel obliged to implement such a spirit in 6 Clare St.' From letters sent to McGreevy throughout the 1930s, it is clear that, for Beckett, the bowler was a loaded symbol and held a very particular set of personal and social meanings for him. He uses it as shorthand for the effect on his brother of his obedient behaviour: '[Frank] went home after 3 years in India and went into the office. And now look at him. With a car and a bowler-hat' (*LI*, 112). In Beckett's assessment, these markers of material security and success gesture to a distinctly glum state of affairs. According to the dismissive logic of this phrase, whatever the financial security suggested by the car, the bowler deprives Frank of his individuality and marks him as a conformist. Particularly during the 1930s, when he enjoyed little or no literary success, Beckett's compulsion to write made him a stranger to his family, who saw it as a refusal of his duties. In letters of the time, he telescopes those loathed duties into the object of the bowler, which he imagines as a sort of social ball and chain, and later carries this formulation into his creative writing.

The English painter and photographer Nevill Johnson was a contemporary of Beckett's and from a similar background. Like Beckett, he experienced a rather fraught period before taking the step of establishing his own creative identity, a move that involved both physically and imaginatively distancing himself from his family. In his autobiography *The Other Side of Six* (1983), he describes a last bid to satisfy his family's middle-class expectations, declaring in the same breath the failure of this gesture as an 'act of affirmation'.[22]

> One bleak morning I visited a hatter's shop and emerged in a few moments half shamed, half laughing wearing a bowler hat. Perhaps, thus covered,

---

[22] Nevill Johnson, *The Other Side of Six: An Autobiography* (Dublin: The Academy Press, 1983), p. 33.

> success would attend me? My father and brother wore them habitually. Let it be understood that I tried; it was just that my skull was the wrong shape for this adornment. I glanced up repeatedly to the driving mirror then pulled impulsively to the curb where I got out to the pavement and removed this expensive item from my head. I placed it upon the ground and crushed it with my foot. In this manner did I commit almamatricide.[23]

In the final punning portmanteau of Johnson's description, the flattening of the bowler is also an attack on the middle-class hopes of his parents embodied in the hat: his alma mater is the school to which they had sent him, while 'matricide' suggests an attack on his mother and, by implication, on his bowler-hatted father.

The narrator of Beckett's 1946 novella *The Expelled* recalls the day when his father brought him on a similarly ill-timed visit to a hatter, before his head, and therefore his mind, was fully formed. As in Johnson's memoir, the scene is freighted with a premonition of inevitable failure and parental disappointment, and in the act of remembering, both sons note the distinct sense of shame and humiliation that accompanied their ceremonial adornment with a cap that evidently will not fit.

> When my head had attained I shall not say its definitive but its maximum dimensions, my father said to me, Come, son, we are going to buy your hat, as though it had pre-existed from time immemorial in a pre-established place. He went straight to the hat. I personally had no say in the matter, nor had the hatter … It was forbidden me, from that day forth, to go out bareheaded, my pretty brown hair blowing in the wind. (*GIV*, 249)

Neither Johnson nor Beckett could satisfy familial expectations, but both eventually used this to advantage in their works, where they focused on the outsider, the dispossessed. Johnson drew on the symbolism of headwear when he celebrated the potential creative advantage of this alienated perspective: 'Belonging blurs the truth and clarity is a lonely man, a man with several hats, all conferring some anonymity.'[24]

The bowler in Beckett and Johnson's accounts symbolises a filial and professional rite of passage typical of middle-class men in the early twentieth century. The bowler hat represented an initiation into a respectable, conformist future. It is notable that Beckett introduces the bowler in 'Malacoda' (1935) and *Murphy* (1935–36), the first poem and novel written after the death of his father. The timing of this introduction informs his

---

[23] Johnson, *The Other Side of Six*, pp. 32–33.
[24] Nevill Johnson quoted in Eoin O'Brien and Dickon Hall, 'Nevill Johnson's Dublin', *Irish Arts Review*, 19 (Winter, 2002) 68–75, p. 73.

identification of the bowler with a set of paternal and patriarchal expectations, and, in line with the guilt-ridden logic of a grieving son, guarantees that the fictional sons in question will disappoint such expectations. To emphasise this disappointment, a great number of Beckett's characters are possessed of skulls that are, like Johnson's, 'the wrong shape' for the symbolically regular bowler. The narrator of Beckett's 1946 novella *The End* is relieved to divest himself of the hat 'which was paining' him (*GIV*, 278–79). Similarly, the eponymous hero of *Molloy* (1955) takes off his hat to give his skull 'the benefit of' the rain, his 'skull all cracked and furrowed and on fire, on fire' (*GII*, 56). Malone describes the effects on Macmann's once black bowler of long familiarity with his head.

> The hat, as hard as iron, superbly domed above its narrow guttered rim, is marred by a wide crack or rent extending in front from the crown down and intended probably to facilitate the introduction of the skull ... And though the edges of the split brim close on the brow like the jaws of a trap, nevertheless the hat is attached, by a string, for safety, to the topmost button of the coat, because, never mind. (*GII*, 222)

This last image is an example of the paradoxical simultaneity with which bowlers in Beckett are both shackle and toy. Beckett consistently undermines the patriarchal sense of continuity that is inscribed in the bowler, with hats that are loose enough to fly off the child's head, yet pinch him as an adult: at no time does the son grow into the hat, thus becoming the man his parents had wished for.

In 1931, May Beckett had a dreadful argument with her son. She had read some of his writing while he was out of the house, and when he returned she was incandescent. She ordered him out of the family home, and it was to be months before the two were reconciled. The theme of ejection from the family home is at the heart of two novellas written in 1946. In *First Love*, the narrator returns from the bathroom to find his room locked and his belongings in a little heap before the door. Having tried every door in the house and found them all locked, he leaves by the street door, and, standing outside, pictures the inhabitants of the house listening for his departure, gathering together to celebrate when they hear the front door close behind him. In *The Expelled*, the narrator is ejected in a rather more direct manner. Having been unceremoniously thrown down the steps in front of the house, he is comforted by the sound of the door slamming, 'For that meant they were not pursuing me down into the street, with a stick, to beat me in full view of the passers-by' (*GIV*, 232, 248). From this point on, it is largely a matter of course that

Beckett's characters are dispossessed and far from a home to which they cannot return. Although these characters reject or are rejected by their family, social standing and professional obligations, many continue to wear bowler hats. It is made explicit, moreover, that a great number of these bowlers are the hats bought for the characters by their fathers, but the time has long past when the bowler's hard shape and what Robinson describes as its symbolic 'orthodoxy' could mould the mind beneath it to the expectations of family and society.[25] None of Beckett's protagonists has a conventional working life. Work is openly and bitterly disdained in his writing. Beckett most explicitly gives vent to his view of work as drudgery in his first novel *Murphy* and first play *Eleutheria* (1947). Although composed a decade apart, central to both works is a sour assessment of employment. While pretending to his girlfriend, the prostitute Celia, that he spends his days 'on the jobhunt', Murphy is privately convinced of the pathological basis and deleterious effects of work: 'For what was all working for a living but a procuring and a pimping for the money-bags, one's lecherous tyrants the money-bags, so they might breed' (*GI*, 48). In *Eleutheria*, Beckett's unwilling hero Victor Krap manages to dodge the demands of his fellow characters for an explanation of his way of living until the third and final act, when he relents and tells them he wants no part of their kind of life, 'for I've taken it into my head that it's always a question of the same drudgery, at every rung of the ladder'.[26]

The suggestion that the working man must sacrifice something of his best to fit the mould recurs in Beckett's 1946 novella *The End*, where the modern urban worker's uniform, the briefcase and bowler, are seen as craven signs of debasement by the narrator. In an inversion of the normal model in Beckett, where the bourgeois father is disappointed by his social pariah of a son, here the roles are reversed.

> One day I caught sight of my son. He was striding along with a briefcase under his arm. He took off his hat and bowed and I saw he was as bald as a coot ... He went bustling along on his duck feet, bowing and scraping and flourishing his hat left and right. The insufferable son of a bitch. (*GIV*, 283)

Marjorie Perloff has argued that the caustic manner in which the narrator observes his son but does not hail or make an effort to engage with him echoes the experience of those in Occupied France, where 'fathers

---

[25] Robinson, *The Man in the Bowler Hat*, p. 26.
[26] Beckett, *Eleutheria*, trans. Michael Brodsky (New York: Foxrock, 1995), pp. 160–1.

and sons or best friends turned against one another and pretended to be strangers for fear of being caught by the Gestapo.'[27] Since the bowler-hatted bourgeois is consistently derided by Beckett, I think this scene is more likely another attack on the self-serving, rule-bound venality represented by the bowler in Beckett's writing.

In *The Man in the Bowler Hat*, Robinson proposes that Beckett and the Surrealist painter René Magritte use bowlers in a similar, revelatory way: to show their audience, the mid-century middle-class, some hidden truth about themselves. Bowlers featured in Magritte's paintings from 1926 to 1966. Lifted from the pages of fashion magazines, Robinson argues that Magritte's bowlers are 'figures of fashion', modern readymades 'as banal as his other generic objects – his pipes and rocks and eggs and balusters'.[28] I suggest that Magritte uses the bowler hat to establish a smooth surface of bourgeois convention, beneath which teems violence and desire. Magritte's bowler-hatted Modern Everyman, despite his generic and unremarkable exterior, conceals under his hat the potent claims of magical daydreaming and destructive impulse. The conventional respectability of Magritte's figures masks a latent chaos and, like any mask, suggests the dramatically transformative potential of its removal. The bowler was a powerful personal symbol for Magritte. As Petra von Morstein has noted, his 'depictions of men in bowler hats are much like photographs of himself wearing a bowler hat'.[29] This has been captured by several photographers, including Steve Schapiro's series for *Life* magazine in 1964, when he photographed Magritte standing in front of his painting *La Golconda* (Figure 2).

That Magritte acknowledged and courted recognition of the similarity between the featureless nobodies of his paintings and his own profile in the hat indicates a crucial difference between the function of this object for him and for Beckett, whose sole personal relation to the bowler was the vehemence of his refusal to wear one. Beckett's bowlers conceal or cap no secret desires for his characters, and on the contrary, gesture to the bourgeois conventions associated with the hat.

---

[27] Marjorie Perloff, '"In Love with Hiding": Samuel Beckett's War', *The Iowa Review*, 35 (Spring, 2005), 76–103, p. 97.
[28] Robinson, *The Man in the Bowler Hat*, p. 125, 126.
[29] Petra von Morstein, 'Magritte: Artistic and Conceptual Representation', *The Journal of Aesthetics and Art Criticism*, 41 (Summer, 1983), 369–74, p. 372.

Figure 2 Steve Schapiro, 'René Magritte at MOMA, 1965'.
Courtesy of Steve Schapiro.

Because of its solid shape and material – felt reinforced with mercury in a process known as shellacking – the bowler was known as the 'iron hat'.[30] Beckett opens his poem 'Malacoda' with the lines:

> thrice he came
> the undertaker's man
> impassible behind his scutal bowler
> to measure
> is he not paid to measure (*GIV*, 29)

'Malacoda' was written the summer after Beckett's father died. These lines convey the horror of handing over the loved one's corpse to the undertaker. The narrator is affronted, not only by the intrusion of a stranger during a period of mourning, but more acutely by the dehumanised professionalism and blank impersonality of someone 'paid to measure', qualities embedded in his bowler hat. In a similar vein, Robinson reads Magritte's bowler-hatted figures in terms that reveal wary disdain for the type of man who would wear a bowler: 'Here was a machine hat, designed like a bolt cap, on a machine body, the stereotyped modern man, the herd creature we were always in danger of becoming.'[31] In 'Malacoda', Beckett emphasises the bowler's hardness when he describes it as 'scutal'. From the Latin for shield, the scutal bowler is the bourgeois helmet. Two rare groups that scorned the bowler were bohemians and aristocrats. For different reasons, both were antagonistic towards the middle-classes: bohemians because they defined themselves against bourgeois conventions, aristocrats because they went in horror of middle-class intrusion in their social lives. In a curious coincidence, the tone of Beckett's disdain for the bowler-hatted undertaker's man in 'Malacoda' recalls nothing so thoroughly as the expression of social distaste in P.G. Wodehouse's *Ring for Jeeves* (1953), which refers indignantly to a 'frightful outsider in a bowler and made-up tie'.[32]

It is a common interpretative gesture for the hat to be read as a symbol of psychological individuality. In her cultural history of clothing, *The Language of Clothes* (1983), Alison Lurie advances the argument that the hat is a symbol of the mind it conceals: 'Traditionally whatever is worn on the head, whether or not it grows there naturally, is a sign of the mind beneath it. The hat, therefore, like the hair, expresses ideas and opinions.'[33] In identifying the mindset of his characters with their uniformly shaped and coloured hat, Beckett may have been influenced by Gustave Flaubert's

---

[30] Robinson, *The Man in the Bowler Hat*, p. 16.
[31] Robinson, *The Man in the Bowler Hat*, p. 131.
[32] P.G. Wodehouse, *Ring for Jeeves* (London: Random House, 2009), p. 84.
[33] Alison Lurie, *The Language of Clothes* (Feltham: Hamlyn, 1983), p. 176.

Bouvard et Pécuchet (1881). Vivian Mercier suggested a link between Estragon and Vladimir and Bouvard and Pécuchet in his 1955 review of *Waiting for Godot*, immediately discounting this link as a mistake in the same breath by noting that Beckett's characters lack the trust in education and progress that gives Flaubert's novel its momentum.[34] A more tenable argument for Mercier's parallel may be found in the opening exchange between Flaubert's characters on the subject of hats, as they simultaneously sit on the same bench and continue to mirror each other by taking off their hats in a single uninterrupted motion.

> To wipe their foreheads, they removed their hats, which each man placed next to him. The short man noticed the name *Bouvard* written in his neighbour's, while the latter made out the word *Pécuchet* in the cap belonging to the fellow in the coat 'Fancy that!' he said. 'We both had the idea of writing our names in our hats.' 'I should say so! Someone could walk off with mine at the office!'[35]

The new friends subsequently devote themselves to a comically haphazard search for the meaning they long to discover in a range of different forms of knowledge, all of which are ultimately disappointing. A passage in *Molloy* seems to evoke the failed quest of Flaubert's novel:

> Yes, I once took an interest in astronomy, I don't deny it. Then it was geology that killed a few years for me. The next pain in the balls was anthropology and the other disciplines, such as psychiatry, that are connected with it, disconnected, and then connected again, according to the latest discoveries … Oh I've tried everything. In the end it was magic that had the honour of my ruins, and still today, when I walk there, I find its vestiges. (*GII*, 35)

It is notable that Bouvard and Pécuchet are copy clerks, tasked with the mindless reproduction of other people's ideas. Robert Walser's characters, many of whom are similarly employed as copyists, share this enthusiasm for abandoning their jobs and engaging in eccentric pursuit of more authentic or original ideas. Bouvard and Pécuchet's friendship is initiated with the realisation that they have both taken the precaution of inscribing their names on their hats lest someone take theirs by accident, the implication being that this happened rather frequently. The almost promiscuous interchangeability of bowler hats also comes to the fore in its use as a comic prop, as we will see in the following section.

---

[34] Vivian Mercier, 'A Pyrrhonian Eclogue,' *The Hudson Review*, 7 (Winter 1955), 620–24, p. 622.
[35] Gustave Flaubert, *Bouvard and Pécuchet*, trans. Mark Polizzotti (Illinois: Dalkey Archive Press, 2005), p. 3.

Comic Bowlers

'We can distinguish by the taste of the hat, the mode of the wearer's mind.'[36] Beau Brummell's pithy identification of hat with mind provides much of the anarchic potential of a swapped bowler in the music-hall tradition, particularly when combined with the freedom of the popular stage to disrupt such stifling social norms as class divisions and everyday etiquette. This freedom was also asserted by the cinematic comedy that had its roots in the disorder of the music hall, and Beckett, like Flaubert, draws upon this potential disruption and confusion in his use of the bowler. Beckett's bowlers also follow another tradition in music-hall and silent film comedy: that of misappropriating an object associated with work for shabby and purposeless play, but as we will see, Beckett made the bowler his own.[37] He would have found himself bombarded by bowler hats in popular and high art forms alike during his youth. The bowler was introduced as a key prop in Wodehouse's *Jeeves* stories, written from 1915 to 1974, was worn by the mysterious figures of Magritte's paintings from the mid-1920s and by the incompetent detectives of Hergé's *Tintin*, Thomson and Thompson, who first appeared in 1932. As a child, Beckett's uncle Howard brought him to the cinema in Dun Laoghaire and Dublin, passing on an enduring enthusiasm for Charlie Chaplin, Laurel and Hardy, Buster Keaton and Harold Lloyd. At college in his early twenties, Beckett often went to variety shows in the city centre. 'Turns' such as the hat-swapping routine that Beckett incorporated in *Waiting for Godot* had been adapted for the screen by performers with their roots in the popular stage.

Given its ubiquity, the bowler offered comedians an item of costume that was also a prop with staggeringly wide references. The bowler was most extensively used as a comic prop by Laurel and Hardy. Stan Laurel wore a 'flat-brimmed Irish children's bowler' and is quoted by Robinson on this 'comic accessory': 'the bowler hat to me has always seemed to be a part of a comic's make-up for as far back as I can remember. I'm sure that's why Charlie wore one. Most of the comics we saw as boys wore them.'[38] Their bowler-switching routine, where first one and then both performers

---

[36] Quoted in Robinson, *The Man in the Bowler Hat*, p. 15.
[37] Beckett's interest, until late in his life, in the comic potential of swapping items of clothing is indicated in the memoir of André Bernold, who befriended Beckett when he was a student and Beckett in his seventies: 'We would swap our spectacles, an idiotic idea of mine that had become one of our rituals, and clown around for a few moments.' See André Bernold, *Beckett's Friendship: 1979–1989*, trans. Max McGuinness (Dublin: Lilliput Press, 2015), p. 27.
[38] Robinson, *The Man in the Bowler Hat*, pp. 80, 82, 76.

lose their hats and engage in an increasingly desperate scramble to retrieve them, formed the basis of the 1927 film *Hats Off*, which builds from a confusion about their own two hats, in which they kick each other's hats into the street, to the frantic climax of a giant battle in the street, with a crowd of men fighting to recover their misplaced hats.[39] For Laurel and Hardy, no less than Bouvard and Pécuchet, wearing one's own hat matters. Other hats simply do not fit, and, as Robinson explains: 'Stan's and Ollie's bowlers, like Charlie's, are so identified with them, so often in place in the most outlandish circumstances, that losing them requires their immediate recovery at whatever cost. Without their hats they are lost.'[40]

The only costume specification in *Waiting for Godot*, casually delivered in a footnote halfway through the first act, is that all four characters wear bowlers. The first reviews and critical studies of the play noted that Beckett's characters make good use of their bowlers in a series of turns that come straight from the music-hall and silent film repertoire, and that the stage business of the play as a whole owes a lot to the popular stage.[41] Beckett himself recommends such a reading when Estragon and Vladimir trade disparaging descriptions of the tedium they, and their audience, are experiencing in the first act.

> ESTRAGON It's awful.
> VLADIMIR Worse than the pantomime.
> ESTRAGON The circus.
> VLADIMIR The music-hall. (*GIII*, 28)

During the many lulls of the play, as the dialogue stalls and they seem at a loss as to how to proceed, Estragon and Vladimir are as exposed as a music-hall two-hander gone wrong. Hesitation and confusion, it will be noted, have a very different value on the 'low' and 'high' stages. Just as Beckett lent these markers of theatrical failure a new quality when he borrowed elements from popular comedy, including the bowler hat, so did he shift the symbolic value of the bowler from that of class, which Robinson

---

[39] This routine has been attributed by the film critic Glenn Mitchell to the director of silent comedies, Leo McCarey, but it may well have migrated from the popular stage to the screen, like many other comic routines and devices. See Glenn Mitchell, *The Laurel and Hardy Encyclopaedia* (London: Batsford, 1995), p. 128.
[40] Robinson, *The Man in the Bowler Hat*, p. 85.
[41] See Mercier, 'A Pyrrhonian Eclogue', 622; Martin Esslin, 'The Theatre of the Absurd', *The Tulane Drama Review*, 4 (May, 1960), 3–15; Ruby Cohn, *Samuel Beckett: The Comic Gamut* (New Brunswick: Rutgers University Press, 1962), especially her final chapter; Frederick J. Hoffman, *Samuel Beckett: The Language of Self* (New York, 1964), xiii; Hugh Kenner, *Samuel Beckett: A Critical Study* (London: Calder, 1962), p. 13.

identifies as the main source of its comic potential, to a range of different uses, as we shall see.[42]

In *Beckett/Beckett*, Vivian Mercier's 1977 study of the tension between certain antinomies in Beckett's work, Mercier observes that the lace or string attaching bowler to greatcoat 'is a mark of the fox-hunting man, who is otherwise likely to lose his headgear while jumping a hedge or a ditch'.[43] This is an accurate description of the historical provenance of the bowler before it migrated to the city, but the lace is necessary in Beckett's work because very few of his characters' hats fit well. For those characters whose hats were bought for them as boys by their fathers, the associated gesture by the father of tying the bowler to his son is a further means of fixing the boy to a professional, respectable future. But if this kind of hat functions as ballast, anchoring the child in reality and curtailing his youth, it is a plaything for the man. Such hats offer many playfully impractical uses, not least of which is derived from the originally pragmatic connection of the hat to the coat, making a peculiar doll of these tramp-like figures and providing them with seemingly endless entertainment. The exemplar of this game is of course Molloy:

> I took off my hat and looked at it. It is fastened, it has always been fastened, to my buttonhole, always the same buttonhole, at all seasons by a long lace. I am still alive then. That may come in useful. The hand that held the hat I thrust as far as possible from me and moved in an arc, to and fro. As I did so, I watched the lapel of my greatcoat and saw it open and close. (*GII*, 9–10)

Later, Molloy throws his hat from him 'with a careless lavish gesture and back it came, at the end of its string or lace, and after a few throes came to rest against my side' (*GII*, 56). The punning homonym of 'throws' and 'throes' shows that Molloy is not the only one enjoying the distractions offered by his hat. This tendency, where useful objects are transformed by idle misuse into playthings, characterises Beckett's material canon in his early and middle periods.

Thinking Caps

Beckett plays on the rigidity of the 'iron hat' in a different sense when he uses the bowler to convey the tedium and grind of hard-headed,

---

[42] Robinson, *The Man in the Bowler Hat*, pp. 64–66, 75–76, 78.
[43] Vivian Mercier, *Beckett/Beckett* (New York: Oxford University Press, 1977), pp. 46–72, p. 51.

rational, pragmatic or logical thought. He does so with particular verve in his early writing, a period in which he was much given to intellectual exhibitionism. This tendency persists in Beckett's treatment of the bowler as a thinking cap. A bowler that is stiff with pride in the process of reasoning is treated ruthlessly in Beckett's writing, where, without exception, it is headed straight for misfortune. The 'turn' of using the bowler as a thinking hat was not Beckett's invention – he saw many comedians on stage and screen remove their hats to scratch their heads in bewilderment – but he translated the figure of speech into an object in order to undermine this now symbolically loaded object by subjecting it to ridicule and attack. Indeed, the many descriptions of hats pinching the heads of Beckett's fictional characters may be an extension of this pun: the small hat indicates a not particularly flamboyant intelligence in the same way that Bertie Wooster refers to hat size when bragging about his valet's keen mind: 'You see? "There is one possible solution, sir" – just like that. For your information, Catsmeat, Jeeves takes a size fourteen hat, eats tons of fish and moves in mysterious ways his wonders to perform. Speak, Jeeves.'[44]

In his analysis of the hat-swapping routines of *Waiting for Godot*, Robinson argues that Beckett's characters quite literally change their minds as often as they change their hat. In this formulation, 'thought' and 'the consciousness that produces it' are contained within the character's hat and may never be assumed 'as part of one's natural makeup'.[45] If the hat so defines the mind of man, then divested of it he is mindless. This seems to be the relation between Lucky's hat and his performance of thinking.

> VLADIMIR [*to Pozzo*] Tell him to think.
> POZZO Give him his hat.
> VLADIMIR His hat?
> POZZO He can't think without his hat.
> ...
> You must put it on his head. (*GIII*, 35)

Yet while it is true that Lucky needs to be wearing his hat to think, the other characters must remove theirs. By taking off their hats, Vladimir and Estragon air their thoughts, but they must replace them to share the fruits of their mental efforts.

---

[44] P.G. Wodehouse, *The Mating Season*, in *The Jeeves Omnibus 3*, 3 vols. (London: Hutchinson, 1991), pp. 175–367, pp. 202–3.
[45] Robinson, *The Man in the Bowler Hat*, p. 161.

ESTRAGON That wasn't such a bad little canter.
VLADIMIR Yes, but now we'll have to find something else.
ESTRAGON Let me see. [*He takes off his hat, concentrates.*]
VLADIMIR Let me see. [*He takes off his hat, concentrates. Long silence.*]
Ah! [*They put on their hats, relax.*] (*GIII*, 57)

So although all four characters wear bowlers in *Waiting for Godot* and use them as thinking hats, they do so in different ways. Whereas Pozzo instructs Vladimir and Estragon to give Lucky his hat because Lucky is unable to think without wearing it, the other characters must remove their headgear to think. This inconsistency spoils both Robinson's argument, and that of Hugh Kenner, who expresses the contrasting view: 'bowler hats are apparently *de rigueur*, and … are removed for thinking but replaced for speaking'.[46] It is not possible to make a general claim about the relevance of covered or uncovered heads to mental activity: the hat is an accessory to thought, and without it, these characters simply could not think.

Mary Bryden has pointed to Beckett's fondness for making clichés literal by describing the effect of removing and squashing Lucky's bowler as 'preventing him from further talking through his hat'.[47] By using the bowler as a thinking hat, Beckett illustrates the attractions, distractions and perils of thought for his characters. By turns absorbed, entertained, confused and wrong-footed by their intellectual efforts, many of Beckett's characters are seen to be in thrall to a distinctly detrimental activity. Pozzo, in this respect, may have been doing Lucky a favour by trampling on his hat. If Lucky can no longer antagonise and bewilder with his chaotic thoughts, both Lucky and Pozzo will be better able to accept their situation. The abandonment of thought by the destruction of a thinking hat also features in *Murphy*. With the death of the eponymous hero, the curse that had prevented Cooper from sitting down or taking off his hat is broken. No less energetic than Nevill Johnson when he rejected his parents' bourgeois expectations of him through an attack on his bowler, Cooper seizes the opportunity to destroy with his rear the pretensions of his head.

> He placed his ancient bowler crown upward on the step, squatted high above it, took careful aim through his crutch, closed his eye, set his teeth,

---

[46] Hugh Kenner, *Samuel Beckett: A Critical Study*, p. 138.
[47] Mary Bryden, 'Beckett, Böll, and Clowns', in *Borderless Beckett – Beckett sans frontières 2006*, ed. Minako Okamuro, Naoya Mori, Bruno Clément, Sjef Houppermans, Angela Moorjani and Anthony Uhlmann (Amsterdam: Rodopi, 2008), pp. 157–72, pp. 167–68.

flung his feet forward into space and came down on his buttocks with the force of a pile ram. No second blow was necessary. (*GI*, 163–64)

Beckett himself had more than a passing acquaintance with the distressing trials and false comforts of intellectual activity. In the poem 'Gnome', written in 1934, three years after quitting his lecturing post in Trinity, Beckett attacked the institution of academia and its 'loutishness of learning' (*GIV*, 9). Beckett's early works of poetry and fiction, however, are characterised by an eagerness to overwhelm his readers into submission with bravura displays of intellectual acrobatics. The remarkable shift in register from the tediously knowing cleverness of his early work to the uncertain and bewildered tone of his middle and later periods indicates the efforts he made to rid his writing of intellectual pride, mastery and authority. Beckett's friend, the poet Anne Atik, relates how in later life he 'feared erudition swamping the authenticity of a work, and constantly warned against that danger for other artists, having had to escape it himself'.[48] In a 1961 interview, Beckett said 'I'm no intellectual. All I am is feeling. *Molloy* and the others came to me the day I became aware of my own folly. Only then did I begin to write the things I feel.'[49]

Whenever Beckett's narrators or heroes are tempted to trust, like Flaubert's Bouvard and Pécuchet, in the various disciplines devised through the ages to gloss the chaos of life, the iron hat is the ideal object of attack. The first man to wear a bowler hat was William Coke. When the prototype he had commissioned returned, he tested the hat by jumping on it several times, and as it withstood his weight, he bought it.[50] In Beckett's writing, the bowler not only invites similarly enthusiastic tests of its strength, but is also used on several occasions to imply the obdurate quality of the mind underneath it. An analogy is suggested between the ostensibly indestructible bowler and iron-cast displays of intelligence that turn out to be similarly vulnerable. The danger of thinking is neatly represented by the mental unravelling of Watt and Moran, both of whom seek to understand the logic and order of their fictional worlds. At the end of this painful process, they find that very little makes sense to them anymore. By contrast, the case of Molloy illustrates the pleasure of abandoning thought, a pleasure that is also expressed in an exchange at the start of the second act of *Waiting for Godot*, where Vladimir tells Estragon,

---

[48] Anne Atik, *How It Was: A Memoir of Samuel Beckett* (Berkeley: Shoemaker and Hoard, 2005), p. 52.
[49] Interview with Gabriel d'Aubarède, quoted in Mercier, *Beckett/Beckett*, p. 160.
[50] Lock & Co. Hatters, London, 'History of Hats', www.lockhatters.co.uk/historyhats-content.aspx [accessed 25 August 2010] (para. 1 of 8).

'We're in no danger of ever thinking any more' and Estragon responds with, 'Then what are we complaining about?' (*GIII*, 56).

When we read Beckett's bowler-hatted characters from the head down, we see that he manipulates this iconic modern object to his own purposes, and invests it with the qualities of conformity and certainty that he rejected as a man and artist. The pattern of Beckett's use of bowler hats describes an arc that reflects his own professional advancement as a writer. This object which Beckett identified with conventional employment and the habit of rational thought disappears from his writing at the end of the 1950s, by which time he could at last be sure that he would no longer have to support his writing career with other work, such as the teaching he loathed, or translations he did of necessity and later disowned. Gerry Dukes's description of Estragon and Vladimir's bowlers as 'relics of old decency' encapsulates why Beckett so roughly treated the hat in his writing.[51] The bowler in Beckett's work indicates variously the hard-headed bourgeois, the fool who has faith in thinking and the relief of the man who has given it up. By making the bowler hat a relic of the mores and habits of the Protestant middle-class of his youth and relentlessly subjecting this object to disdain or violence, Beckett inscribes in his writing the distinct impression that middle-class work and thought are a mug's game. Robinson describes hats as 'stressed words in the grammar of costume'.[52] In Beckett's poetry, fiction and drama, the bowler is evocative of stifling professional expectations, rigorous and unimaginative thought, all of which Beckett violently rejected, a refusal he enacts in the rough treatment of bowler hats in his writing.

Old Boots

Unlike the bowler hat, which originated in the nineteenth century and has all but disappeared from contemporary daily dress, the boot has much older origins and has never left us. Its self-evident function is and has ever been to protect and cover the foot.[53] The extraordinary longevity of the boot indicates how ideally suited its design has remained across civilisations and centuries. The venerable provenance of the boot does not

---

[51] Gerry Dukes, 'The *Godot* Phenomenon', in *Samuel Beckett 100 Years: Centenary Essays*, ed. Christopher Murray (Dublin: New Island, 2006), pp. 23–33, p. 29.
[52] Robinson, *The Man in the Bowler Hat*, p. 16.
[53] Blanche Payne, Geitel Winakor and Jane Farrell-Beck, *The History of Costume: From Ancient Mesopotamia Through the Twentieth Century*, 2nd edn (New York: Harper Collins, 1992), p. 21.

mitigate its rather humble and despised status. It does, however, give it a compelling resonance. More resonant still is an old boot, which we understand in a glance or touch to have loyally served the foot, or feet, it once contained. Unlike bowler hats, which Beckett uses as playthings, degrading and undermining their symbolic social value, old boots are already debased and pathetic objects.

Humble Relics

A curious complex of affection, pity and disgust tends to characterise our reaction to old boots, inspired perhaps by a visceral response to the material of deteriorated leather, which we know to be skin that has been preserved and then worn by another creature into a state of decay. Old boots also provoke an uneasy fascination because while they declare their manifest subordination to man, falling apart from the strain of carrying him over the earth, shabby and worn-down old boots emphatically declare the even greater frailty and vulnerability of the body they protected. Gazing at or reading descriptions of worn leather, tangled or missing laces, or a flapping sole, we are led to speculate on the state of the feet that trudged and tramped the boots in question into such disrepair. The sixteenth-century playwright Thomas Dekker drew on his audience's sympathy for old boots or shoes as intimate, steadfast objects when he described a character that had been rejected by another as having been 'laid at one side like a paire of old shooes'.[54] The implicit pathos of a worn-out boot or shoe is also evoked in a saying attributed to Gustave Flaubert: 'In the sight of an old pair of shoes there is something profoundly melancholy.'[55]

Many of the old boots in Beckett's writing from the 1930s to the 1980s are indeed charged with a melancholic resonance. Their dents and discoloration tell the stories of the journeys made in them. They are humble relics of the restlessness and physical suffering that dominate the experience of many of Beckett's characters. In *Waiting for Godot*, Vladimir finds a moral about human nature in the painful fit of Estragon's boots, chastising his companion for complaining about the boots hurting, when Estragon has neglected to take them off every day: 'There's man all over for you, blaming on his boots the faults of his feet' (*GIII*, 5). The play opens with Estragon struggling with his boot and declaring, 'Nothing to

---

[54] Thomas Dekker, *The Shoemakers' Holiday*, ed. Jonathan Gil Harris (London: Methuen, 2008), 1:1.143–4, p. 15.
[55] Michael Ann Holly, 'Mourning and Method', *The Art Bulletin*, 84 (Dec, 2002), 660–669, p. 660.

be done.' It is unclear, in these first moments, whether his comment refers exclusively to the boot, but it seems comprehensively to have defeated him. The stage directions present boots as tricky objects, which are not to be underestimated: '*Estragon, sitting on a low mound, is trying to take off his boot. He pulls at it with both hands, panting. He gives up, exhausted, rests, tries again. As before. Enter Vladimir*' (*GIII*, 3).

In the opening pages of *Molloy*, the narrator revises his original impression of one of the wayfarers, altering the details of this man in an imaginative act that transforms him from a respectable figure to a tramp. He does so by eliminating the positively loaded social symbols of respectable clothing, Pomeranian and cigar, and replacing them instead with a stray dog and old boots, both of which act as markers of loneliness in this passage, which gathers momentum in its evocation of social isolation until it anticipates the desperate encounters between the figures of *How It Is*:

> But was not perhaps in reality the cigar a cutty, and were not the sandshoes boots, hobnailed, dust-whitened, and what prevented the dog from being one of those stray dogs that you pick up and take in your arms, from compassion or because you have been straying with no other company than the endless roads, sands, shingle, bogs, and heather, than this nature answerable to another court, than at long intervals the fellow-convict you long to stop, embrace, suck, suckle, and whom you pass by, with hostile eyes, for fear of his familiarities? (*GII*, 8)

To date, relatively few critics have explored boots in Beckett's writing.[56] A brief note in *The Grove Companion to Samuel Beckett* notes that he once claimed that the name Godot had its origins in the French slang for boots, 'godillots' and 'godasses'. In naming the play after a personified source of hope that proves elusive, if not illusory, and whose failure to appear dampens Estragon and Vladimir's determination to wait without changing their behaviour, Beckett emphasises the dependence of his two central characters on their idea of Godot. It is apt, then, for the name Godot to have been taken from popular words for boots, for there is hardly any item more important to a tramp than a sturdy and reliable pair of boots. Such a sense of their practical usefulness as well as their near-ubiquity in

---

[56] See Edward Bizub's associative link between Beckett's Huguenot heritage and Golgotha in the use of boots in *Waiting for Godot*: 'Beckett's Boots: the Crux of Meaning', *Samuel Beckett Today/ Aujourd'hui*, 25 (2013), 267–79. See also Dieter Wellershoff's argument for the recurrence of a single pair of shoes in the trilogy: Wellershoff, 'Toujours moins, presque rien: essai sur Beckett,' *Cahier de l'Herne* trans. R. Denturck (Paris: L'Heme, 1976), pp. 169–82.

his writing presumably moved *The Grove Companion* to describe boots as 'essential accessories' for Beckett's protagonists (*GC*, 70). Similarly, Watt's personal history, enthusiastically demanded by a minor character at the start of the novel written from 1941 to 1945, is condensed into a description of Watt's memorable need for a single boot: 'I met him one day in the street. One of his feet was bare. I forget which. He drew me to one side and said he was in need of five shillings to buy himself a boot. I could not refuse him' (*GI*, 185). *Malone Dies* also features the story of a single boot belonging to the titular hero. In contrast with Mr Nixon's charitable granting of Watt's unusual request, however, Malone's story illustrates a rather less generous trait in mankind.

> One boot, originally yellow, I forget for which foot. The other, its fellow, has gone. They took it away, at the beginning, before they realised I should never walk again. And they left the other, in the hope I would be saddened, seeing it there, without its fellow. Men are like that. (*GII*, 242)

Mismatched and Ill-fitting Boots

There are remarkably few matching pairs of boots in Beckett, and over time, such mismatched pairs may be expected to cause their wearers to suffer. The many odd combinations of boots of different sizes, or pairs made up of a boot and shoe, are described in great detail in Beckett's writing, and give occasion for a compulsive and darkly comic type of play as we watch or imagine characters repeatedly putting them on and taking them off, or swapping them between feet, in the hope that one day they will miraculously fit better. A moment after lamenting his missing boot, Malone admits that 'it did not greatly resemble – but it is wrong of me to dwell upon it – the one I have preserved' (*GII*, 242). Mr Knott, master of the strange house in which Watt serves, is described in a frenzy of indecision about whether to put on 'his boots, or his shoes, or his slippers, or his boot and shoe, or his boot and slipper, or his shoe and slipper' (*GI*, 343). The utterly engrossed pleasure of Mr Knott in acting out his compulsion in this extended scene is infectious, and is passed on to Watt in the form of an increasingly addictive and extreme enumeration of the seemingly limited, but in practice almost endless combinations and orders of words and things around him.

The mystery of Watt's request for money to buy a single boot within the first pages of the novel is solved towards its end, where we discover that he wore a boot on one foot and a shoe on the other.

> Watt wore, on his feet, a boot, brown in colour, and a shoe, happily of a brownish colour also. This boot Watt had bought, for eight pence, from a one-legged man who, having lost his leg, and a fortiori his foot, in an accident, was happy to realise, on his discharge from hospital, for such a sum, his unique remaining marketable asset. He little suspected that he owed this good fortune to Watt's having found, some days before, on the seashore, the shoe, stiff with brine, but otherwise shipshape. (*GI*, 348)

Watt's good fortune is less certain given the sizes of his eclectic footwear: 'In this boot, a twelve, and in this shoe, a ten, Watt, whose size was eleven, suffered, if not agony, at least pain, with his feet, of which each would willingly have changed places with the other, if only for a moment' (*GI*, 348). Such descriptions seem calculated to mock, in their merciless thoroughness, the hopeless efforts of Beckett's characters in wishing their odd pairs of boots even.

Beckett often takes pleasure in giving detailed accounts of his characters' bad feet, in tones which recall the hapless Mr Toots in Dickens's *Dombey and Son* (1848). Heartbroken, Toots has neglected his usually immaculate grooming and dress: 'If you could see my legs when I take my boots off, you'd form some idea of what unrequited affection is.'[57] Beckett's keen interest in bad feet may have partly had its origins in personal experience. His youthful tribute to Joyce of wearing shoes of the same narrow style and size, although Joyce had much smaller and daintier feet, is well known.[58] In *Dream of Fair to Middling Women*, written in 1932, Belacqua purchases 'mighty nailed boots for climbing', but ignores his friend's advice of wearing extra socks, bandaging his feet well and soaping the boots to soften the leather. His feet had been 'sound and strong' that morning, but he tiptoes home barefoot, on 'bloated' and 'bloody' feet, cursing the boots and bestowing them as a gift on a servant who pawns them for drink.[59] Knowlson has quoted Mario Esposito on the source of this passage in an ill-fated Italian hiking trip taken by Beckett:

> He [Beckett] damaged his feet badly and spent the rest of his sojourn in the house of a peasant woman who had let us two rooms in her house. Every few hours she bathed his feet in hot water and herbs which she said would cure him, and did. He got angry with me and a doctor who lived in the same house for joking about him ... On returning to Ireland he wrote me

---

[57] Charles Dickens, *Dombey and Son*, ed. Peter Fairclough (London: Penguin, 1985), p. 769.
[58] See Knowlson, Cronin, Georges Belmont, 'Remembering Sam', in *Beckett in Dublin*, pp. 111–28, 114–15.
[59] Beckett, *Dream of Fair to Middling Women* (New York: Arcade, 1992), p. 129.

two letters which I have, apologising for his rude behaviour to me and the doctor. (*DF*, 73)

Old Boots as Still Lifes

Beckett's interest in boots is not solely concerned with the damage they can do to his characters' health. He also creates certain boots with a painter's eye for colour and detail. Those in *Krapp's Last Tape* (1958) are a 'surprising pair of dirty white boots, size ten at least, very narrow and pointed' (*GIII*, 221). This eye-catching detail has led many commentators to read Krapp's identity from the feet up. Mary Bryden, among others, has suggested that Krapp's white boots are those of a sad and washed-up clown, while Vivian Mercier suggests that Krapp's boots instead recall the 'former cricketer' or 'ex-dandy'.[60] Beckett also draws on colourful boots to conjure an appropriate visual field in the blind space of radio theatre. The colour of Holloway's galoshes in the 1957 radio play *Embers* is given, with great lyricism, twice: 'Vega in the Lyre very green. [*Pause.*] Vega in the Lyre very green' (*GIII*, 199).[61]

Bedridden and dying though he may be, Malone is shocked by the unorthodox footwear of his mysterious visitor in an old-fashioned black suit: 'It was then I saw he was wearing brown boots, which gave me a shock as no words can convey' (*GII*, 265). This is an exaggerated version of the narrator's reaction to the bar manager's brown shoes in *Mercier and Camier* (1946): 'Some purists might have preferred, with his pearl-grey trousers, black shoes to the tan he wore' (*GII*, 472). Malone's horror is more violent even than Moran's disparagement of the ugly suit and shoes of the stranger he will shortly murder: 'He wore a thick navy-blue suit (double breasted) of hideous cut and a pair of outrageously wide black shoes, with the toe-caps higher than the uppers. This dreadful shape seems only to occur in black shoes' (*GII*, 144–45). The 'hideous' portrait of the speaker of *How It Is* is similarly established by enumerating the many flaws in his physical appearance: 'pale staring hair red pudding face with pimples protruding belly gaping fly spindle legs sagging knocking at the knees wide astraddle for greater stability feet splayed'. These

---

[60] See Mary Bryden, 'Clowning with Beckett', in *A Companion to Samuel Beckett*, pp. 358–71; Vivian Mercier, *Beckett/Beckett*, p. 56.
[61] Vega is the brightest star in the constellation Lyra, and is almost directly overhead during the summer in Ireland. See James Stokley, 'Cross Glitters Overhead', *The Science News-Letter*, 42 (August 1942), 138–39, p. 138.

natural flaws are topped with a correspondingly hideous outfit, a visual affront for which he alone might be held responsible: 'green tweeds yellow boots' (*GII*, 429). Beckett also displays a painter's attention to detail when describing the efforts made by Belacqua in *More Pricks than Kicks*, the collection of stories written from 1931 to 1933, to clean from the boots of the guard the mess he has just vomited up on them: 'Contriving two swabs of the Twilight Herald he stooped and cleaned the boots and trouser-ends to the best of his ability. A magnificent and enormous pair of boots emerged' (*GIV*, 128).

The second act of *Waiting for Godot* opens with Estragon deliberating like an aesthete over the pair of boots that are discovered on stage, refusing to commit himself to the colour of either the boots in front of him or the pair he left in the same place the evening before.

> ESTRAGON Mine were black. These are brown.
> VLADIMIR You're sure yours were black?
> ESTRAGON Well they were a kind of grey.
> VLADIMIR And these are brown. Show.
> ESTRAGON [*picking up a boot*] Well they're a kind of green. (*GIII*, 60)

Indeed, Beckett's interest in the visual effect of old boots is most keenly evident in the last moments of the first act of *Waiting for Godot*, when Estragon resolves to discard his boots and carefully places them at the front of the stage, where they remain for the interval.

> [*Estragon gets up and goes towards Vladimir, a boot in each hand. He puts them down at edge of stage, straightens and contemplates the moon.*]
> ...
>
> VLADIMIR Your boots, what are you doing with your boots?
> ESTRAGON [*turning to look at the boots*] I'm leaving them there. [*Pause.*] Another will come, just as ... as ... as me, but with smaller feet, and they'll make him happy. (*GIII*, 45)

Beckett indicates that the curtain falls at the end of the first act, and it is a matter of directorial discretion whether to position Estragon's boots within or outside the stage curtain. If the boots are left on stage in front of the curtain at the very edge of the stage, they fill a visually provocative and generically nebulous role between the acts for those members of the audience who have not made a dash for the bar or bathroom. The brief staging of Estragon's boots during the interval implies that Beckett's meagre drama in either act serves only to tell us the story of these ruined objects. Within reach of the audience, they are simultaneously abandoned yet framed by the curtain behind and the empty space around them, calling attention to their curious visual dynamic.

These abandoned boots have a sculptural self-sufficiency that makes them extraordinarily expressive. Discarded boots such as these offer a potent illustration of Beckett's fascination with the inscribed, embedded history of things as they migrate from person to person and place to place. Still warm from the actor, Estragon's boots hold the shape of the feet that have moulded them, and resonate with that strange poignancy typical of a still life, *une nature morte*. It is apt, then, that when Estragon fusses over the precise arrangement of the boots at the end of the first act, he carefully aligns them as though he were preparing a still life study. If, however, the curtain closes over to conceal the boots during the interval, it means that the second act opens by dramatically revealing the boots on an empty stage: '*Estragon's boots front centre, heels together, toes splayed*' (*GIII*, 49). Whatever the directorial decision, the first act will end and second begin with a focus on Estragon's boots, a privileging of these objects that may recall one of Vincent van Gogh's series of still life paintings of old boots, an affinity that has already been briefly noted by *The Grove Companion*.[62]

In a friend's account, the pairs of old boots Van Gogh bought at flea markets to paint were on occasion not battered enough for his purposes, so he would pull them on and trudge through the muddy streets of Paris until he deemed them sufficiently deformed with the character he sought.[63] Van Gogh's still life studies of such boots are notable for the extraordinary degree of attention he pays to the line and colour of the ruined material and lopsided, mismatched features of such boots. His application of oils in greasy, fleshy layers and sensitive attention to details such as laces and signs of wear in the leather, together with his discreet use of light and colour makes these still lifes a miracle of intensity in miniature. The lack of background or rival elements to contextualise or distract from the boots in these sparse compositions signals the central importance of boots as painterly subjects for Van Gogh. His decision, moreover,

---

[62] 'Estragon's boots suggest Van Gogh's various paintings of *souliers* (a similar pair, "lacerated and gaping", is among the "insignia" of "Text 8")' (*GC*, 71). In *The Truth in Painting*, Jacques Derrida has written compellingly about Van Gogh's paintings of boots in terms that are strikingly applicable to the boots in Beckett's writing: 'These objects concern us. Their detachment is obvious. Unlaced, abandoned, detached from the subject (wearer, holder or owner, or even author-signatory) and detached / untied in themselves (the laces are untied)'. See Derrida, *The Truth in Painting*, trans. Geoff Bennington and Ian McLeod (Chicago: The University of Chicago Press, 1987), p. 261.

[63] The friend was Francois Gauzi (1861–1933), a fellow student of Van Gogh's at Cormon's studio. See Gauzi, 'Vincent van Gogh (1886–87)', in *Van Gogh in Perspective*, ed. Bogomila Welsh-Ovcharov (New Jersey: Prentice-Hall, 1974), pp. 33–34.

to position them in the centre of the painting, facing out or at a slant, creates a visual dynamic where they fix the viewer with a regard every bit as searching as his or her own, eyeing them directly or looking at them askance, as the case may be. In a letter to his brother Theo in December 1882, Van Gogh wrote that 'what matters is to grasp what does not pass away in what passes away', and it is clear that this is a quality he wanted to capture in his painting.[64] Beckett evidently shared this fascination with the sensuality of wear and tear, especially as a mnemonic for the passage of time and mortality, and for both artists the means of procedure is that of salvaging the object. Old boots are literally the basest elements of dress, taking on the shape of a foot as the old skin of leather moulds itself around the living foot. They are thus intimately associated with that foot. Like an empty glove, the well-worn boot registers the deterioration of foot and boot, flesh and leather, and of all material things as life passes. To a greater degree than any other item of dress, the old boot is thus a humble relic. To stage or describe an abandoned pair of boots is to evoke the simultaneous fragility and determination of the missing walker, the traces of whose journey through life we observe in the worn and empty boots they have left behind.

The gloomy subjects of Van Gogh's 1886 *Shoes* (Figure 3) are as 'lacerated and gaping' as those in the eighth of Beckett's *Texts for Nothing* (*GIV*, 322–23), with their uppers apparently falling apart in weariness, and their laces a tangled, disorganised mass. This pair is moreover composed of two left boots, making them as perversely ill-suited for walking as the footwear of many of Beckett's characters. In Beckett's writing, as in Van Gogh's paintings, an unlaced, flapping old boot has a particular semiotic quality, a plangently inflected logic of inevitable material and physical decay. Such worn-out old boots draw attention to themselves as impediments to the very function they were designed for, suggesting by implication that the character wearing such footwear will not be going far.

Beckett had a plain two-room house built in Ussy-sur-Marne in 1953, which became his retreat outside Paris when he wanted to escape the distractions of the city in order to write. Inside this spartan house, all was functional, clean and orderly, with everything in its place. In preparation

---

[64] Van Gogh, letter to Theo van Gogh, between Wednesday 13 and Monday 18 December 1882, The Hague. See *Vincent van Gogh: The Letters*, ed. Leo Jansen, Hans Luijten, Nienke Bakker (Amsterdam & The Hague: Van Gogh Museum & Huygens ING, 2009). http://vangoghletters.org/en/let294 [accessed 22 December 2015].

Figure 3 Vincent van Gogh, *Shoes* (1886).
Courtesy of Van Gogh Museum and Foundation, Amsterdam.

for his 1996 documentary study of Beckett, the filmmaker Seán O'Mórdha visited Ussy in 1983 to develop a plan for shooting and noticed under Beckett's kitchen table three or four pairs of tough walking boots, all very worn, but well maintained, symmetrically arranged in a neat line. I discussed this with O'Mórdha, whose description recalled Van Gogh's 1886 group study *Three Pairs of Shoes* (Figure 4). O'Mórdha did not include Beckett's boots in the film because he felt it would be a breach of privacy, given the peculiar intimacy of well-worn boots or shoes. Instead, he used a comparable image: a long shot of the inside of the shed where Beckett's gardening tools including rakes, shovels, hedge clippers and an old fashioned hoe, were hung up on nails in lines as neatly as the boots in the kitchen.[65] The shot is mesmerising, and the objects seem to speak eloquently of the thorough, methodical nature of the man. O'Mórdha said

---

[65] Knowlson also comments on the precision of this arrangement in *Samuel Beckett: As the Story Was Told*, describing Beckett's gardening tools as being 'ranged meticulously in two long rows, large tools like a scythe, rakes, forks and spades on the row above, small tools, like a hand fork, garden shears and trowels on the row beneath' (*DF*, 389).

Figure 4 Vincent van Gogh, *Three Pairs of Shoes* (1886).
Courtesy of Fogg Art Museum, Harvard University.

that Beckett, with whom he was friendly, 'never threw out a thing that could be used again'.[66] It seems to me that this is not unlike his creative practice, where his poor materials are used again and again during a fifty-five-year creative period.

In Beckett's writing, walking is equated with living, and life is imagined as a *via dolorosa*. In *The Practice of Everyday Life* (1984), the social philosopher Michel de Certeau asserts that 'To walk is to lack a place.'[67] All Beckett's characters who can, walk. The incapacitated narrator of *Malone Dies*, trying to piece together how he came to be in the strange bed in which he finds himself, observes: 'But what is the last thing I remember, I could start from there, before I came to my senses again here? That too is lost. I was walking certainly, all my life I have been walking, except the first few months and since I have been here' (*GII*, 177). Similarly, in the bizarre 'birth' that is imagined in *Texts for Nothing 9*, a hunched little old man, shod in heavy boots, tramps out and into a life of walking.

> [I]t would be the first step on the long travelable road, destination tomb, to be trod without a word, tramp tramp, little heavy irrevocable steps, down the

---

[66] Personal interview with O'Mórdha, 18 October 2010, Dublin.
[67] Michel de Certeau, *The Practice of Everyday Life*, trans. Steven Rendall (Berkeley, Los Angeles, London: University of California Press, 1988), p. 103.

long tunnels at first, then under the mortal skies, through the days and nights, faster and faster, no, slower and slower, for obvious reasons (*GIV*, 325).

Walking and restlessness are such important elements of Beckett's writing that three of the four chapters in this book explore this theme from different perspectives, while the remaining chapter concentrates on two characters (of whom Malone is one) who have both been imprisoned by immobility. Beckett's old boots register the imperative of leave-taking for his peripatetic characters, the very condition of whose lives is defined as a pointless journey. Much of Beckett's fiction is dominated by the motif of a figure covering great distances on foot, but this motif evidently cannot be transferred to the stage. Even if his characters cannot leave the confines of the stage or their fictional shelters, however, pacing is an obsessive and very necessary occupation.

Old Boots and Death

Beckett's treatment of death has received considerable attention. A number of critics have responded eagerly to the ribald disdain for life expressed by several of Beckett's characters by recuperating such instances as an acceptance of mortality. In his far-ranging 1993 study, *Beckett's Dying Words*, Christopher Ricks celebrates this aspect of Beckett's writing:

> So that although it makes sense to read Beckett, as many do, as a writer who is oddly criss-crossed, a writer who manages to be excruciatingly funny despite his possessing a deeply dispiriting apprehension of life, the opposite makes sense too: the conviction that Beckett's apprehension of death is not dispiriting, but is wise and fortifying, and therefore is unsurprisingly the lens of his translucent comedy.[68]

---

[68] Christopher Ricks, *Beckett's Dying Words: The Clarendon Lectures, 1990* (Oxford: Oxford University Press, 1993), p. 20. A similarly affirmative reading of Beckett's treatment of death features in several essays in *Beckett and Death*, ed. Simon Barfield, Philip Tew and Matthew Feldman (London: Continuum, 2009). Death is figured as a positive term in Beckett's compositional process by Mark Nixon, and as providing opportunities for political, aesthetic, philosophical and linguistic aporetics by Shane Weller, Paul Stewart, Sean Lawlor and Elizabeth Barry. Simon Critchley and Alain Badiou have also insisted on the central importance of a transformative ethics where death becomes a positive term in Beckett's work. Critchley focuses on what he describes as Beckett's ethical comedy, while Badiou argues that the imperative for Beckett's characters and narratives to continue constitutes an affirmative ethical position. See Simon Critchley, *Very Little ... Almost Nothing: Death, Philosophy, Literature* (London: Routledge, 1997); Alain Badiou, *On Beckett*, ed. Nina Power and Alberto Toscano (Manchester: Clinamen, 2003); *Beckett and Ethics*, ed. Russell Smith (London: Continuum, 2009).

In paying tribute to such an affirmative formulation of death, however, Ricks seems to have in mind the American poet Robert Lowell rather than Beckett. Twelve pages before the above passage, Ricks quotes Lowell's masterful docking of the cliché: 'All's well that ends', and observes, 'This acknowledgement, life yielding to death, is a wording grimly glad to be suddenly cut short.'[69] To my mind, Ricks's lines on the fortifying wisdom and translucent comedy of Beckett's writing on death is more apt as a response to Lowell's 'emergency amputation'. Death is designated by Beckett, not so much as the inevitable end of life by which standard all else seems futile, and is therefore relegated to the stuff of comedy, but rather as an impossible return to the peace before life. Death is therefore most strongly marked by grief, not desire. Beckett's narrators and characters, moreover, do not express envy for those gone before them so much as mourn their absence.

In several works, Beckett explicitly associates old boots with death. Old boots are expressive objects for partings, as they so tangibly declare the distance travelled in them, but, having served their purpose are left behind like a shed skin. The sound of boots, moreover, implies leave-taking. In *Endgame*, the blind Hamm argues against Clov leaving the shelter, warning, 'Outside of here it's death', but he is struck later in the play by the sound of Clov's boots, as each step taps out the threat of imminent departure (*GIII*, 97).

> HAMM [*irritably*] What's wrong with your feet?
> CLOV My feet?
> HAMM Tramp! Tramp!
> CLOV I must have put on my boots.
> HAMM Your slippers were hurting you?
> [*Pause*.] (*GIII*, 133)

Endgame takes its place among several other works in which Beckett uses the sound of footsteps to achieve certain effects. The dragging feet and panting of Maddy Rooney trudging along to meet the train are such an example in the radio play *All That Fall*, as is the repeated sound of 'Henry's boots on shingle' in *Embers* (*GIII*, 157, 197). Beckett specifies that the manic pacing of the four figures around a small space in *Quad* (1981) should, at times, be clearly audible, impressing upon the audience the unceasing motion of the figures: 'Percussion intermittent in all combinations to allow footsteps alone to be heard at intervals' (*GIII*, 480). In

---

[69] Ricks, *Beckett's Dying Words*, p.8.

That Time (1974–75) the Listener remembers the almost silent tread of the attendant in the Portrait Gallery, 'drowsing around in his felt shufflers not a sound to be heard only every now and then a shuffle of felt drawing near then dying away' (*GIII*, 418). The Speaker of *A Piece of Monologue* (1977–79) does not move, but his noticeable 'white socks' encourage us to imagine the precisely delineated movements of this figure narrated in the piece as occuring in near silence (*GIII*, 453). Similarly, Beckett first dresses the old man and child of the late prose piece *Worstward Ho* (1981–82) in the outfit worn by so many of his wandering characters: 'Black greatcoats to heels. Dim black. Bootheels', but then takes their boots away, leaving them barefoot and, by implication, with far less distance to cover (*GIV*, 474, 476).

Those characters whose feet are bootless and footsteps are soundless are inevitably close to death. The three solicitous figures of *Come and Go* (1965) that leave the stage in sequence must do so silently because of their 'light shoes with rubber soles' (*GIII*, 387). *Footfalls* (1975) is organised around this conceit. Her life spent attending to her ailing mother, May compulsively walks up and down a lit strip onstage, her footstep a 'clearly audible rhythmic tread'. The sound of her steps is an essential element in this soothing compulsion, and she tells her confused mother that she 'must hear the feet, however faint they fall' (*GIII*, 427, 429). The comforting effect of hearing her footfalls, it is implied, is in registering the ground she covers as she paces. Cronin reports Beckett as having told him that Beckett's own father had 'walked himself to death' (*LM*, 29). The final directions of *Footfalls* stage this claim. As if to further emphasise the finality of May's disappearance, having walked herself into thin air, *Footfalls* is one of Beckett's few plays that calls for a curtain at its conclusion. The figure of May, barely there in her life, her tattered gown giving the impression of no more corporeality than a handful of feathers, simply dissolves and vanishes at the end of this short play.

Another explicit illustration of Beckett's suggestion that all the walking done by his characters is towards death occurs in the late prose piece *Ill Seen Ill Said*. At the heart of the story is a grieving old woman who, in her haste to reach the mysterious 'zone of stones', repeatedly raises her skirt to her calf, revealing her boots and stockings. In this study of urgent, repeated visits, possibly to a grave, the deterioration of the old woman's boots is memorably condensed into a single image: a deformed buttonhook removed from her boot and hanging on the wall by a nail like a painting.

> Weeping over as weeping will see now the buttonhook larger than life. Of tarnished silver pisciform it hangs by its hook from a nail ... The oval

handle is wrought to a semblance of scales. The shank a little bent leads up to the hook the eye so far still dry. A lifetime of hooking still lessened its curvature … Since when it hangs useless from the nail … Silver shimmers some evenings when the skies are clear. Close-up then. In which in defiance of reason the nail prevails. Long this image till suddenly it blurs. (*GIV*, 455)

This buttonhook is not itself beyond repair, but the old woman is beyond repairing it. As frequently happens in Beckett, the resonance of this object derives from a play on words: the buttonhook, like Estragon's jettisoned boots, has been 'hung up'. In Estragon's case, this action teasingly suggests great changes in the second act of the play, but the corresponding scene in *Ill Seen Ill Said* forecasts nothing but sterility and death.

Old Boots and the Twentieth Century

We are primed to identify in Beckett's boots echoes of the displacement and forced exile that characterised the experiences of many in Europe during the twentieth century. Marjorie Perloff has explored the affinities between the fictional world of *Waiting for Godot* and the Second World War through a comparison of the French and English passages in which Vladimir and Estragon speak of wandering in the Pyrenees:

> In the original French version, Beckett specifies more fully: 'Nous irons,' Gogo tells Didi, 'dans l'Ariège,' and he adds, 'J'ai toujours voulu me balader dans l'Ariège.' The joke here is that the Ariège was hardly a place suitable for wandering. Also known as 'Le Chemin de la Liberté' … it was the chief World War II escape route from France to Spain – a route chosen to avoid all official checkpoints and any likely contact with German patrols.[70]

Beckett's biographers relate his personal experiences of living 'on the hoof' during the war.[71] He and his partner, Suzanne, spent six weeks on the run after their last-minute escape from Paris in 1942, too panicked and pressed for time to pack and bring things with them. They sought assistance from a series of friends and acquaintances, hiding and sleeping by day and tentatively moving towards Roussillon during the night. Once there, Beckett worked as a labourer to provide their food:

> Soon Beckett established a routine of going to work on a more or less daily basis on the Audes' farm. The farmer was generous with food …

---

[70] See Perloff, '"In Love with Hiding": Samuel Beckett's War', 76–77.
[71] See also *DF*, 321; *LM*, 328–29.

> In exchange, Beckett worked without being paid in the fields, woods or vineyard. Often accompanied by Suzanne, he would walk the four kilometres down to the farm, mostly taking a little-known path to avoid running into unexpected German patrols. (*DF*, 324–25)

During his long trek to safety with Suzanne when fleeing Paris, or when working in the fields, woods or vineyards in Roussillon, it is likely that sturdy footwear was often on Beckett's mind. Indeed, Beckett seems to have found old boots peculiarly expressive objects for this experience of the disruption of war on a personal level. Knowlson has remarked the emphasis in Beckett's wartime and post-war writing 'on feeling and in *not* knowing'.[72] Beckett may not have written directly about the war in his creative works, but they are suffused with the spirit of confusion, want and dim threat that he experienced as a daily reality in Occupied France. As Cronin observes: 'Wars quickly establish their own normality. For almost six years Beckett's normality had been that of a country where almost everybody's life was torn or disrupted by the exigencies of conflict' (*LM*, 342). In setting him up as the saviour of post-war literature, Theodor Adorno claimed that 'Beckett turns existential philosophy from its head back on its feet.'[73] He might have substituted the phrase 'into its boots'.

There are, however, very few direct references to the war in his work: Beckett was in fact extraordinarily reluctant to voice his experiences or those of others during the war. In his account of translating Beckett's letters, George Craig notes the dramatic switch to a policy of 'understatement' between the first volume of Beckett's letters, covering the years 1929–40, and the second volume (1941–56).

> Beckett's work in the Resistance has been described in some detail; but never by him. The horrors of war and Occupation are vividly present to him: he will not write about them. What we know of his loyalty to his friends will tell us what their death means to him; he will not. What we see is a sort of crack in the surface of his writing; we have ourselves to imagine what lies beneath it … Beckett talks, unforgettably, of the need to express: but expressing is not turning on a confessional tap.[74]

---

[72] James Knowlson and John Haynes, *Images of Beckett* (Cambridge: Cambridge University Press, 2003), p. 38.
[73] Theodor Adorno, 'Trying to Understand Endgame', trans. Michael T. Jones, *New German Critique*, 26 (Spring–Summer 1982), 119–150, 130.
[74] George Craig, *Writing Beckett's Letters*, *The Cahiers Series*: 16 (Paris: Sylph, 2011), p. 29.

In a 1956 interview with Israel Shenker, Beckett famously set out what he was attempting to achieve in his writing with uncharacteristic candour: 'My little exploration is that whole zone of being that has always been set aside by artists as something unusable – as something by definition incompatible with art.'[75] To do this, Beckett had to find a way of writing from nowhere.

In the introduction to this book, I suggested that Beckett's body of work is the final iteration of a certain European cultural and intellectual tradition. Upon his death, the *Irish Times* published a piece by John Banville, which paid tribute to Beckett as the representative of an era that had now concluded:

> In the death of Samuel Beckett a long generation finds its end. For all the seeming iconoclasm of his work, he was the product of his age, that age which nurtured Joyce and Yeats and Eliot, Proust, and Rilke, and Thomas Mann. They were the moderns (with a lower-case m we can just about squeeze them all in under that heading), yet to a man they took the classical as their touchstone and their model. Now they are all dead ... The novels and the plays make a sort of broken Ark of the Covenant, wherein we find preserved the jumbled remnants of our culture: a snatch of Schubert, a memory of Milton's cosmology, a night, tempestuous and bright, such as Kaspar David Friedrich loved. This is the shattered song of our time.
>
> For if Beckett represents continuity with the classical world, he also bears witness to the ending of an era.[76]

Just as Cronin identified Beckett as 'The Last Modernist', Amit Majmudar, in a similar rhetorical turn, has named George Steiner 'the last European'.[77] In terms of the register of their writing, there could scarcely seem two less compatible figures than Beckett and Steiner, but the implications of their having each been identified as the terminal point of closely related cultures bears examination. Like Steiner, Beckett's cultural inheritance

---

[75] Israel Shenker, 'An Interview with Beckett', *New York Times*, 5 May 1956, Section II, 1, 3; reprinted in *Samuel Beckett: The Critical Heritage*, ed. Lawrence Graver and Raymond Federman (London: Routledge and Kegan Paul, 1979), pp. 146–149, p. 148. In *Arts of Impoverishment*, Leo Bersani and Ulysse Dutoit interpret Beckett's deliberately impoverished art rather differently. They consider Beckett, with the painter Mark Rothko and filmmaker Alain Resnais, to be challenging the established canons of art and authority. See Bersani and Dutoit, *Arts of Impoverishment: Beckett, Rothko, Resnais* (Cambridge: Harvard University Press, 1993), p. 8.
[76] John Banville, 'Samuel Beckett Dies in Paris Aged 83', *Irish Times*, 25 December 1989, p. 18.
[77] Amit Majmudar, 'George Steiner, Last of the Europeans', *Kenyon Review* 34, No. 4 (Fall 2012), 178–187, p. 187.

spanned the intellectual and creative achievements of Europe: this was the subject of his undergraduate education at Trinity College Dublin, and for the rest of his life, he pursued his reading with the avidity of an autodidact. It is unlikely that Europe will again produce a writer or scholar as immersed in its heritage as Beckett or Steiner. While Steiner has been a tireless polymath, I hope to have shown in this chapter that Beckett's sense of coming at the end of a period and culture finds expression instead in his creative translation of indigence into a new literary form. This is the literary salvage we see in practice when Beckett writes about bowler hats and old boots: a form of writing that looks back on a shattered world and contents itself with hoarding the remaining scraps and fragments, cradling them until the anticipated end.

In this chapter I have tried to suggest how Beckett puts a pair of objects to use in his wider project of setting his writing apart: the shabby bowler hat gives away Beckett's characters as failed sons and citizens, far from the kind of men their families, like Beckett's own, would have wished them to become, while extended descriptions and set pieces with old boots mark the importance for characters who are at home nowhere, of having the means of moving on to the next place. The bowler hats and old boots in Beckett's writing forcefully convey the fundamental homelessness of his characters; ultimately, this loss or lack of home means that they can speak of nowhere and nothing with authority. Beckett's testimony to the painter Jack B. Yeats, written for a Paris exhibition by the eighty-three-year-old painter, included the line 'The artist who stakes his being is from nowhere, has no kith', and this claim is one he carried out, to a remarkable degree and with exemplary effect, in the imaginative no-man's-land he subsequently carved out for himself.[78] I have described bowler hats and old boots as relics to emphasise how they are symbolically oriented towards the past, to what has been left behind or is no more. As an iconic twentieth-century item of dress, the bowler hat carries with it a host of associations, but for Beckett, the most germane of these are the social and cultural values he disdained and rejected as a young writer: Protestant Irish middle-class piety, professionalism and, above all, unquestioning adherence to habits of thought and behaviour. Old boots, on the other hand, have a single overriding symbolic value, and function as a *memento mori*: elegiac objects that are evocative of pathos and mortality. As a relic of the social values rejected by Beckett, the

---

[78] Beckett, 'Hommage à Jack B. Yeats / Homage to Jack B. Yeats', in *Disjecta: Miscellaneous Writings and a Dramatic Fragment*, ed. Ruby Cohn (New York: Grove, 1984), pp. 148–49, p. 149.

bowler hat comes in for enthusiastically rough treatment in his writing from the 1930s to 1950s, and in undermining or flattening it, he illustrates precisely his opinion of conventional respectability and hard-headed thought. By contrast, old boots are abject, humble relics. It is the very ordinariness of old boots, their banal utility and the readiness of their material to display signs of age and decay, which gives them such poetic resonance.

Bowler hats and old boots are also relics in the sense that they are both valuable objects in Beckett's establishment of a singular form of writing. These objects first feature in his poetry and fiction of the 1930s, and by following their various iterations over the years and between media, it is possible to chart the ways in which Beckett modified the literary blank canvas that he had set out to create in the 1930s. He did so by deliberately wrenching his writing free of the hold of tradition and place. Beckett's many years without literary success gave him the freedom to write as he wished, and without a readership for his poetry and novels in the 1930s, Beckett's writing steadily gained the quality of a voice speaking to itself. This was also the period when he first began to write in French.[79] Beckett had a natural facility for French and, as is clear from the elaborate games-playing of his letters from the 1940s and 1950s, writing in French did nothing to dampen his linguistic capacity. However, in adopting French as the language of composition for many of his works, and negotiating the distance between French and English in his subsequent self-translations, he had evidently wrong-footed himself as a writer, and deliberately destabilised his creative process. Beckett was asked about his turn to French on many occasions, and he supplied a range of different explanations. One was his aim to write 'sans style', a statement that calls to mind the abundance of style and the comfortable, not to say swaggering, authorial posturing of his early work in English, written under the influence of Joyce and self-consciously aligned with European modernism.[80] Another was his desire to 'impoverish' himself 'still further'.[81] However, as Sinéad Mooney has astutely noted, 'if Beckett's switch to French is repeatedly linked to reduction, weakening, and self-impoverishment, other scattered comments made by him on the topic suggest that writing in French was as

---

[79] After settling in Paris in 1937, Beckett began to write poetry in French, telling Tom McGreevy in 1938, 'I have the feeling that any poems there may happen to be in the future will be in French'. During the Second World War, Beckett began to write fiction in French too. (*LI*, 614).
[80] Beckett's quote appears in Niklaus Gessner, *Die Unzulänglichkeit der Sprache: eine Untersuchung über Formzufall und Beziehunglosigkeit bei Samuel Beckett* (Zurich: Junis Verlag, 1957), p. 32.
[81] Michael Edwards, 'Beckett's French', *Translation and Literature*, 1 (1992), 68–83, p. 77.

much an assertion of self as an abdication.'[82] In the 1930s, Beckett's work also developed its characteristically skewed realism, where jobs, homes and families are overlooked in favour of the scavenging vagabondage of isolated, misanthropic figures who wander on the edges of towns, or, more often, in woods and on back roads. I suggest that Beckett's elective estrangement from authorial fluency by writing in a non-native language or through self-translation is directly comparable to his adoption of the poor materials under study in this book. As a writer who continuously and provocatively challenged the limits of his writing throughout his career, the paradoxically liberating appeal of reducing his artistic palette in these two ways is not to be underestimated. Although he grumbled about it, I believe that Beckett adopted self-translation as his dominant method of composition. Like the limited number of worn-out things to which he showed such stubborn attachment, it was a form of literary impoverishment that, in fact, held surprisingly fertile resources and offered the prospect of a distinctively new form of writing.

These discoveries are both analogous with the agricultural practice of gleaning, which Beckett experienced while working as a labourer in Roussillon in 1942. He found himself walking tilled fields after the crops had been harvested, searching for any vegetables that might have been left behind. Many years later, Beckett recalled his discovery of an overlooked potato while gleaning, and described it, with none of his characteristic understatement, as a 'triumph' (*DF*, 323). When we try to understand why Beckett wrote as he did, focusing on subject matter that had hitherto been ignored in prose and monologue forms that eschewed literary convention, we could do worse than picture him as a gleaner, walking along drills of turned earth, head bowed and intent. In his introduction to the second volume of Beckett's letters of the 1940s and 1950s, Dan Gunn notes the repeated references to gardening and specifically to digging in the letters, which cover the period when Beckett spent much time in his house in Ussy-sur-Marne outside Paris. These references reveal his sense of the strong affinity between the manual labour of turning the ground to move beneath its surface, and the imaginative labour of sitting at his desk and similarly attempting to unearth material (*LII*, lxxii–lxxiv). Beckett also made this comparison between writing and digging himself, in a letter written from Ussy to his friend Ethna MacCarthy in 1959: 'My silly old body is here alone with the snow and the crows and the exercise-book

---

[82] Sinéad Mooney, 'Beckett in French and English', in *A Companion to Samuel Beckett*, pp. 196–208, p. 196.

that opens like a door and lets me far down into the now friendly dark.' (*LIII*, 195)

Beckett's attempts over the years to achieve more with steadily fewer literary resources may have offered ways of keeping himself interested in the process of writing, but more than anything, those attempts convey Beckett's intense, ascetic view of the purpose and what he described in *Proust* as the 'excavatory' nature of art (*GIV*, 539). In this manner, Beckett set about recasting bowler hats and old boots, the detritus of his century, as relics. Fugitive writing, in its disavowal of certainty and authority, and exploration of subjects that were hitherto dismissed or overlooked, is intimately preoccupied with salvage, and is a literary form of gleaning. Beckett recovered from annihilation marginal stories, accounts of victims, ignored and isolated things that would otherwise never see the light of day and thus made of his own sense of estrangement an imaginative home for himself, a unique space in and from which to write. Battered bowlers and old boots are crucial elements in establishing the necessary conditions for the new and distinct form of literature Beckett sought to create: a mode of writing that would not speak for any audience, and not of any society, but rather concern itself with the portrayal of dispossession, failure and confusion. Like the contents of the suitcase Dovlatov's emigré narrator brings with him, bowler hats and old boots are relics from a vanished world, and while they evoke the shattered past, they can never recover it in its entirety.

CHAPTER 2

Heirlooms

Greatcoats, Widow's Weeds, Feminine Hats, Rocking Chairs, Beds

Sites of Memory

Beginning the day after his mother's death, the French literary philosopher Roland Barthes kept a record of his grief on small pieces of paper he carried about with him. These assorted bits of paper were published posthumously as his *Mourning Diary* (2011). Among these scattered notes, Barthes muses over his compulsion to include his mother in his writing, and identifies what he hopes to achieve: by writing a tribute to her, he would save her from the perfect extinction that awaits all but literary creations.[1] This belief in the power of literature to shore up the memory of deceased loved ones was evidently shared by Beckett. Knowlson has described Beckett's demonstration, even in the last months of his life, of 'feelings of love for his mother and remorse at having, as he saw it, let her down so frequently', and how these feelings were so 'intense, almost volcanic', that his relationship with her remained a taboo subject for Beckett and his biographer (*DF*, 670). Beckett's writing prompted bewilderment in his father and outrage in his mother. It was one of his expressed regrets that both parents died before he achieved any substantial acclaim as an author, because he felt that he had been a failure as a son. Beckett's cousin Sheila Page voiced the same regret: 'If only they could have lived to have seen the success that he's been. But they used to think: "if only he'd write something we could understand"' (*BR*, 12).

Beckett may have been only dimly aware of his motives when he returned, over and over again, to memories of his parents for his characters'

---

[1] Roland Barthes, *Mourning Diary*, annotated Nathalie Léger, trans. Richard Howard (London: Notting Hill Editions, 2011), p. 113, 234.

dress and props and for the imaginative setting of much of his writing, but this recurrent use of parental heirlooms builds up memorials to his parents while profoundly altering the emotional register of his writing. The space dedicated to these heirlooms in Beckett's work can be described as sites of memory, privileged sites established through idiosyncratic and intimate items of his parents' dress, and through the maternal domestic space and paternal walking landscape with which either parent is so firmly identified. By focusing on items of dress often worn by his parents, and on those settings in which they spent much of their time, Beckett taps into the two means by which memory is mediated, according to the philosopher Edward Casey: through the body and through place. Casey has challenged the hegemony of older models of memory that privilege notions of calling images and impressions of the past 'to the mind's eye' in favour of 'a more nuanced model', in which body and place are seen to hold memories. Casey argues that 'concrete places retain the past in a way that can be reanimated by our remembering them', and that 'Body memories are not just memories *of* the body but instances of remembering places, events, and people *with* and *in* the lived body.' Beckett's writing follows the pattern described by Casey, where 'body and place, both ensconced in the life-world of the rememberer, assume an unaccustomed prominence'.[2] The landscape traversed in walks with his father, and the maternal bedroom, rocking chair or bed, embed traces of Beckett's parents in the spaces of his writing. Beckett's use of greatcoats and widow's weeds, moreover, emphasises physical intimacy in the function of parental objects in his writing, for greatcoats and widow's weeds are both 'wrapping materials' that carry with them the conventional beliefs and thoughts of a particular time and place, as well as the specific and ghostly expression of literal embraces by Beckett's mother and father.[3]

Beckett's turn towards memories of his parents after their deaths is a remembering, however, that is subject to control, an imaginative recollection in which invention and memory work together. It is notable that like Casey, the neuroscientist Gerald Edelman also prefers the active term 'remembering' to 'memory'. Edelman has insisted that memory is not a mechanical but a 'dynamic' process, and should not be considered 'a fixed storage of all the variants of a scene, say of a familiar room visited

---

[2] Edward Casey, *Remembering: A Phenomenological Study*, xi.
[3] On 'wrapping materials', see *Wrapping and Unwrapping Material Culture: Archaeological and Anthropological Perspectives*, ed. Laurence Douny and Susanna Harris (Walnut Creek: Left Coast Press, 2014).

on multiple occasions'.[4] In *Second Nature* (2006), Edelman suggests that 'every act of perception is to some degree an act of creation, and every act of memory is to some degree an act of imagination'.[5] The translator Michael Hamburger has made a similar observation. During the writing of his memoirs, Hamburger noted his discovery of the intimate relationship between memory and invention, and described memory as 'a darkroom for the development of fictions'.[6] Similarly, the Argentinian writer Jorge Luis Borges, Beckett's near-contemporary, includes in 'Tlön, Uqbar, Orbis Tertius' (1941), his story of an illusory and carefully invented world, a comment about the need and power of memory that bears quite closely upon Beckett's use of parental heirlooms. Having been called into existence by a mass effort of imagination, aspects of the world of Tlön must be continuously remembered, and reimagined, in order to remain standing:

> Things … tend to grow vague or 'sketchy', and to lose detail when they begin to be forgotten. The classic example is the doorway that continued to exist so long as a certain beggar frequented it, but which was lost to sight when he died. Sometimes a few birds, a horse, have saved the ruins of an amphitheatre.[7]

The impact of the returning beggar, birds and horse to parts of the imagined world of Tlön, where their presence sharpens the details of the places they visit, is comparable to the impact of the recurring parental heirlooms of greatcoats, feminine hats, widow's weeds, rocking chairs and maternal beds. Something that Borges celebrates in the above lines is, of course, the ability of words to transcend the falling into ruin of the ostensibly far less transient material world. Beckett's parental heirlooms realise this mysterious power of literature through the incantatory effect of their repeated use. Beckett's discreet, patient and devoted gestures of dressing so many of his male characters in greatcoats and female characters in striking hats, and of setting so much of his writing in spaces identified with either of his parents, is a tribute that precisely evokes the insistence of grieving memory, while inscribing traces of his father and mother into the fabric of his writing. By these means, he also transfers to his characters or narrators the hazy compulsion to salvage shards of memory.

---

[4] Gerald M. Edelman, *Second Nature: Brain Science and Human Knowledge* (New Haven: Yale University Press, 2006), p. 59.
[5] Edelman, *Second Nature: Brain Science and Human Knowledge*, p. 100.
[6] Hamburger, 'Translator's Note', in W.G. Sebald and Jan Peter Tripp, *Unrecounted: 33 Texts and 33 Etchings*, p. 3.
[7] Jorge Luis Borges, 'Tlön, Uqbar, Orbis Tertius', in *Collected Fictions*, trans. Andrew Hurley (London: Penguin, 1998), p. 78.

The act of remembering, and the attempts to recover fragments of the past from erasure and annihilation by time and forgetfulness, occupy an increasingly central position in Beckett's work over the course of his writing life. Beckett's fictional, poetic and dramatic narratives are all characterised by the loss of ground that follows the experience of being overwhelmed by partial memory, and by the effort to uncover more of the moment glimpsed. When speaking to Knowlson about the many imperfectly or incorrectly remembered quotes in *Happy Days*, Beckett observed, 'I suppose all is reminiscence from womb to tomb.'[8] The sites of memory in Beckett's work cause his writing to become iterative and fragmentary in form, as the structure and register of his narratives take on the quality of the efforts, rewards and perils of compulsive remembering. Beckett's writing is thus suffused with the poignant haziness of the attempt to recover fleeting, vanished moments. This chapter demonstrates that Beckett's work is centrally preoccupied with the recovery of memories through parental heirlooms, and that after lingering descriptions and extensive use in many works, such heirlooms acquire the resonant potential Philip Larkin had in mind when he spoke of certain objects that 'link us to our losses'.[9] Beckett was also engaged in an extended meditation on the nature of literary invention. His authorial procedure here is to offer his characters access to memories of their mourned loved ones through heirlooms that are intimately identified with his own parents. This manipulation of the emotional landscape of his grieving characters indicates the degree to which Beckett drew on personal memories and emotions in the writing process. By dressing his characters in his parents' clothes and placing them in scenarios that are versions of the places in which his parents were most often to be found, Beckett links his characters to his own losses.

Heirlooms

The objects examined in this chapter are all items of dress or furniture that were worn and used by Beckett's mother and father, and are used by Beckett to inscribe, with great tenderness, traces of both parents into his writing. An heirloom is a 'piece of personal property that has been

---

[8] Beckett, letter to Knowlson, 11 April 1972, quoted in Knowlson, 'Beckett's "Bits of Pipe"', in *Samuel Beckett: Humanistic Perspectives*, ed. Morris Beja, S.E. Gontarski and Pierre Astier (Columbus: Ohio State University Press, 1983), pp. 16–25, p. 16.
[9] Philip Larkin, 'Reference Back' in *Collected Poems*, ed. Anthony Thwaite (Victoria: Marvell and Faber, 2003), p. 111.

in a family for several generations' or anything 'inherited from a line of ancestors, or handed down from generation to generation'.[10] The form of salvage explored in this chapter is Beckett's recovery from annihilation of the buried treasure of memories of his parents through objects and places explicitly and intimately identified with them. Both sets of parental heirlooms announce a curious aesthetic choice: despite their rather grand middle-class home in Foxrock, Beckett elected to remember and associate his parents with worn-out or bizarre objects. His mother May, née Roe, grew up in Roe Hall in Co. Kildare, an imposing house on sixty-five acres of grounds with a large staff of servants and gardeners (*DF*, 3). As a result, May Beckett brought exacting standards to the domestic order of Cooldrinagh, making strict demands of her family and servants alike. Despite her noted fastidiousness, she is identified in Beckett's writing with the odd hats she was fond of, the mourning dress she wore after her husband's death and the enclosing domestic spaces of rocking chairs and beds. Similarly, Beckett's father, a successful quantity surveyor and 'gregarious clubman', is identified with the old greatcoat in which he liked to walk the land surrounding Cooldrinagh, on his own or accompanied by his young son (*LM*, 30).

These heirlooms correspond quite closely to Beckett's relationship with his parents: while greatcoats offer Beckett's characters solace and playful distraction, maternal objects reflect the more severe and passionate nature of Beckett's relationship with his mother. It is not remarkable that Beckett's characters might display elements of the genial or abrasive manners attributed to his father and mother, or favour the long walks and eccentric hats either parent was noted for. Beckett does not, however, simply pass on aspects of his parents' natures to his fictional, poetic or dramatic characters. Rather, his characters are given literary realisations of the very objects worn or used every day by his parents, and in which, as a result, memories of Beckett's father and mother are embedded. Beckett's narratives, moreover, often take place in the spaces identified with each parent, allowing his characters to move in and through the same imaginative landscapes in which memories of his parents were located.

A consistent feature of Beckett's formulation of the relationship between child and parent is how fraught it is on either side with guilt. In all the biographies, he is reported to have spoken of his sense of having let his

---

[10] *OED*, a, b.

parents down. The attitude of parent to child is marked by a similar sense of harm done for which it is pointless to seek pardon. Hamm in *Endgame* and V, the mother in *Footfalls*, each ask forgiveness of their charges:

HAMM [*coldly*] Forgive me.
[*Pause. Louder.*]
I said, Forgive me. (*GIII*, 100)

V   I had you late. [*Pause.*] In life. [*Pause.*]
Forgive me again. [*Pause. No louder.*]
Forgive me again. (*GIII*, 428)

Neither Hamm nor V receives an answer, because, it is implied, their crime as parents is to have passed on life, a difficult gift to return.

Beckett outlived his parents and brother, and made himself available to care for all three of them as they moved towards their deaths. He found himself at liberty to observe the members of his family as he attended to their needs as they were ill or dying, and after their deaths, the solitary nature of his occupation gave him ample time to sift through his memories of caring for them in this way. The experiences of nursing his parents and brother fed into Beckett's work, particularly in terms of his sensitivity to the potential power struggle and tyranny in the relationship between invalid and nurse. The illnesses and deaths of his family, particularly his parents, were powerfully inspirational. In conversation with Knowlson, Beckett described periods of personal bereavement yielding to a different form of mourning, in which he distanced himself from his grief and dispassionately considered his memories of the deceased in order to translate these memories into material for his writing: 'It was one of the key features of Beckett's aesthetic that what he once described to me as "the cold eye" had to be brought to bear on a personal experience before it could be used in a work of art' (*DF*, 384).

Such an unsentimental appropriation of life for art certainly characterises Beckett's liberal quotation from his cousin Peggy Sinclair's poorly written love letter to him in 'The Billet Doux of the Smeraldina-Rima'. This story was written in 1932, a year after Peggy died from tuberculosis, and was published in 1934 in *Dream of Fair to Middling Women*. Like Bill Beckett, Peggy Sinclair wore a green coat, but there is a world of difference between Beckett's treatment of the green coats of his cousin and father in his writing. This may be largely attributed to sensitivity acquired during the passage of time, as Beckett included his father's greatcoat in his writing a decade after Peggy's. There is a tenderness in his treatment of items of dress associated with his parents in later works that is utterly lacking in the early stories of *Dream of Fair to Middling Women*, but is present in his return to Peggy Sinclair's green coat in *Krapp's Last Tape*, over two decades later: 'What remains of all that misery? A girl in a shabby green coat, on a railway-station platform?' (*GIII*, 224).

Most accounts of Beckett's treatment of memory take as their starting point his comments in *Proust* (1930) about the difference between voluntary and involuntary memory, and go on to trace this paradigm in Beckett's later creative writing.[11] In *Proust*, Beckett sums up Proust's entire literary project as 'a monument to involuntary memory and the epic of its action', and distinguishes sharply between voluntary and involuntary memory. Beckett describes voluntary memory in Proust's writing as 'a concordance to the Old Testament of the individual', and 'the uniform memory of intelligence' that 'presents the past in monochrome'. Proust's treatment of involuntary memory, by contrast, is valorized as 'explosive', and 'an unruly magician' that 'will not be importuned. It chooses its own time and place for the performance of this miracle' (*GIV*, 522, 523). The emphatic nature of these comments has greatly influenced consideration of Beckett's approach to memory in his own writing. It should not, however, simply be presumed that Beckett's celebration of Proustian involuntary memory in this early critical work led him to adopt a similar technique in his own later creative work. Dirk Van Hulle and Mark Nixon have established that two years after the publication of *Proust*, Beckett expressed criticism 'of Proustian involuntary memories, Joycean epiphanies and Woolfian "moments of being"'.[12] In each writer's work, time is arrested, if not abolished, by a character's transcendental moment of insight or access. This is frankly unthinkable in Beckett's own writing. His characterisation of memory in *Proust* as a laboriously wordy, intellectual, visual and, crucially, disembodied process is not reflected in the fiction and drama that he would subsequently write.

Three years after writing *Proust*, Bill Beckett died. It was to be eight years before Beckett introduced his father's greatcoat into his writing, in *Watt*, and with it he deployed the fragmentary, embodied and persistent

---

[11] See, for example, Adam Piette, *Remembering and the Sound of Words: Mallarmé, Proust, Joyce, Beckett* (Oxford: Clarendon Press, 1996), pp. 81–82, p. 250; Attilio Favorini, *Memory in Play: From Aeschylus to Sam Shephard* (New York: Palgrave Macmillan, 2008), p. 9, p. 186; Anthony Cordingley, 'Beckett's Ignorance: Miracles/Memory, Pascal/Proust', *Journal of Modern Literature*, 33.4 (June 2010), 129–52, pp. 145–49.

[12] Dirk Van Hulle and Mark Nixon, *Samuel Beckett's Library* (Cambridge: Cambridge University Press, 2013), p. 74.

form of remembering, which was to characterise his treatment of memory throughout the rest of his work. Memory in Beckett is a nebulous and melancholic fog that presages no epiphanies, but rather overwhelms his characters with the poignant loss of dead loved ones or failed relationships. It is also, without exception, and increasingly so in Beckett's later writing, more arbitrary and fleeting than Proust's immersive, overwhelming and complete sensual recovery. Perfect recall is such an impossibility for Beckett's characters that it is mocked by the narrator of *The Unnamable*: 'what a memory, real fly-paper' (*GII*, 375). Beckett's father died in 1933 and his mother in 1950: from each of these points, Beckett clears a space in his work for the heirlooms of this chapter, organising characters' costumes and set-pieces around objects closely associated with either parent. The individual circumstances of his parents' deaths were instrumental in determining how Beckett adapted memories of them for his writing. Bill Beckett's sudden death was a shock and stole him from his family. The paternal figures in Beckett's writing, as a result, are untainted by association with illness or decrepitude. The converse was true of Beckett's mother, whose long widowhood was succeeded by the steady deterioration caused by Parkinson's disease before the relief of, what seemed to Beckett at least, a long overdue death. Maternal figures in his work tend to be ancient, harrowed, physically weak, and with distressed, wandering minds.

Paternal Heirloom

Beckett's relationship with his father was so close that William Beckett 'carried his son's recent letters on his person until the day he died'.[13] After his father's death, Beckett began to dress his characters in the greatcoat Bill Beckett had worn for the long walks he loved, and continued to do so throughout the rest of his writing career, over more than five decades. This gesture indicates Beckett's sensitivity to the poetics of often-worn items of dress that are left behind after death and remain like a shed skin of the body that once inhabited them. Such objects serve as tangible, tactile mementos, retaining traces of the dead wearer's shape and allowing an otherwise impossible proximity with the deceased. As heirlooms, greatcoats also have an overwhelmingly practical function, protecting the person who inherits them on the part of the original, now absent, owner. In

---

[13] Lois Gordon, *The World of Samuel Beckett: 1906–1946* (New Haven: Yale University Press, 1996), p. 92.

wearing his father's greatcoat, Beckett's characters acquire, by a process of associational transference, characteristics of the Bill Beckett who emerges from the biographies and memoirs. These include his temperament: genial, self-contained and contented, largely passive and mildly bewildered but prone, on occasion, to short-lived flashes of surprising anger or violence (*DF*, 10). That many of Beckett's characters display such traits may, in part, be ascribed to their inherited costume. Unthreatening, unquestioning, uncomprehending, greatcoat-wearing characters understand little and demand less from life. Like Bill Beckett, these figures have a horror of physical suffering and remove themselves from the scene of births with particular alacrity, but even in more peaceful times seem to be engaged on endless walks. As the narrator of *From an Abandoned Work* (1954–55) puts it: 'I have never in my life been on my way anywhere, but simply on my way' (*GIV*, 341).

The anecdote of Beckett's birth is well known from biographical and critical studies, as from his own writing. The portrait of Bill Beckett tramping the fields while his wife was in labour emphasises how his father, a man of his time, was not comfortable with the physical brutality of birth. It also indicates something of the attitude inherited by Beckett on the subject. He devotes a considerable part of *Company*, written in the late 1970s, to the subject. Although the father leaves the house after breakfast 'with a flask and a package of his favourite egg sandwiches for a tramp in the mountains' and returns ten hours later when it is dark, he learns to his 'dismay' that 'labour was still in swing'. With considerably more sympathy for father than mother, the passage ends by noting that, 'Though footsore and weary he was on the point of setting out anew across the fields in the young moonlight when the maid came running to tell him it was over at last. Over!' (*GIV*, 429–30). This sardonic 'Over!' identifies the moment of birth as the beginning, rather than end, of pain. It may be over for the mother, and a matter of relief for the father, but for the child, birth is a shocking and brutal initiation into the suffering of life.

Biographical accounts of Bill Beckett have addressed at some length his confusion and bewilderment with the interests and behaviour of his younger son. Beckett thought that his decision to attempt to become a writer rather than pursuing a career in the family business or as a university lecturer was a source of disappointment to his father, and spoke of his regret and guilt at having caused this:

> My father was a very kind man. Interested in my progress. I always felt guilty at letting him down. When I was working in Trinity College,

teaching in TCD, that gave him a great deal of pleasure. He was absolutely non-intellectual … Then when I resigned and gave the whole [teaching] thing up, he was very disappointed. (*BR*, 12–13)

Beckett spoke about this at length with Knowlson, who suggests that the final two lines of Joyce's poem 'Ecce Puer', 'O Father forsaken / Forgive your son!', epitomised for Beckett his guilt about having 'forsaken' his family when he suddenly resigned from his lecturing post at Trinity in 1932, since, when discussing his resignation with Knowlson at the age of eighty-three, Beckett 'began to recite part of it aloud, unprompted, just as he remembered it' (*DF*, 157–58). Beckett expressed a similarly keen regret over his resignation from lecturing to W.A. Watts, then Provost of Trinity, in 1986. Watts organised a meeting to ask if Trinity might name the new college theatre under construction after Beckett, in his honour. In Watts's recollection Beckett opened their conversation 'by saying that he owed Trinity an apology for his sudden departure, so sudden it seems that he hadn't returned his room keys'.[14] Knowlson has also described how Beckett agreed to accept an honorary doctorate from Trinity in 1959 not because he wanted to, or felt that he deserved such formal academic recognition, but because 'although both his parents to whom the degree would have mattered most were dead, it may have seemed like a belated justification for a decision which at the time had so bitterly disappointed them' (*DF*, 465). If Bill Beckett was disappointed by his son, he did not voice it. Their relationship seems to have been marked by a silent and unwavering, if largely passive, sense of mutual support. There is a remarkably unthreatening and uncompetitive quality to Beckett's relationship with his father. The famous scene at the Forty-Foot bathing area, with a father calling his young son from below to 'Be a brave boy', and jump into the water from 'the tip of the high board' is recorded in *Company* and acknowledged by Beckett's critics as an incident from his life, but apart from this, demands of ideal masculine or adult behaviour are never made of sons by fathers in Beckett's writing, and by all accounts seem never to have been made of Beckett by his own father (*GIV*, 432).

First Love and *The Expelled*, two of Beckett's novellas written in 1946, refer to lifesaving paternal gifts of money, fictional bequests that recall accounts of Bill Beckett's soft touch as he discreetly slipped money into his son's hands when May was not looking (*GIV*, 231, 235, 254). Deirdre

---

[14] William Watts, *A Memoir* (Dublin: The Lilliput Press, 2008), p. 138.

Bair recounts Beckett's dire financial straits after his resignation from Trinity and with no evident prospects as writer, teacher or translator:

> Bill had secretly begun to send Beckett small amounts of money at regular intervals, and though he was ashamed of himself for taking it, his need was so great that he had no choice. 'Sam must never want,' Bill was heard to remark from time to time, but always out of earshot of his wife. While May waited grimly for her son to return home, beaten because he could not survive financially, her husband was surreptitiously sending just enough money to keep this from happening.[15]

This support continued after Bill Beckett's death. Financial arrangements made in his will paid Beckett a regular allowance of £200 a year, the value of which Cronin establishes by comparing it to the contemporaneous civil service salary of £180 plus a cost of living bonus, noting that from a similar income, Flann O'Brien 'had to maintain his widowed mother and eleven siblings' (*LM*, 196–97).

In this way, Bill Beckett made it possible for his son to devote himself to the slow business of creating his own voice as a writer. Bill Beckett's generous acceptance of his odd son's endless adolescence and literary pretensions made a saint of the father in Beckett's memory; and the better the father, the worse the son, as guilt became one of the defining emotions with which Beckett thought of and remembered him. In his astute analysis of Beckett's literary references to his father, Cronin summarises the relations between father and son:

> All Samuel Beckett's writings about his father have this curiously protective quality; and more strangely still he sees this gregarious clubman as essentially lonely and almost beyond communication … And, of course, guilt. 'That was always the way, walk all over the mountains with you talking and talking and then suddenly mum and home in misery and not a word to a soul for weeks, sulky little bastard, better off dead.' (*LM*, 30)[16]

Bill Beckett died suddenly of a heart attack in June 1933, aged sixty-two. After his collapse, Beckett stayed by his father's bed watching over him, and also 'shaved him and washed him' (*DF*, 170). Both Knowlson and Cronin quote from Beckett's poignant letter to McGreevy soon after his father's death: 'I can't write about him. I can only walk the fields and climb the ditches after him' (*LI*, 165). However, as Cronin put it: '[H]e

---

[15] Deirdre Bair, *Samuel Beckett: A Biography* (London: Vintage, 1990), pp. 150–51. Bair's account above is supported if tempered by similar accounts in the two other, more measured, biographies. See *LM*, 173 and *DF*, 163.
[16] Cronin quotes from Beckett's *Embers* (*GIII*, 201).

would write about him many times. The sense of some ultimate sadness, even injustice in his father's life would never leave him; and he would mourn for that life as well as for his death; but the memory of few fathers has been better served' (*LM*, 191).

In a letter to his lover Pamela Mitchell in December 1954, shortly after his brother Frank's death, Beckett spoke of the walks he had been taking, and said 'the real walk is elsewhere, on a screen inside, old walks in a lost country, with my father and my brother, but mostly with my father, long ago'.[17] Even before his father's death, Beckett had come to associate walking alone with nostalgia for the satisfactions of childhood, and wrote to McGreevy in 1931 that 'for me, walking, the mind has a most pleasant and melancholy limpness, is a carrefour of memories, memories of childhood mostly' (*LI*, 93). Until the very end of his life, when he was too physically weak to do so, Beckett took regular, long walks. His comments to Mitchell and McGreevy suggest that he thought of walking as a movement back in time, and into an interior landscape dominated by memories of his father. By dressing his characters in greatcoats and placing them in landscapes that recall the back roads and hills he walked with his father, Beckett locates his works in the intimate imaginative space in which his nostalgic reflections took place, and that irrecoverable time spent at his father's side to which he sought to return.

Greatcoats

Beckett's itinerant greatcoat-wearing old men ramble throughout the pages of his fiction from *Watt* (1941–45) to *Stirrings Still* (1983–87), often holding the hand of a small child, as in *Worstward Ho* (1981–82), his penultimate prose work. During the period in which Beckett first established the dilapidated qualities of the greatcoat in *Watt*, many examples abounded in Ireland, as they did in post-war Europe.[18] The following image of the Dublin character Johnny Forty-Coats was taken while Beckett was writing *Watt* (Figure 5).

---

[17] SB, letter to Pamela Mitchell, December 27, 1954, quoted in Knowlson, 'A Writer's Homes – A Writer's Life', p. 21.
[18] André Bernold proposes a number of possible post-war French models for the costumes of Beckett's characters, including Robert Doisneau's photograph 'Coco, rue Xavier Privas' (Bernold, *Beckett's Friendship: 1979–1989*, p. 55). This photograph was taken, however, a decade after Beckett finished writing *Watt*, in 1952. Beckett's greatcoat-wearing men more closely resemble the despondent figures in long dark coats that haunt the photographs of the Hungarian-born American photographer André Kertész (1894–1985).

Figure 5 Independent Newspapers, 'Dublin character PJ Marlow also known as Johnny Forty Coats' (1943).
Courtesy of the National Library of Ireland.

As early as the third page of *Molloy*, this item makes an appearance, adorning the two men observed by the narrator, 'one small and one tall', a pairing of physical types that echoes Laurel and Hardy and presages Vladimir and Estragon: 'The air was sharp for they wore greatcoats' (*GII*, 5). The greatcoat is such a key part of his characters' attire that on three occasions Beckett uses it to identify the central figure and mark him out from other background characters who, unlike the outcast, outmoded, contrarian protagonist, alter their dress according to the seasons. The fugitive main character of *Film*, written in 1963, is identified by his 'Long dark overcoat (whereas all others in light summer dress)' (*GIII*, 372). In *Ohio Impromptu* (1981), the subject of Reader's narrative is described wearing 'his long black coat no matter what the weather' (*GIII*, 474), while in 'One Evening', we learn that the protagonist 'wore a greatcoat in spite of the time of year' (*GIV*, 421). Such lonely, sad men are evidently loath to divest themselves of their greatcoats, even when their weight and warmth must be a source of discomfort. The two characters of *Mercier and Camier* share a greatcoat. At one point they spread it out on wet grass and use it as a blanket to protect them from a chill, prompting Mercier, sitting on his half of the coat, to insist that 'clover is nothing to it' (*GI*, 424).

The greatcoat is an essential part of Beckett's iconography, its worn deformities and copious pockets providing both a literal expression of his characters' vagrancy and destitution and a frequent source of their diverting play. The most potent use of the greatcoat in Beckett's writing, however, is to house and evoke memories of his father. Seamus Heaney makes use of the same device in 'The Butts', his elegy to his father published in the 2010 collection *Human Chain*. Colm Tóibín has described *Human Chain* as a book of 'shades and memories, of things whispered, of journeys into the underworld, of elegies and translations, of echoes and silences'.[19] In 'The Butts', Heaney seeks to recall his father's corporeal presence, to recover him as he was in life, through the suits left empty by his death. Heaney eloquently marks his father's physical absence in the first stanza by describing his suits hanging in the wardrobe as 'broad / And short / And slightly bandy-sleeved'.[20] In the fourth stanza, the suits sway 'Like waterweed disturbed' and disorient the narrator as he reaches in among them, bringing to the surface memories of his father. These memories are tactile: he sniffs at the stale smoke and sweat still clinging to the fabric of the suits, and works his hand into the 'forbidden handfuls' he expects to find in the pockets. The 'cold smooth pocket-lining' yields no tangible mementoes, but the sensation of a 'kind of empty-handedness' and a 'paperiness' recovers for the narrator visceral memories of washing his father's body in the last days of his life. In sorrow, Heaney notes every dent and discoloration of the 'thornproof and blue serge' material, but by

---

[19] Colm Tóibín, 'Book of the Week', *The Guardian*, 21 August 2010.
[20] Seamus Heaney, 'The Butts', in *Human Chain* (London: Faber and Faber, 2010), pp. 12–13.

exploring the feel and smell of his father's suits, Heaney gains a poignantly fleeting access again to the body that once filled them.[21] Beckett's characters experience a more intimate contact with the dead: several describe their greatcoats as paternal hand-me-downs. By wearing these greatcoats, Beckett's characters perform the intimate gesture of a son putting on an item of dress that has been moulded from wear by the mourned shape of their father. It is this physical proximity to dead fathers that lends greatcoats their potent sensual and emotional resonance in Beckett's writing.

The greatcoat, 'a large heavy overcoat; a top-coat', was according to the *OED* an essential item of dress for a man of any social standing throughout the nineteenth century and into the early twentieth century. In her study of clothing in Ireland from 1860 to 1930, Anne O'Dowd observes that in all places but the west coast and some isolated areas, the typical coat worn 'was often a large and heavy great coat, reaching to the ground and with a large cape attached to cover the shoulders. It was commonly known as a 'trusty' or cóta mór'.[22] This sense of the greatcoat as a 'venerable' item of dress is emphasised by the journalist George Sala in his mid-nineteenth-century complaint about the recent fashionable trend in London for replacing the once standard greatcoat with a wide range of other coats. Sala's tribute identifies many of the features that make the greatcoat so useful for Beckett:

> ... the long, voluminous, wide-skirted garment of brown or drab broadcloth, reaching to the ankle, possessing unnumbered pockets; pockets for bottles, pockets for sandwiches, secret pouches for cash, and side-pockets for bank-notes ... Your father wore it before you, and you hoped to leave it to your eldest son. Solemn repairs – careful renovation of buttons and braiding were done to it, from time to time. A new great-coat was an event – a thing to be remembered as happening once or so in a lifetime.[23]

In her study, *Dress in Ireland* (1989), Mairéad Dunlevy links the evolution of the greatcoat with early nineteenth-century improvements to transport by carriage and coach that resulted in greater mobility for men.[24] By the mid-nineteenth century, a number of Irish tailors had developed their own styles of greatcoats, the most popular of which proved to be John Getty McGee's 1866 design: the ulster. McGee promoted the ulster

---

[21] Heaney, 'The Butts', pp. 12–13.
[22] Anne O'Dowd, *Common Clothes and Clothing 1860–1930* (Dublin: National Museum of Ireland, 1990), p. 9.
[23] George Sala, *Gaslight and Daylight* (London: Chapman and Hall, 1859), p. 60.
[24] Mairead Dunlevy, *Dress in Ireland* (London: Batsford, 1989), p. 152.

as 'the best storm defier ever produced'.[25] The ulster was the greatcoat of choice for many, including Arthur Conan Doyle's Sherlock Holmes, and it remained popular into the twentieth century. One of the features of McGee's ulster, according to Jack McCoy, was its 'large number of pockets'.[26] It is most likely that Bill Beckett's greatcoat was an ulster, but sadly, no photograph of him wearing it seems to exist, for as a professional and member of several gentlemen's clubs, it is extremely unlikely that Bill Beckett would have posed for photographs in the shabby article he wore for his walks. As McCoy further notes, very few ulsters have been 'preserved in historic dress collections' because they were so highly prized by their owners that they 'were worn out rather than relinquished for exhibition'.[27]

The greatcoat is once called a 'topcoat', in *Company*, is referred to simply as a 'coat', in *Mercier and Camier* and *Ohio Impromptu*, and features as the 'same old coat' in the radio play *Cascando* and prose works *All Strange Away* and *Fizzles 3*, written in the early 1960s, and in Beckett's final pieces of fiction, including *Ill Seen Ill Said* and *Stirrings Still*. However, the striking coincidence of colour, length, weight, warmth and shabby details such as mismatching buttons or frayed material in all the coats worn by Beckett's male characters gives rise to the overwhelming impression that there is in reality only one greatcoat, pulled out of the same imaginary wardrobe for use by Watt, Mercier and Camier, Vladimir and Estragon, Molloy, Macmann, the Unnamable's cast of 'moribunds', and still holding up well enough to serve the later characters of Beckett's fiction, film and drama for stage and radio.

The emphatic register of Sala's praise for the greatcoat is echoed by an advert taken out by McGee on 11 February 1870 in the *Belfast News-Letter*, when the ulster is described in a testimonial as 'the best driving Coat I ever possessed'. Bill Beckett's greatcoat was most likely a driving coat before it became a walking coat. Cronin describes it as 'Originally

---

[25] Dunlevy, *Dress in Ireland*, p. 152.
[26] Jack McCoy, 'The Ulster Coat', *Irish Arts Review (1984–1987)*, 2.4 (Winter, 1985), 18–23, p. 19.
[27] McCoy, 'The Ulster Coat,' p. 23. Although Bill Beckett's greatcoat was most likely an ulster, and it evidently provided the source for the greatcoats worn by so many of Beckett's characters, it is worth noting that the specific design of the greatcoat fluctuates over time, with the addition or loss of details such as velvet collars according to the demands of the narrative or character. The greatcoat may additionally have served as a comic tribute to Proust, who was closely identified with the shabby, fur-lined coat he wore at all times of the day, and while writing at night, in bed. See Lorenza Foschini, *Proust's Overcoat: The True Story of One Man's Passion for All Things Proust*, trans. Eric Karpeles (London: Portobello Books, 2011), pp. 94–101.

a motoring coat of the sort that was necessary before the First World War, it finally became his walking garb, indeed, as it deteriorated over the years, his "walking rags"' (*LM*, 29). Bill Beckett was an enthusiast for motorbikes and cars, as was his son in his youth, and if he had not already acquired a sturdy overcoat before his marriage in 1901, it is likely that he purchased his greatcoat for use while driving the motorbike and sidecar bought soon after his marriage, and the succession of cars acquired later, including a Delage and the De Dion Bouton that features in *Company* and *The Old Tune*, Beckett's 1960 translation of Robert Pinget's play *La Manivelle*.[28] The provenance of the car reflects that of the first greatcoat to appear in Beckett's writing, in *Watt*. Watt's greatcoat is a hand-me-down from his father, who bought it in turn 'second-hand, for a small sum, from a meritorious widow ... when Watt's father was a young man, and motoring in its infancy, that is to say some seventy years before' (*GI*, 347). Once Bill Beckett's greatcoat had fallen out of shape and was no longer presentable enough for driving, he wore it instead for his regular walks over the fields and mountains near the family home, right up to his sudden death in 1933.

It is to fond memories of walking hand in hand with his father that Beckett most frequently returned when describing happy elements of his childhood. Cronin and Knowlson each include details of the routes taken by Bill and Samuel Beckett in their biographies, and stress the enormous emotional impact of these walks on Beckett. Their descriptions also highlight the degree to which Beckett subsequently drew on such walks in his writing. Cronin's account of these walks recalls several prose works, including *Malone Dies, From an Abandoned Work* and *Company*.

> Even when Sam was quite small they would set out hand in hand up the Glencullen Road with the sea behind them gradually coming into view, the Three Rock mountain ahead to the left and the equally rocky eminence known as Prince William's Seat directly in front. His father taught him the names of these mountains and of the islands and promontories of the sea, as well as of the lights and lightships that became visible after dark. (*LM*, 29)

The silhouette of an old man and child walking hand in hand in silence together is the most perfect approximation of contented companionship in Beckett's work. These figures register a degree of happiness and peace unavailable to adult couples or to isolated characters. It is partly

---

[28] Beckett's cousin Sheila Page describes Bill Beckett's car as a Delage (*BR*, 10), but Eoin O'Brien suggests that the car was a De Dion Bouton. See O'Brien, *The Beckett Country*, p. 9.

for this reason that the lonely characters in Beckett's late, nostalgic prose are so preoccupied with memories of walks with a father figure, as in *Worstward Ho*:

> Hand in hand with equal plod they go. In the free hands – no. Free empty hands. Backs turned both bowed with equal plod they go. The child hand raised to reach the holding hand. Hold the old holding hand. Hold and be held. Plod on and never recede. Slowly with never a pause plod on and never recede. Backs turned. Both bowed. Joined by held holding hands. Plod on as one. One shade. Another shade. (*GIV*, 473)

Cronin's claim that Beckett once told him his father had 'walked himself to death' gives a different resonance to the many calculations of distances travelled by Beckett's itinerant characters in his works (*LM*, 29). The description of a ghostly paternal figure still walking the same route in *Company* charts the slow process by which a person becomes identified with a particular landscape: 'Father's shade to right and a little to the rear. So many times already round the earth. Topcoat once green stiff with age and grime from chin to insteps' (*GIV*, 434). This poignant description recalls Flann O'Brien's considerably more jaunty suggestion in *The Third Policeman* (written from 1939 to 1940) that the road travels up into the soles of a regular walker's feet, making him sluggish and hastening his death.[29]

The loving relationship with his father and the lyrical features of the terrain they covered together result in a protective paternal landscape of hill and mountain in Beckett's writing.[30] Physical memories of their walks are embedded in the colours of the greatcoat, which echo the colours of the mountains and fields, while its well-worn fabric is as yieldingly soft as the bracken Bill Beckett jocosely swore to his doctors that he would lie and fart in forever more if he were to recover from the sudden heart attack that killed him several days later (*LM*, 191). Several characters and narrators describe their greatcoats as originally of a green colour that over time has faded and lightened to yellow or darkened to black, but the colour green remains to the fore in such descriptions. A visual record of the landscape is by this means inscribed in the greatcoats, and by wearing this garment almost to the exclusion of any other, the characters themselves

---

[29] Flann O'Brien, *The Third Policeman* (London: Folio, 2006), p. 95.
[30] By contrast, Paul Lawley identifies the paternal in Beckett with the 'shore-scape' and 'seascape', arguing that this exposed landscape is consistently associated with fathers in his work. See '"The Rapture of Vertigo": Beckett's Turning-Point', *The Modern Language Review*, 95.1 (January 2000), 28–40, p. 31 and 'Samuel Beckett's Relations', *JOBS*, 6.2 (Spring 1997), 10–13, pp. 11–13.

become closely identified with this paternal terrain. Beckett's gallery of greatcoat-wearing characters are thus enclosed in a sweep of fabric that not only protects them from the elements, but swaddles them in a host of sensual and tactile associations largely taken from memories of his father's walking coat, and of walks with his father. Eoin O'Brien has shown in *The Beckett Country* that the landscape through which Beckett walked with his father features prominently in much of his writing. I want to extend this and suggest that Beckett's frequent evocation of this landscape establishes a distinctly paternal terrain in his work, embedded with memories of his father, and of the greatcoat his father wore to move over hill, mountain, quiet roads, through fields and the racecourse, and past gorse, bracken and sea. Warm descriptions of such walks with his father when Beckett was in his late twenties feature in his letters to friends written from the family home in Foxrock in the 1930s, providing a reprieve from his complaints and often expressed wishes to be elsewhere.

Part of the reason Beckett's characters rarely take off their greatcoats is that one of the most important functions of these garments is to provide a distinctly paternal kind of swaddling: several greatcoats vicariously, if imperfectly, satisfy the desire of many of Beckett's characters to be hugged by their dead fathers, for these paternal heirlooms offer a similarly tender comfort to characters as that provided by the fathers who once wore them. Unlike the severe, rather distant and physically undemonstrative love offered by maternal figures, the bodies of fathers in Beckett's work are identified as sources of comfort and life-affirming warmth. The narrator of *The End* describes such a moment on a walk with his father. 'It was evening, I was with my father on a height, he held my hand. I would have liked him to draw me close with a gesture of protective love, but his mind was on other things' (*GIV*, 292). In *The Calmative*, the narrator is well aware that it is less the story of Joe Breem than the reassuring paternal voice and contact that puts him to sleep: 'He might have simply told me the story, he knew it by heart, so did I, but that wouldn't have calmed me, he had to read it to me … evening after evening the same pictures, till I dozed off on his shoulder' (*GIV*, 263). A tender moment in the second act of *Waiting for Godot* sees Vladimir provide his coat as a blanket for the sleeping Estragon, having sung him to sleep. More poignantly, one of the first images described in *That Time* is of the Speaker seeking warmth and comfort from his greatcoat: 'huddled up on the slab in the old green greatcoat with your arms round you whose else hugging you for a bit of warmth to dry off and on to hell out of there and on to the next' (*GIII*, 418).

The greatcoat also provides repeated occasions for digressions and play, the two most famous examples of which are in *Watt* and *Malone Dies*, both of which share interesting characteristics. By the time the greatcoat makes its way onto Macmann's shoulders in *Malone Dies*, it has acquired more buttons and deteriorated slightly since Watt wore it. In long, rambling, mirror accounts of their coats, Watt and Macmann are both described as being nearly fully covered from head to foot by their greatcoats. We are told that patches of velvet or shag still attach to the collars, and that although old and battered, both coats are damaged only at their end, seat or elbows. Greatcoats that were once black are now green and tending to yellow. The cloth is felt-like, holding the shape of the body, embracing the wearer and retaining those shapes made by a 'spasm.' Each greatcoat is also heavy and never washed, except as a result of encounters with rain, snow, sleet and canal water. These digressive descriptions of greatcoats are a marvellous example of ludic activity at a narrative level and display an extraordinary coincidence of tone and descriptive detail, a marked tendency of Beckett's writing between *Watt* and *How It Is*. Malone concludes his account of his greatcoat with the dismissive phrase 'So much for this coat', and in subsequent works there are no such detailed descriptions of greatcoats: although the greatcoat continues to envelop a host of different characters in Beckett's later works it receives little or no comment (*GII*, 222). Instead, from this point on, it is taken for granted as a staple of the extraordinarily limited wardrobe used by Beckett for his characters.

The impermeability of the greatcoat and possibilities afforded for play by its pockets and lapels make it an essential, exuberant prop in *Molloy*. Molloy informs us that his coat, like that of many another tramp or homeless man, is lined with sheets of newspaper to keep him warm. His newspaper of choice for this improvised lining is the *Times Literary Supplement*, since the obtuseness of its prose is matched by a comparable resilience to natural phenomena:

> And in winter, under my greatcoat, I wrapped myself in swathes of newspaper, and did not shed them until the earth awoke, for good, in April. The *Times Literary Supplement* was admirably adapted to this purpose, of a neverfailing toughness and impermeability. Even farts made no impression on it. (*GII*, 25–26)

The pockets and lapels of his greatcoat also provide a great source of distraction and play for Molloy. Discovering that his hat is fastened to his buttonhole by a lace, he moves his hat in an arc before him, watching his lapel open and close in time, and remarks: 'I understood now why

I never wore a flower in my buttonhole, though it was large enough to hold a whole nosegay. My buttonhole was set aside for my hat. It was my hat that I beflowered' (*GII*, 10). Later, Molloy occupies himself for many pages with the distribution of his store of sucking stones among the pockets of his greatcoat. Sitting in his greatcoat by the sea, gazing at the stones spread out before him 'in anger and perplexity', Molloy considers increasing the two pockets of his coat to fourteen to accommodate the orderly circulation of his stones, perhaps by dividing the existing pockets with safety pins.[31] His task is not made any easier by the 'usual' abundant contents of his left pocket, which include some silver, a horn and a vegetable knife, as well as what he describes as 'occasional objects' but refuses to name (*GII*, 65, 66).

In the works that follow *Molloy*, the lapels and pockets of greatcoats are no longer used for distracting play and the garments are no longer described with tangible affection, bringing to an end their use as ludic or comforting objects. Symbolically, the greatcoat is cast off and hung up in *From an Abandoned Work* (1957):

> But not my long coat, just my jacket, I could never bear the long coat, flapping about my legs, or rather one day suddenly I turned against it, a sudden violent dislike. Often when dressed to go I would take it out and put it on, then stand in the middle of the room unable to move, until at last I could take it off and put it back on its hanger, in the cupboard. (*GIV*, 346–47)

After this scene, greatcoats assume a different order of symbolic value. In the prose written in the 1960s, greatcoats are barely described. Instead, they function as shorthand for an earlier mode of characterisation and narrative organisation that was centrally focused on an old man wearing a greatcoat for his long walks. References to 'the same old coat' in works of this period convey Beckett's reluctance to continue writing in this vein, even when he resumes the motif of the journey. The first distinct image in the story *All Strange Away* (1964) is 'Out of the door and down the road in the old hat and coat like after the war, no, not that again.' *Fizzles 3* (early 1960s) similarly describes 'the trunk horizontal, the legs asprawl, sagging at the knees, same old coat, the stiffened tails stick up behind', and this phrase is repeated in the radio play *Cascando* (1963): 'come on ... same old coat ... he goes down' (*GIV*, 349, 408; *GIII*, 347).

---

[31] Molloy's distribution of his sucking stones is considered at greater length in the conclusion to this book.

Having been hung up in *From an Abandoned Work*, greatcoats are not properly taken out of the wardrobe again until works written in the 1970s. In these dramatic and fictional works, set in empty spaces haunted by obsessive memory and the tender melancholy of what has been lost, descriptions of greatcoats are attenuated in comparison to the lengthy digressions on their colour and shape in earlier periods, and yet, curiously, these late indistinct sweeps of dark fabric are more poignantly and strangely resonant than those earlier comforting or ludic greatcoats. Later greatcoats seem to have grown in the wardrobe, or perhaps the wizened characters that wear them have shrunk. The length of a greatcoat is remarked in the play *That Time* (1976) with the repeated lines: 'back down to the wharf with the nightbag and the old green greatcoat your father left you trailing the ground' (*GIII*, 424). The same feature is emphasised in *Company*: 'By the time you open your eyes your feet have disappeared and the skirts of your greatcoat come to rest on the surface of the snow' (*GIV*, 438–39). In *That Time*, *Company* and *…but the clouds …*, all written in the 1970s, Beckett seems to emphasise the bagginess of the greatcoat as it swamps its wearers to make tangible the grief felt for the absent body that once filled it. In such texts, the greatcoat becomes a poetically charged icon of loss, a metonym for mourned loved ones and past lives that haunt Beckett's later writing.

No longer delicately coloured, endlessly distracting and comforting, the baggy black greatcoats of the 1980s most closely resemble shrouds. The 'Dark greatcoat reaching to the ground' in *Ill Seen Ill Said* evokes an emphatically physical sense of loss, particularly in the passage where the greatcoat hangs starkly empty yet is embodied with the symbolic value of mourning, to the point of physically resembling a dead body: 'A black greatcoat. Hooked by its tails from the rod it hangs sprawling inside out like a carcass in a butcher's stall. Or better inside in for the pathos of the dangling arms' (*GIV*, 457, 466). In the elegiac prose works *Worstward Ho* (1983) and *Stirrings Still* (1983), greatcoats are used to evoke memories of walks across a paternal terrain. In *Worstward Ho*, there is a return to the motif of a man and child walking hand in hand, but these 'plodding shades' are identified only by their coats: 'Black greatcoats to heels. Dim black.' Similarly, the figure of *Stirrings Still* is described as wearing a greatcoat while he is visited by memories of the dead in his room: 'Same hat and coat as of old when he walked the roads. The back roads. Now as one in a strange place seeking the way out. In the dark' (*GIV*, 474, 488).

The evolving qualities of Beckett's greatcoats across many decades and media reflect the development of his characters. Early greatcoats that are presented as well-worn hand-me-downs have an abundance of functions and keep Beckett's characters and narrative occupied for many pages. Such pleasurable digressions fade as greatcoats lose many of their distinguishing characteristics. This mirrors what happens to Beckett's characters, whose idiosyncrasies and techniques for keeping themselves entertained or distracted are similarly attenuated. Losing their distinguishing features but still going, Beckett's seemingly indestructible greatcoats announce on a material level the continued experience of his characters, all of whom Beckett once described as 'falling to bits'.[32] It is to the evidence of decay that Hamm points when raucously demonstrating to Clov that they are still alive: 'But we breathe, we change! We lose our hair, our teeth! Our bloom! Our ideals!' (*GIII*, 99) The deterioration of the greatcoat from *Watt* to *Stirrings Still* shows it to be as subject to the mutations of time and change as the body – and indeed, as memory itself, its many dents and discolorations exemplifying materially what happens to Beckett's treasured paternal memories as they are revisited throughout his oeuvre.

Maternal Heirlooms

Beckett's singular maternal portraits are organised around hats, mourning dress, beds and rocking chairs, all but the rocking chair explicitly based on those of his own mother. Odd hats and widow's weeds are directly drawn from her wardrobe and build up a piecemeal portrait of May Beckett, while also establishing a certain type of maternal figure in Beckett's writing. Hats of elaborate and often striking design suggest the eccentric and mysterious personality of his maternal characters, while the complementary objects of beds and rocking chairs eloquently express complex depictions of motherhood. If life-giving maternal power is conventionally expressed through beds, the welcome release of death is symbolically manifested through rocking chairs, objects that lull characters to death. The familiarity of the maternal objects of rocking chairs and beds no doubt adds to their impact. Readers and audience members will be encouraged by these objects to recall various literary conventions of benign, nurturing aged mothers or grandmothers, or indeed, their negative counterpart, a certain kind of anti-maternal figure: the stepmother, witch or crone who

---

[32] Israel Shenker, 'An Interview with Beckett (1956)', in *Samuel Beckett: The Critical Heritage*, p. 461.

works to frustrate the ambitions of the hero. Beckett's maternal miscellany also highlights the affinities between the figures of the mother and writer in his work: a consequence, I suggest, of the Janus-like role of both figures in presiding over the beginning and ending of life.

Like Beckett, Roland Barthes had no children. Barthes planned to write a memoir of his mother and although he never completed the project, in *Camera Lucida* (1993), he describes the partial and disappointing results of his efforts to recall his mother through photographs. Her possessions, on the other hand, allow Barthes to awaken in himself a visceral and immediate recollection of her smell and touch. His observation that 'clothing is perishable, it makes a second grave for the loved being' explains why this may be the case.[33] Barthes uncovers his mother's memory in things that belonged to her, including her powder box, a low chair in her bedroom and the crêpe de chine fabric of her clothes. These intimate, everyday objects are directly comparable to May Beckett's floral or feathered hats, her bed and rocking chair, and layers of black clothes.

Scattered throughout the biographies of Beckett are references to the garden at Cooldrinagh and to his mother's pleasure in tending to it. May Beckett was an avid gardener, and the lemon verbena, sweet-pea and lavender that charm Beckett's characters all grew abundantly in her garden. Cronin notes Beckett's use of this space in *Molloy* when describing the Beckett home.

> Cooldrinagh is ... the model for Moran's house in *Molloy*, even to the lemon verbena to whose scent he refers, a flower which, by the time Sam was a toddler, already grew in profusion round the hall door, giving forth 'a fragrance in which the least of his childish joys and sorrows were and would for ever be embalmed.' (*LM*, 12)

In a rather more literal way, the flowering veronica hedge at the back of the house held the memory of an argument between Beckett and his mother in 1932. Describing this scene, Knowlson refers to Beckett arriving home 'very drunk indeed … He quarrelled with his mother and began to throw plates from the kitchen table. Finally he threw a pudding into the veronica hedge near the kitchen door' (*DF*, 169). Beckett's work is keenly attentive to the physical and sensual experiences of its characters, but contains notably few descriptions of smell. Those smells that do arise are generally of decay, sewage or the unpleasant odours of an ageing

---

[33] Roland Barthes, *Camera Lucida: Reflections on Photography*, trans. Richard Howard (London: Vintage, 1993), p. 64.

or ill body. Pleasant scents of flowers or herbs are a rare sensual treat.[34] One such fragrance presages Watt's vision of his dead father, when 'alone in a rowing-boat, far from land, he suddenly smelt flowering current' (*GI*, 226). Yet in every other instance, the smell of flowers is put in the service of a maternal memory or portrait. When Molloy cycles over and kills an old dog, he is taken home by the maternal figure Lousse to replace the dog as her companion. Molloy's description of Lousse's garden focuses on her many lavender plants:

> Till nothing was left but this monotonous voice, in the deepening night and the smell of the damp earth and of a strongly scented flower which at the time I could not identify, but which later I identified as spike-lavender ... And if I had not lost my sense of smell the smell of lavender would always make me think of Lousse, in accordance with the well-known mechanism of association. (*GII*, 43)

In the second half of the same novel, Moran savours the smell of one of May Beckett's favourite flowers: 'Contentedly I inhaled the scent of my lemon-verbena' (*GII*, 88). A maternal portrait in *How It Is* draws on the same flower and the comforting, hazy warmth of fond memory, as the narrator recalls 'we are on a veranda smothered in verbena the scented sun dapples the red tiles yes I assure you' (*GII*, 418).

Beckett's relationship with his mother was notoriously vexed, and accounts of maternal disputes pepper the first volume of his *Collected Letters*. In 1937, after an argument with his mother that precipitated his leaving home and settling in Paris for good, Beckett famously wrote to Tom McGreevy:

> I am what her savage loving has made me, and it is good that one of us should accept that finally ... I simply don't want to see her or write to her or hear from her ... And if a telegram came now to say she was dead, I would not do the Furies the favour of regarding myself even as indirectly responsible. Which I suppose all boils down to saying what a bad son I am.

---

[34] There are a number of flowers in Beckett's work, but only those associated with mothers have a pleasant fragrance. White flowers feature in *From an Abandoned Work*, and there are potted crocus bulbs in *How It Is* and in two of Beckett's novellas, *First Love* and *The End*. In both novellas the plants die. *How It Is* also features a vase of marguerites. Flowers appear in several poems, with green tulips in 'Enueg II' and yellow tulips in 'Sanies II', lilies in 'Malacoda' and daffodils in 'thither'. No smell is mentioned for any of these flowers. The enueg is a poetic form for the expression of matters that vex the poet. In 'Enueg I' Beckett focuses on the image and smell of the rafflesia, conflating sex and death in its red flower and reference to hymen. The misogyny here is specifically directed against wives or lovers rather than mothers and does not negate the subtle tribute of Beckett's associations of maternal figures with the scent of flowers elsewhere in his work. See Raymond Thompson Hill, 'The Enueg', *PMLA*, 27.2 (1912), 265–296, p. 265.

Then Amen. It is a title for me of as little honour as infamy. Like describing a tree as a bad shadow. (*LI*, 552–53)

The bold tone of disdain here contrasts starkly with the regret and hurt expressed in many of Beckett's other letters, often also to McGreevy. This dismissive swagger does nothing to hide the evidently passionate relationship between mother and son.

In Beckett's writing, forceful maternal love is returned by the child who demands full possession of the mother. The eponymous hero of *Molloy* pauses a moment from a disparaging attack on his mother to 'give her credit' for being a 'uniparous whore', a swerve that damns her with faint praise for not inflicting the suffering of life on another being, while also claiming her love and attention for himself alone (*GII*, 15).

> My mother. I don't think too harshly of her. I know she did all she could not to have me, except of course the one thing, and if she never succeeded in getting me unstuck, it was that fate had earmarked me for less compassionate sewers. But it was well-meant and that's enough for me. No it is not enough for me, but I give her credit, though she is my mother, for what she tried to do for me. And I forgive her for having jostled me a little in the first months and spoiled the only endurable, just endurable, period of my enormous history. And I also give her credit for not having done it again, thanks to me, or for having stopped in time, when she did. (*GII*, 14)

All of Beckett's central characters share the privileged status of the single child. The supporting cast, such as the Lynch family in *Watt* and Lambert family in *Malone Dies*, have siblings, but Mahood's extended family in *The Unnamable* is the sole example of such throughout Beckett's writing. If mothers are to encompass the gamut of life and death and to be held responsible for both, it is crucial that there is no rival sibling to distract passionate maternal love from the anti-heroic son or beleaguered daughter.

If Beckett savaged his mother in his work, after he had moved to France, he became a model of the devoted son, particularly during her last illness, when distance eased hurt and pity seems to have got the better of lingering resentment. Knowlson has described the 'complex, highly emotional nature of [Beckett's] relationship with his mother', and writes of how the guilt that tends to follow the death of a close loved one was 'heightened in his case by the remorse that he felt at not having been the dutiful son that she wanted' (*DF*, 383). This bond of guilt recalls Beckett's comments about his father, but maternal and paternal loves manifest themselves in very different ways in Beckett's writing, where the love of a mother for her child is a far more conflicted and overpowering phenomenon than that of a father, and is returned in similar form. Maternal love is often characterised by Beckett as a confrontation where either mother or child seeks to subdue the other with their intensity of feeling. His characters often seem helplessly paralysed by maternal love, or, conversely, may be suddenly, intransigently galvanised by a determination to visit their estranged mothers, as is memorably the case for Molloy:

> I needed, before I could resolve to go and see that woman, reasons of an urgent nature, and with such reasons, since I did not know what to do, or where to go, it was child's play for me, the play of an only child, to fill my mind until it was rid of all other preoccupation and I seized with a trembling at the mere idea of being hindered from going there, I mean to my mother, there and then. (*GII*, 11)

While this formulation of the dynamic between mothers and sons has a likely basis in Beckett's relationship with his own mother, I am more interested in tracing the ways he uses objects with maternal associations to establish a distinctive set of maternal portraits than in speculating about his personal relationships.[35]

Ladies' Hats

May Beckett was fond of her hats and they feature prominently in descriptions of her. Her niece Caroline Beckett said of May, 'I never remember her wearing any other colour than black. And she always wore a hat' (*BR*, 10). This recollection is echoed by Cronin's account:

> Nearly always wearing flowered hats, she was a well-known figure at dog and donkey shows or driving round the roads of Foxrock in her little trap. These flowered hats, worn in the garden and frequently round the house as well as out shopping, were one of the best-known things about May in the locality. (*LM*, 22)

Deirdre Bair, whose biographical study of Beckett focuses keenly on the intense relationship between mother and son, identifies May's hats as her sole gesture of frivolous femininity: 'She kept her hair tightly coiled against her head, fastened with savage-looking iron pins, hiding it first

---

[35] It is worth noting here the distance between Beckett's heirlooms and the objects that feature in writers' lives and are subsequently collected or studied in the mode of literary biography. In Foschini's *Proust's Overcoat*, Proust's black, mink-lined coat is an object of desire for collectors, and fuels Foschini's engaging narrative – but the resonance of this object is entirely personal. Beckett's heirlooms, by contrast, as part of his material canon, serve to establish his imaginary world and distinctive aesthetic.

beneath her nursing cap, then under a succession of fashionable hats – her one vanity.'[36] Sidestepping the antagonism of Bair's account, it is indeed striking that May Beckett, by all accounts a rather stern woman, would display such sustained preference for unusual and extravagant hats, particularly when she wore only black for so many years. It is possible, of course, that her wide-brimmed hats did not serve a primarily decorative function, but were worn to shade her eyes during gardening and when visiting the shops, church or neighbours in her donkey and trap.

In her study of the semiotics of clothes, Alison Lurie notes that the symbolic meaning of women's hats has traditionally been oriented towards 'social role rather than social status':

> Throughout most of the nineteenth century all respectable wives, widows and spinsters wore not one but two symbolic head coverings. Except for young unmarried girls, an indoor cap of muslin or silk, trimmed with lace and/or ribbon, was an essential part of the everyday costume. It was donned on arising, and could be dispensed with only for formal evening entertainments … When the middle-class woman left her house, even to walk in the garden, she put on a hat or bonnet – over her cap if she wore one. She thus shielded her pure and private thoughts, covering them with an elaborate and conventional representation of contemporary public femininity. A well-dressed female who appeared out of doors without her hat, or indoors without a cap (if she was old enough to wear one), was assumed to be emotionally distracted, mentally disturbed or of loose morals.[37]

May Beckett was by all accounts old-fashioned, wilful and eccentric, so it is not perhaps surprising for her to have adopted habits of dress that accorded with a Victorian attitude.

Knowlson describes how life in Cooldrinagh was strictly regulated in line with a Victorian set of social practices and etiquette. Control and order of the domestic space were of the utmost importance to May Beckett: 'Everything had to be properly done as she attempted to live up to the standards of the big house in which she had been brought up, although with fewer staff' (*DF*, 20). Describing the Beckett home, Cronin attempts to establish if it was typical of other middle-class Protestant families in Foxrock, and concludes: 'There is no reason to suppose that the domestic arrangements in Cooldrinagh were any more pretentious than they were in other similar households, but certainly some of May's general strictness of characters and demeanour were reflected in them' (*LM*, 24).

---

[36] Bair, *Samuel Beckett*, p. 6.
[37] Alison Lurie, *The Language of Clothes*, pp. 176–77.

Knowlson quotes May's harassed-sounding parlour maid about her mistress's obsession with decorum: 'I used to do all the rounds with little finger bowls if they had grapes or anything. Little doilies and little glass dishes that you had to leave with a little drop of water to wipe their fingers.' These standards were also extended to the Beckett children, as recalled by Sheila Page, Beckett's cousin:

> May Beckett had very strict standards of behaviour and the children had to conform or risk her anger and punishment ... So the children stood up whenever a visitor came into the room, opened doors for guests, pulled out chairs for them at dinner, and were scrupulously polite in greeting people and answering their questions: 'our table manners were terribly Victorian'. (*DF*, 20, 21)

On this subject, Eoin O'Brien has observed: 'That May Beckett was a disciplinarian with Victorian principles is beyond doubt, and that young Sam spent many a summer evening supperless in bed, no doubt deservedly so, is clearly recorded, but not in bitterness.'[38]

Striking and delicate hats are an integral element of the costume of a number of female characters in Beckett's plays, as is indicated by the specificity and detail of the costume descriptions in such stage directions. There are sixteen female roles in Beckett's stage and radio theatre, five of which are organised to a remarkable degree around the hats of the characters.[39] In *Happy Days* and the radio play *All That Fall*, Winnie and Maddy steadfastly attend to the horror of their days, the former armed with the remnants of her 'classics', the latter with her earthy humour. Despite their own ailments and problems, both women urge on their flagging male companions: Mr Slocum, a passing motorist and former 'admirer' of Maddy offers her a lift, but is reluctant to assist her generous frame up into his car from behind, until she advises, 'As if I were a bale, Mr Slocum, don't be afraid.' It is with the same tone that Winnie encourages her erstwhile missing husband, who has appeared in the last moments of the play and is attempting to crawl towards her, 'Come on, dear, put a bit of jizz into it, I'll cheer you on.' When Maddy later finds herself crouching with slapstick difficulty and indignity to get out of Mr Slocum's car,

---

[38] Eoin O'Brien, 'Zone of Stones: Samuel Beckett's Dublin', *Journal of the Irish Colleges of Physicians and Surgeons*, 16.2 (April 1987), 69–77, p. 74.

[39] Of these sixteen roles, four are disembodied voices, without significant physical description (*Eh Joe, Ghost Trio, Rough for Radio I* and *II*), two consist of close-ups of a female face, excluding head (*Not I* and *... but the clouds ...*), and four explicitly call for the characters to be bareheaded (*Play, Footfalls* and *Catastrophe*). Hats are pivotal elements of the five female roles in *Happy Days, All That Fall* and *Come and Go*.

she is cautioned by the boy helping her: 'Mind your feather, Ma'am', a note that adds an incongruous and comically delicate feathered hat to our image of the fat old woman awkwardly trying to back out of the car (*GIII*, 164, 307, 166). The feathered hat, because of its suggestion of gentility and decorum, increases the humour of Maddy's predicament. Winnie also wears a hat with a feather – and the implicit social propriety serves, similarly, to point up the strangeness of her scenario. Vivian Mercier has remarked of *Happy Days*, 'Any actress worth her salt believes that, even under the extreme handicaps of Act II, she can still convince an audience not merely that she is a lady – Winnie wears a hat – but that under all that pile of sand she is still a woman.'[40] Mercier's observation arises from Beckett's play with the propriety of ladies' hats to establish a comic dissonance in the play where the central character remains inappropriately wedded to the etiquette associated with her hat despite the precarious and isolated situation in which she finds herself. Wearing a delicate headpiece with a crumpled feather, Winnie expresses anxiety about being powerless to put on or take off her hat as polite social codes dictate. In the first act, Winnie speaks of the symbolic importance of her 'ornate' hat with 'crumpled feather' in terms that echo both Lurie's account, and popular conceptions of May Beckett: 'To think there are times one cannot take off one's hat, not if one's life were at stake … How often have I said, Put on your hat now, Winnie, there is nothing else for it, take off your hat now, Winnie, like a good girl, it will do you good, and did not' (*GIII*, 279, 283–84).

The physical characteristics of maternal figures with broad-brimmed hats in *How It Is* and *Film* match those of Beckett's own mother, who was thin and had a keen gaze, but there is another type of maternal figure in Beckett's work: physically imposing, often fat, determined to help the male characters they encounter, by force if necessary. In this, they may recall May Beckett, who frequently set out on charitable visits to her less fortunate neighbours around Foxrock in her donkey and cart.[41] These women attempt to bridle and detain Beckett's male characters, imprisoning them in their homes and subduing them with care, as one would a dependent child or pet. One such female character that profits from her broad-brimmed hat is the energetically and naïvely philanthropic Lady Pedal in *Malone Dies*. Her vividly coloured and eccentrically designed hat takes precedence in the physical description that introduces her: 'She

---

[40] Mercier, *Beckett/Beckett*, p. 182.
[41] See *BR*, 9–10; *LM*, 18–19, 21–22.

was a huge, big, tall, fat woman. Artificial daisies with brilliant yellow disks gushed from her broad-brimmed straw hat. At the same time behind the heavily spotted fall-veil her plump red face appeared to pullulate' (*GII*, 277). Lady Pedal's halo-shaped hat declares her charitable intentions. Having insisted on an excursion to the island that disrupts their normal routine and discomfits the inmates, Lady Pedal attempts to jolly them along by singing a song. When this fails to raise their spirits, she orders her servant Ernest to distribute a hamper of buns she has brought for the group, soon before Lemuel produces his hatchet.

Broad-brimmed feminine hats also signal the mystery of maternal characters in Beckett's writing. One way Beckett establishes the overwhelming, all-encompassing nature of maternal love is by giving his narrators the perspective of a child, thereby emphasising the power of the mother over her charge. This is particularly evident in Beckett's repeated recourse to a photograph of himself as a child, praying at his mother's knee (Figure 6).

Staged for May Beckett's friend Dorothy Kay, who wanted to paint such a scene, this photograph is reproduced in the biographies and is evoked by Beckett in *How It Is* (1964) and *Film* (1967), with an unbroken emphasis in both texts on the almost unbearable intensity of maternal affection directed at the child. In *How It Is* 'the huge head hatted with birds and flowers is bowed down over my curls the eyes burn with severe love I offer her mine pale upcast', while in *Film* a series of photographs is ripped up in turn by the protagonist (*GII*, 418). The first image is of a babe in arms: 'Mother's big hands. Her severe eyes devouring him. Her big old-fashioned beflowered hat.' Dorothy Kay's photograph is next: 'On a veranda, dressed in loose nightshirt, kneeling on a cushion, attitude of prayer, hands clasped, head bowed, eyes closed. Half profile. Mother on chair beside him, big hands on knees, head bowed towards him, severe eyes, similar hat to 1' (*GIII*, 381). The mothers of *How It Is* and *Film* glower down at their charges behind the brims of their hats. This costume decision affirms the mystery of these characters: by shielding the eyes and obscuring their features, such hats register the impenetrability and intimidating remoteness of the maternal gaze.

The three female characters in *Come and Go* profit from their 'Drab nondescript hats with enough brim to shade faces' to make a chiaroscuro of their furtive series of tableaux as they whisper to each other in pairs each time the third in their trio leaves the bench on which they sit and wanders offstage (*GIII*, 387). All three women in *Come and Go* are preoccupied with the seemingly terminal and darkly secret illnesses of their two dear friends, but unaware of their own. Their hats shield their expressions while

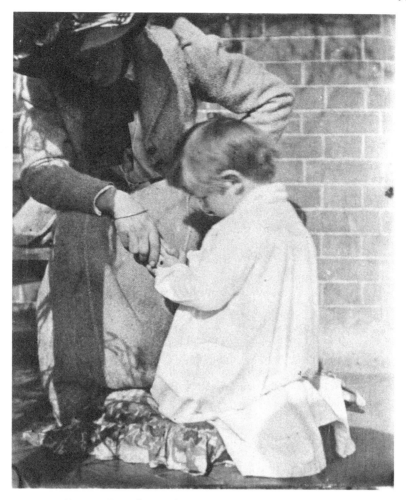

Figure 6 Dorothy Kay, 'May and Samuel Beckett' (c. 1908).
Courtesy of Harry Ransom Humanities Research Centre, University of Texas.

whispering to each other, creating a beautifully sculptural image onstage. The costume and theme of *Come and Go* also indicate the degree to which Beckett's later works identify older women with death and mourning. It is in *Rockaby* (1980), fifteen years later, however, that Beckett brings together the theme, stage properties and costume of his play to establish the central role of his late female characters as one of grieving.

Widow's Weeds

The female character of *Rockaby* is in widow's weeds, echoing the costume of mourning worn by May Beckett for almost two decades. In conversation with Knowlson, Beckett describes how his mother devoted herself to her husband's memory: 'My father died in 1933 and my mother died seventeen years later. She was seventeen years a widow. In fact, she hardly left off mourning for the whole time' (*BR*, 6). In these years, May Beckett wore only black, commemorating the ceremony that marked the end of her husband's life for the remainder of her own. This determination to visibly mourn her husband for so many years may have been instrumental in Beckett's identification of maternal figures with the visual trappings of grief. In letters to McGreevy written three years after his father's death, Beckett notes the unabating nature of his mother's grief, reporting that 'Mother remains alertly bereaved, which is not meant to be an unkind description of a behaviour she cannot help', and later that 'Mother is the picture of misery, one of her periodical attacks' (*LI*, 352, 361). Cronin describes the degree to which May Beckett insisted on maintaining an air of sombre decorum in Cooldrinagh after Bill's death:

> She had decided that full, traditional, high Victorian mourning must be observed and she created an atmosphere of gloom in the house which Sam found depressing and irksome. Even his piano playing had to be suspended as not sufficiently solemn, though an exception was made for the setting of Tennyson's 'Crossing the Bar' which his grandmother Beckett had made and which – or so he claimed anyway – he played nightly before dinner. The blinds were kept drawn, everybody was expected to maintain a solemn demeanour and dinner was eaten in an atmosphere of gloomy silence. (*LM*, 192)

May Beckett was born in 1871. Her approach to mourning harked back to a time when grieving was a highly codified matter, with strictly defined dress and behaviour. This code of mourning is described by Lou Taylor in *Mourning Dress* (1983):

> It was Victoria, the middle-class ideal of Christian widowhood, who fanned the cult of mourning, spreading it to all classes of society during her lifetime. After Albert's death she shrouded herself in crape-covered black clothes, her face behind a black veil. She wore versions of these weeds all the rest of her life, the only difference in her dresses being in her waist measurements… During the 1850–90 period mourning became such a cult that hardly anyone dared defy it.[42]

---

[42] Lou Taylor, *Mourning Dress: A Costume and Social History* (London: Allen and Unwin, 1983), p. 122.

Beckett himself was evidently attentive to the codes of dress during such a ritual of mourning, for he reproduces them in *Rockaby*. According to Lou Taylor, the widow's weeds worn by upper and middle-class women in the nineteenth and early twentieth centuries were composed of layers of black material under the pervasive and lingering influence of Queen Victoria's example.[43] Beckett's use of jet embellishment in the costume for *Rockaby* indicates that the protagonist has been a widow for a long time. The stage directions specify the desired visual effect: to sparkle. 'Black lacy high-necked evening gown. Long sleeves. Jet sequins to glitter when rocking. Incongruous flimsy head-dress set askew with extravagant trimming to catch light when rocking' (*GIII*, 461). Taylor notes the social impropriety of such eye-catching detail, unless a substantial period of mourning had already passed: 'If a shiny, faceted, black jewel was worn whilst in deepest mourning instead of one with a matte surface it could be as socially disastrous as coming out of mourning too early.'[44] Atavistic custom and superstition are, for obvious reasons, highly influential considerations in mourning practices, and Taylor attributes the dictate against glossy finishes in mourning jewellery to the 'survival of the most ancient superstitions concerning reflected images of the dead'.[45]

This decision was presumably prompted by the need to create a visually compelling stage image from a figure dressed in black on a dimly lit stage, but the effect of this decorative embellishment is to emphasise the curiously bird-like quality of W, something she shares with other female characters in Beckett's work. The widowhood of the maternal character in *Krapp's Last Tape* is described as her 'long viduity', and while Krapp cannot immediately recall the meaning of this obscure word and is forced to look it up in the dictionary, he is excited to discover its ornithological association, something conveyed to striking effect by John Hurt in the role at Dublin's Gate Theatre in 2013, who flapped the two tails of his rusty black waistcoat like the wings of a flightless bird while pacing delightedly after delivering the following:

> KRAPP [*reading from dictionary*] State – or condition – of being – or remaining – a widow – or widower. [*Looks up. Puzzled.*] Being – or remaining?... [*Pause. He peers again at dictionary. Reading.*] 'Deep weeds of viduity.'... Also of an animal, especially a bird ... the vidua or weaver-bird.... Black plumage of male ... [*He looks up. With relish.*] The vidua-bird! (*GIII*, 225)

[43] See Taylor, *Mourning Dress*, p. 122, pp. 154–62, pp. 224–39.
[44] Taylor, *Mourning Dress*, p. 224.
[45] Taylor, *Mourning Dress*, p. 229.

An image is suggested in these lines of a widow adopting the plumage of mourning. In *Rockaby*, the quivering, glinting black costume of W marks her as a rare and morbid species. Indeed, there is a pronounced imaginative link between Beckett's female characters and birds: Winnie muses that if only the earth would release her, she would 'simply float up into the blue', while the female mouth of Beckett's 1972 play *Not I* is suspended high up on stage, as though it were the third act of *Happy Days* and part at least of Winnie's wish had been granted, and the agitated and insubstantial figure of May in *Footfalls* simply disappears without a trace, a 'tangle of tatters' like an injured bird (*GIII*, 289, 430). Other characters in mourning are similarly sad, delicate and mysteriously bodiless, lacking the physical substantiality of an earthbound set of limbs. These include the old women in 'One Evening' and *Ill Seen Ill Said*. The old woman in 'One Evening' is described as being 'all in black. The hem of her long black skirt trailed in the grass', while her counterpart in *Ill Seen Ill Said* is similarly dressed: 'Save for the white of her hair and faintly bluish white of face and hands all is black' (*GIV*, 421, 451).

The mourning dress of Beckett's maternal characters gestures to the funeral ceremonies for which they originally adopted their black costumes, ceremonies that have determined their identities ever since. Beckett's identification of mothers with death must also have been influenced by his own mother's steady deterioration into ill health and fragility. Unlike her husband, May Beckett died slowly. Her Parkinson's disease meant that she worsened noticeably between Beckett's visits, so that each time he saw her he was struck by death's incremental progress, as he recorded in moving letters from Cooldrinagh during this period. To his friend Georges Duthuit in 1948, two years before her death, Beckett wrote of his mother's blue eyes: 'I gaze into the eyes of my mother, never so blue, so stupefied, so heart-rending – the eyes of an issueless childhood, that of old age … these are the first eyes I think I truly see. I do not need to see others; there is enough there to make one love and weep' (*LII*, 92). In such letters we see that once her will was no longer antagonistically attempting to direct and determine his own, Beckett could sympathise fully with his mother.

In his study of Beckett's use of autobiographical material, *The Author in the Autograph* (1996), H. Porter Abbott suggests the impact of May Beckett's death on her son's writing:

> Before 1950, death in Beckett is generally a matter of dying (by assumption, by accident, by medical malpractice, by being boiled alive, by explosion, by drowning, by suicide, by murder, by decrepitude). After 1950, death is increasingly a matter of mourning. Whether this shift was catalysed by the

death of Beckett's mother, May Beckett, on August 25, 1950, one can only speculate.[46]

Abbott's intuition is astute, although I suspect that his choice of date for such a dramatic turning point is too late, and should acknowledge Beckett's inclusion of the father's ghost wading in the river in *Watt*. What does change during the protracted mourning of his mother for her husband is Beckett's representation of maternal figures. With no longer any prospect of the sort of furious confrontation that precipitated his moving out of Cooldrinagh and to Paris for good in 1937, Beckett could at last include some of the primal force of their relationship in his works.

Maternal Beds

In Beckett's early writing, there is a correlation of domestic space and his representations of the family, which most often take the form of bitterly skewed filial relationships. However, Beckett abandons the domestic space and family portraits in his middle period. Nicholas Grene has observed that '*Endgame* has the last fully represented living space in Beckett's theatre.'[47] The last fictional representation of a domestic space and family occurs in *Molloy*. While the family more or less disappears from Beckett's writing after these works, one privileged space and relationship continues to be represented: the maternal.

May Beckett's bed and bedrooms in Cooldrinagh and New Place, the bungalow she built after her husband's death, were powerfully imaginative spaces for her son. Beckett identified his mother's bedroom in New Place as the scene of his famous epiphany about the purpose and focus of his writing to come, dramatically relocated to a jetty in a storm for *Krapp's Last Tape*. Paul Lawley describes Beckett's efforts to untangle this skein and distinguish between fact and fiction.

> In 1987 he told James Knowlson: 'Krapp's vision was on the pier at Dun Laoghaire; mine was in my mother's room. Make that clear once and for all.' ... In 1986 he had written to Richard Ellmann: 'All the jetty and howling wind are imaginary. It happened to me, summer 1945, in my mother's little house, named New Place.'[48]

---

[46] H. Porter Abbott, *Beckett Writing Beckett: The Author in the Autograph* (New York: Cornell University Press, 1996), p. 149.
[47] Nicholas Grene, *Home on the Stage: Domestic Spaces in Modern Drama* (Cambridge: Cambridge University Press, 2014), p. 144.
[48] Paul Lawley, ' "The Rapture of Vertigo:" Beckett's Turning-Point', p. 29.

Cronin describes May Beckett's bedroom in Cooldrinagh as 'a big room with a bow window facing the Dublin mountains' (*LM*, 2). Knowlson notes that in this room, 'May gave birth to the two boys' (*DF*, 15). Details of his mother's bedroom, including the brass bed and view of the larches and mountains from the bow window, feature on many occasions in Beckett's work, from *Watt* to *A Piece of Monologue* more than thirty years later.

Beckett's most thorough use of a maternal bedroom and bed as the location for a piece of writing is, of course, in *Molloy*, which famously opens by informing the reader that Molloy has usurped his mother's place in her bed: 'I am in my mother's room. It's I who live there now. I don't know how I got there … In any case I have her room. I sleep in her bed. I piss and shit in her pot. I have taken her place. I must resemble her more and more' (*GII*, 3). The protagonist of *Film* also sleeps in his mother's bed. Beckett's explanatory note indicates the degree to which he had come to locate the action of his works in this maternal space as he suggests, almost as an aside, 'It may be supposed that it is his mother's room, which he has not visited for many years and is now to occupy momentarily, to look after the pets, until she comes out of hospital' (*GIII*, 380). In occupying their mother's beds and bedrooms, these characters are subject to the maternal influence and energy that lingers in the space of her bedroom, a force resented by these characters, but also irresistible to them.

The importance of maternal beds and rooms as imaginative spaces is perhaps most succinctly asserted in *Company*, written in the late 1970s: 'You first saw the light in the room you most likely were conceived in' (*GIV*, 429). This identification of a maternal bed with conception and birth also features in *A Piece of Monologue*, the set of which is composed of a 'skull-sized white' lamp and the foot of a coffin-like white pallet bed (*GIII*, 453). In this meditation on the brevity of life and certainty of death, light and darkness assume symbolic resonance. The speaker repeatedly describes the difficult process of birth and the complicated and tentative lighting of the lamp in his room, establishing an imaginative affinity between both creative gestures in a space that is evidently based on May Beckett's bedroom: 'That first night. The room. The spill. The hands. The lamp. The gleam of brass' (*GIII*, 456). There is a recurrent causal association in Beckett's work of the moment of birth with the inevitable moment of death. One of the ways he conveys this is by identifying maternal beds as spaces where life begins and ends for his characters. A keen and persistent fantasy for many of Beckett's characters is the yearning to coffin themselves in their mother's beds and slip back to a time and state before their own births in satisfyingly symmetrical expirations. John Fletcher has suggested that most of Beckett's early heroes regard the womb as a 'protective calm' and life as 'a punishment, a pensum', which makes death 'a second, and perhaps happier birth', because 'it will finally reverse the process that has been so painful to recall and for which life itself has not been sufficient to atone'.[49] 'Birth was the death of him', as *A Piece of Monologue* opens, an apt gloss for many of Beckett's characters (*GIII*, 453).

Maternal figures take centre stage in three of Beckett's plays. In *All That Fall*, *Footfalls* and *Rockaby*, the three female protagonists have daughters rather than sons, and the relationship between mother and daughter is vexed, tainted by what throughout Beckett's work is suggested as the maternal sin of giving birth to a dying creature. Leo Bersani and Ulysse Dutoit make a similar point: 'If being born is a death sentence, then to give birth is a murderous act'.[50] The conception of life as a death sentence informs the corruption and decay that characterizes the physical experience of nearly all Beckett's characters and lies behind the vexed nature of the relationship between mother and offspring in his works, a relationship that is dictated by the brute fact of mortality. Pozzo's image in *Waiting for Godot* of giving birth astride a grave forcefully conveys this sense, present throughout Beckett's writing, of the specifically maternal crime or curse of initiating and perpetuating life, hence death. Beckett's identification of birth as a death sentence and designation of motherhood as a blameworthy act, anticipates the more extreme formulation by the Austrian writer Thomas Bernhard in which every parent must take responsibility for sponsoring the suicide of their offspring.

Where Bernhard's characters deny and decry life, and his narratives engage in a savage cycle of self-destruction, Beckett uses the trope of a regretted life foisted unthinkingly upon his characters to reflect upon the comparable authorial impertinence in the creation of narrative and characters. To date, this has been glossed by critics as a means of excluding women from the act of creation, with the generation of literature therefore happening in a space controlled exclusively by men. Frank Matton, for example, has assessed Molloy's effort to supplant his mother as a bid to exceed the maternal creative effort that brought him into being, in an

---

[49] John Fletcher, 'Malone "Giving Birth to into Death"', in *Twentieth Century Interpretations of Molloy, Malone Dies, The Unnamable*, ed. J.D. O'Hara (New Jersey: Prentice Hall, 1955), pp. 48–60, p. 60.
[50] Bersani and Dutoit, *Arts of Impoverishment*, p. 43.

apparently homosexual form of autogenesis.[51] Fintan O'Toole has similarly described the 'great conceit' of Flann O'Brien's *At Swim Two Birds* (1939) as that of 'literary creation as a form of parthenogenesis'.[52] O'Toole proposes that despite the great differences between O'Brien and Beckett in terms of family background, intellectual temperament and linguistic approach, this idiosyncratic view of literary creation is one of the few shared features of their writing:

> Writing is sex for an all-male, sex-averse society. Its children are conceived without all the bother and awkwardness of having to deal with women. In the bedroom that is the world of his narrators, congress with oneself generates the only life that is available – the life of words and stories.[53]

Matton and O'Toole both advance the argument that Beckett sought to write mothers out of his work by replacing the female body with the self-sufficient male authorial voice that creates in isolation. I propose instead that Beckett's singular formulation of the burden and responsibility of literary invention is to a large extent modelled on the maternal role in creation. Beckett uses maternal beds to mediate the regret of his characters at ever having begun life, and their longing to return to the quiet, darkness and calm before birth. In this scenario, mothers are not supplanted but instead are forcefully claimed by their errant sons. Several of Beckett's narratives are dominated by the characters' descriptions of the small, simple spaces they take up as if longing, by sheer descriptive élan, to dream themselves back into the womb. The protagonist of the post-war novella *The End* obtains great satisfaction from the makeshift nest he contrives in an upturned boat, described as his 'little kingdom' (*GIV*, 292). The narrator of the contemporaneous novella *The Expelled* likewise spends all day in a cab, sleeps in it and tries to convince the cabman to sell it to him without its horse. This trope also features in several prose works from the 1960s: *All Strange Away, Imagination Dead Imagine, Ping* and *Fizzles 1*. The efforts of all these characters fail, but towards the end of *Malone Dies*, before the bedridden Malone's strange description of Macmann's trip to the island, this strategy appears to have been vindicated:

---

[51] Frank Matton, 'Beckett's Trilogy and the Limits of Autobiography', in *Beckett On and On ...*, ed. Lois Oppenheim and Marius Buning (London: Associated University Presses, 1996), pp. 69–82, p. 79.
[52] Fintan O'Toole, 'Oblomov in Dublin', *New York Review of Books*, Volume 56, No. 13, August 13, 2009.
[53] Fintan O'Toole, 'Oblomov in Dublin'.

I am swelling. What if I should burst? The ceiling rises and falls, rises and falls, rhythmically, as when I was a foetus … Leaden light again, thick, eddying, riddled with little tunnels through to brightness, perhaps I should say air, sucking air … I am being given, if I may venture the expression, birth to into death, such is my impression. The feet are clear already, of the great cunt of existence. Favourable presentation I trust. My head will be the last to die. (*GII*, 276)

This desire for a soothing, maternal death is, however, considerably more likely to be satisfied in a rocking chair than a bed.

Rocking Chairs

The rocking chair features in Beckett's work for more than four decades, from *Murphy* to *Rockaby*, its movement explicitly identifying restful sleep with desired death and generating much of the ambivalence around death in his work. The rocking chairs that are associated with death in these texts are notably imagined in maternal terms. In *Molloy*, Moran gives an indication of the odds set against him before he has even left home on his doomed quest for Molloy, by describing the seated attitude of Martha, his servant and an ineffective maternal check on his sporadically savage fulfilment of his paternal duties: 'Martha watched me in silence, lolling in her rocking-chair. Like a Fate who had run out of thread' (*GII*, 115). The throne-like rocker lends Martha a physical air of mastery over Moran, and by associating her with one of the three Greek Fates, ancient spinning women who play out, weave and cut the thread of destiny, Beckett encourages the association of rocking chairs with the hidden and mysterious order of life and death. Two of John McGahern's short stories, in similar fashion, associate old ladies and death with rocking chairs. In 'Eddie Mac', Mrs Kirkwood dies in the rocking chair in which she habitually naps each day. The servant discovers her: 'The chair was still imperceptibly rocking before the window, but the book had fallen, and when she called there was no answer. An intense stillness was in the room.' Similarly, an old woman's death is signalled in 'The Country Funeral' by her now-empty 'brown rocking chair'.[54] Dickens may have had a similar association to both authors in mind when he described Mrs Clennam, the indomitable, wheelchair-bound matriarch of *Little Dorrit* (1855–57), as 'Fate in a go-cart'.[55]

---

[54] John McGahern, 'Eddie Mac'; 'The Country Funeral', *Creatures of the Earth: New and Selected Stories* (London: Faber, 2006), pp. 263–278, p. 265; pp. 369–408, p. 376.
[55] Charles Dickens, *Little Dorrit* (London: Arrow, 2008), p. 319.

Beckett's first rocking chair appears in *Murphy*. The spiritual gain of negation so desired in the novel is achieved by yielding the body to this calming object. The soothing rhythm of the rocker is a habit to which the eponymous hero and, later, his girlfriend Celia become dependent. Murphy describes the comfort he gets from the chair: 'First it gave his body pleasure, it appeased his body. Then it set him free in his mind' (*GI*, 4). Murphy ties himself to his rocking chair in the hope of assuaging and numbing his body, thus attaining mental freedom. Celia discovers him in an undignified heap: bound, upside down and naked, after an accident in which the chair overturned while he was tied into it. At the end of the novel, a gas leak helps Murphy to achieve such peace in this chair that he permanently transcends the cares of mortality, a pattern to be repeated in later rocking chairs:

> The rock got faster and faster, shorter and shorter, the gleam was gone, the grin was gone, the starlessness was gone, soon his body would be quiet. Most things under the moon got slower and slower and then stopped, a rock got faster and faster and then stopped. Soon his body would be quiet, soon he would be free. The gas went on in the w.c., excellent gas, superfine chaos. Soon his body was quiet. (*GI*, 151)

The addictive and stupefying qualities of the rocking chair recur in *Malone Dies*:

> In the first [cell] a young man, dead young, seated in an old rocking-chair, his shirt rolled up and his hands on his thighs, would have seemed asleep had not his eyes been wide open. He never went out, unless commanded to do so, and then someone had to accompany him, in order to make him move forward. (*GII*, 274)

For O, the protagonist of *Film*, the rocking chair offers the only safe space for unhurried examination of his photographs. His chair lulls him into states of inattention, ease, and finally sleep, in the closing scene of the film. In *Rockaby*, Beckett extends the potential of earlier rocking chairs, with the rocker occupying the technical and narrative heart of the play. The rocking chair onstage functions as both the physical set and as a talismanic hand-me-down, for the apparent death that concludes the play is clearly patterned on that of W's mother, who also died in the rocking chair, and who has subsequently haunted her daughter.

Beckett's writing exhibits a shift in register in its treatment of the maternal figure; Molloy's bitterly misogynistic acknowledgement of the powerful claim of his mother upon him gives way to the calmer, kinder maternal portraits of *Krapp's Last Tape* and *How It Is*. Mothers in Beckett's later works such as W in *Rockaby* are delicate creatures that inhabit elegiac spaces: iterative, fragmentary and suffused with the poignant haziness of dim and imperfect recollection, such portraits precisely evoke the insistence of grieving memory:

> let down the blind and down
> right down
> into the old rocker
> mother rocker
> where mother rocked
> all the years
> all in black
> best black
> sat and rocked
> rocked
> till her end came
> …
> dead one night
> in the rocker. (G*III*, 468)

W's shocking 'fuck life' in the closing moments of the play is an amplification of the maternal 'burning to be gone' in *Krapp's Last Tape*. The fall of her head onto her chest at the end of *Rockaby* is thus a vivid note of victory, rather than being merely pathetic or sentimental (*GIII*, 228, 470).[56]

The qualities of the rocking chair that offer succour are evident in its design: 'Pale wood highly polished to gleam when rocking. Footrest. Vertical back. Rounded inward curving arms to suggest embrace' (*GIII*, 462). This tenderness is emphasised throughout the play by W's 'white hands holding ends of armrests', while her intonation of 'those arms at last' articulates the relief of being back in the chair once more (*GIII*, 461). Further indication of the chair's potential to calm and care for W is given in Beckett's description of the quality of its 'rock': 'Slight. Slow. Controlled mechanically without assistance from W' (*GIII*, 462). This suggestion of a body being cradled and gently – if stiffly – rocked, sits neatly with Beckett's portraits of mothers. Unlike the soft, worn material of greatcoats that swaddle so many sons in a tactile and nurturing gesture of paternal affection, rocking chairs offer a rigid and domineering

---

[56] Leslie Hill has argued that W's exclamation somehow initiates life in the closing moments of the play. This is not convincing to me. See Leslie Hill, '"Fuck life": *Rockaby*, Sex, and the Body' in *Beckett On and On …*, pp. 19–26, p. 21, p. 25.

form of comfort, one that is typical of the rather more severe maternal love in his writing.[57]

Authorial Mothers and Silent Fathers

As the source of life, mothers are the origins from which Beckett's characters seek to distance themselves, yet whose approval is sought and whose will cannot be denied. The moment closest to a flouting of maternal will occurs in *Endgame*. Hamm, the aggressively disdainful and worst of sons, has had his parents unceremoniously stuffed into ashbins: punishment, perhaps, for their having brought him into the world. But after Clov announces the death of Nell, Hamm's mother, Hamm asks if he is 'very white' (*GIII*, 138). While this contains sardonic echoes of the Smeraldina in Beckett's early *Dream of Fair to Middling Women*, who similarly asks, 'Ne suis-je point pâle? Suis-je belle?', Hamm's question may also be a form of grieving, articulated in his own gruffly inimitable way.[58] The complex and contentious relationship between Beckett and his mother has been much canvassed by his biographers, and it is clear that this relationship informs his portraits of maternal characters. In an exchange that features several times in Beckett's prose, the shock of a maternal rebuke or withdrawal of affection is evoked. It is described in *Company*:

> Looking up at the blue sky and then at your mother's face you break the silence asking her if it is not in reality much more distant than it appears. The sky that is. The blue sky ... For some reason you could never fathom this question must have angered her exceedingly. For she shook off your little hand and made you a cutting retort you have never forgotten. (*GIV*, 429)

The same scenario is evoked in *Malone Dies*: 'I said, The sky is further away than you think, is it not, mama? ... She replied, to me her son, It is precisely as far away as it appears to be. She was right. But at the time I was aghast' (*GII*, 261). The exchange is most emphatically condensed in its first appearance, in *The End*, 'A small boy, stretching out his hands and looking up at the blue sky, asked his mother how such a thing was possible.

---

[57] The comforting lull of a steady rocking motion has been effectively used by the theatre company Pan Pan, who have seated audiences of *All That Fall* since 2011 in rocking chairs to listen in the dark to the unseen actors perform the play, making the concluding moments of discordant sound and blinding light all the more bracingly powerful.

[58] Beckett, *Dream of Fair to Middling Women* (New York: Arcade, 2006), p. 68. ['Am I not very white? Am I beautiful?' (my translation)]

Fuck off, she said' (*GIV*, 277). Tangible in each of Beckett's retellings is the child's hurt and mother's power. The affably bewildered, tender and slightly pathetic fathers in Beckett have nothing like this maternal force. It is the figure of the mother whose approval is sought in Beckett's work, yet whose influence is violently resisted, and against whom the artist son creates a distinctive identity and signature.

Beckett's depiction of fathers and the father–son relationship is one of companionable silence, whereas mothers ask questions and make demands, thereby provoking their sons into expression. Fathers are rarely heard in Beckett; even when they read a bedtime story to a number of appreciative sons, their voice is mutely inscribed into the fabric of the narrative. Mothers, on the other hand, will not be silenced. From no matter how far away, mothers can be heard, as in *From an Abandoned Work*: 'Then I raised my eyes and saw my mother still in the window waving, waving me back or on I don't know, or just waving, in sad helpless love, and I heard faintly her cries' (*GIV*, 342). Maternal voices hector, encourage, beseech and wheedle throughout Beckett's writing. Their strong presence should alert us to the affinity between Beckett's writing and a maternal, creative voice that insists on being heard, as is the case with the women's voices in *Rough for Radio I* and *II* (written in the late 1950s or early 1960s), *Eh Joe* (1965), *Ghost Trio* and *Footfalls* (both 1975).

This contrast between maternal and paternal influence is also registered on a material level, as we have seen. The paternal is embedded in the reassuring and useful hand-me-down of the greatcoat, while the maternal bed, like the rocking chair, encloses and holds the entire body, signalling the more intensely vexed physical relationship of Beckett's characters with their mothers, registered in their sustained denigration and reviling of the maternal body. In *Women in Samuel Beckett's Prose and Drama* (1993), Mary Bryden rather questionably proposes that Beckett's association of womb and tomb is of a similar order as the exuberantly matriarchal and life-affirming ideas of the feminist theorist Hélène Cixous.[59] Beckett's scatological, traumatic and regretted births cannot be recuperated in this way. The impossible maternal death longed for in his work is not imagined in terms of a union with the mother, but is figured rather as a return to the womb, to which his characters feel a strong proprietorial claim. Far from celebrating the womb as a space in which new life might potentially be nurtured, and from which it might emerge, this space is a contested

---

[59] Mary Bryden, *Women in Samuel Beckett's Prose and Drama: Her Own Other* (Basingstoke: Macmillan, 1993), p. 190.

one for Beckett's characters. Their attitude to the womb more accurately recalls that of the Austrian writer Joseph Roth. According to Michael Hofmann, Roth's translator, he 'reacted to his overproud and overprotective mother, Miriam, or Maria, to the extent that he sometimes claimed to have her pickled womb somewhere'.[60] The devastating combination in Roth's phrase of possessiveness so extreme that the organ has been preserved in an acidic solution and the careless neglect signalled by that shrug of 'somewhere' is much closer to the register in which Beckett's characters speak of the womb.

Beckett's attitude to birth is further complicated by his avowed prenatal memories, which he related at length in conversation with Knowlson in 1989, the year he died.

> I used to lie down on the couch and try to go back in my past. I think it probably did help. I think it helped me perhaps to control the panic. I certainly came up with some extraordinary memories of being in the womb. Intrauterine memories. I remember feeling trapped, of being imprisoned and unable to escape, of crying to be let out but no one could hear, no one was listening. I remember being in pain but being unable to do anything about it. (*DF*, 177)

In a letter to his friend Arland Ussher in 1937, Beckett distilled the above into a swaggering cod-autobiographical account: 'My memoirs begin under the table, on the eve of my birth, when my father gave a dinner party & my mother presided' (*LI*, 474). This same experience finds its way into *Watt*, where it is told from the mother's perspective, a rare occurrence in Beckett's work:

> ... that morning at breakfast Goff turns to me and says, Tetty, he says, Tetty, my pet, I should very much like to invite Thompson, Cream and Colquhoun to help us eat the duck, if I felt sure you felt up to it. Why, my dear, says I, I never felt fitter in my life ...
> The first mouthful of duck had barely passed my lips, said Tetty, when Larry leaped in my wom.
> Your what? Said Mr. Hackett.
> My wom, said Tetty.
> You know, said Goff, her woom.
> How embarrassing for you, said Mr. Hackett.
> I continued to eat, drink and make light conversation, said Tetty, and Larry to leap, like a salmon.

---

[60] *Joseph Roth: A Life in Letters*, ed. and trans. Michael Hofmann (London: Granta, 2013), xi.

What an experience for you, said Mr. Hackett.
There were moments, I assure you, when I thought he would tumble out on the floor, at my feet. (*GI*, 177)

Literary inspiration, debt and affiliation for male writers have often been cast in distinctly oedipal terms. In *Literature in Secret*, Jacques Derrida examines Kafka and Kierkegaard's frustrations with their fathers in order to address what he describes as the pivotal relationship between fathers, sons and writing: 'Literature would begin wherever one no longer knows who writes and who signs the narrative of the call – and of the 'Here I Am' – between the absolute Father and Son.'[61] In *Kafka's Dick*, Alan Bennett gleefully stages this same oppressive patriarchal influence on the artist son's signature. If Derrida thought of the father–son relationship in terms of secrecy, forgiveness and literature, Bennett trumps him when he has Kafka's monstrous father Hermann K say, 'A book is a coffin and in it is your father's body.'[62]

There is nothing in Beckett's work like these formulations of writing as a monument erected by the son to honour the father. Beckett, by marked contrast, draws explicit and illuminating parallels between the processes of birth, writing and defecation. Birth is repeatedly associated with the scatological: Molloy introduces his mother as the woman 'who brought me into the world, through the hole in her arse if my memory is correct. First taste of the shit' (*GII*, 12). So too, however, is writing. Beckett frequently describes the process of writing in scatological terms, in markedly similar terms to those he uses for birth. Mark Nixon has surveyed the shift in Beckett's writing-metaphors from an association with faeces to birth, and cites Beckett's description of submitting work to a magazine as sending them 'three turds from my Central Lavatory' in a letter to McGreevy in 1930. In 1953 to Con Leventhal, however, the metaphor had changed: 'Watt is having a difficult birth but is expected out into the dark of day next week.'[63] Here, Beckett suggests that birth and writing are comparably slow, painful means of bringing life into being. Beckett's negatively inflected awareness of maternal power seems to tie in directly with his own skewed self-portrait as author: mothers and writers foist life, and therefore hardship and death, on their creations. Paul Stewart has also

[61] Jacques Derrida, *The Gift of Death and Literature in Secret*, trans. David Wills (Chicago: University of Chicago Press, 2008), p. 134.
[62] Alan Bennett, *Kafka's Dick* in *Plays Two* (London: Faber and Faber, 1998), pp. 1–116, p. 86.
[63] Mark Nixon, '"Writing Myself into the Ground": Textual Existence and Death in Beckett', in *Beckett and Death*, pp. 22–30, pp. 23–24.

noted the link drawn by Beckett between sexual reproduction and literary production:

> Beckett's aesthetic creation is shadowed by natural forms of procreation, and all the attendant horrors. Although Beckett attempts to turn away from paradigms of creativity that are informed by, or predicated on, natural procreation, the result still remains the same: the creation of a suffering being. This is compounded by the fact that Beckett, as author, must elicit speech and possibly even meaning from this new suffering being; and the means to that end are further suffering. In such a way, artistic creation is implicated within the same ethical considerations as sexual reproduction.[64]

In the conclusion to this book, I will consider the implications of Beckett's singular equation of literary creativity and procreation in greater length, and hope to offer a possible answer to Stewart, who ends his book with a question: 'Why, almost to his deathbed, did Beckett keep creating? Why did he not just stop?'[65]

The creative function of mothers sees them blamed for the infliction of suffering that characterizes life in Beckett's writing, and as a result mothers are often singled out for bitter invective. However, if birth condemns unknowing creations to a sham life, this neatly matches Beckett's own idiosyncratic formulation of authorial invention. In Beckett's writing, as we have seen, many maternal figures wear widow's weeds, and we are given to understand that the mother's function as a custodian of grief is directly related to the maternal role in creation. The ultimate maternal gift, as it is presented in Beckett, is not life, but the certainty of death, granting an end to the misery inflicted on all living creatures. In the next two chapters, we will see how Beckett was preoccupied by the cruelty he saw as implicit in literary creation. To have created life, even if only from words, was an act that deeply troubled him, and if he jocularly referred to his books as 'abortions', he also sought to expiate the guilt of having brought them to life by returning his characters to the peace and rest of nothingness from which he had roused them.[66]

---

[64] Paul Stewart, *Sex and Aesthetics in Beckett's Work* (New York: Palgrave Macmillan, 2011), p. 196.
[65] Stewart, *Sex and Aesthetics in Beckett's Work*, p. 198.
[66] Bernold, *Beckett's Friendship: 1979–1989*, p. 31.

CHAPTER 3

Props

Bicycles, Wheelchairs, Crutches, Sticks

Literary Prosthetics

Pascal might have had Beckett's writing in mind when he claimed that 'Our nature consists in motion; complete rest is death.'[1] Their relative ease or frustration of movement is a central concern for Beckett's characters, just as the tension between motion and stasis is a crucial factor in the narratives of every medium and period throughout Beckett's work. Four lines that span Beckett's career indicate this importance of movement. The poem 'Serena III' from *Echo's Bones and Other Precipitates* closes with the lines: 'keep on the move / keep on the move' (*GIV*, 27). Similarly, Malone speaks of parents moving babies unceasingly about the house in which he finds himself, 'to prevent their forming the habit of motionlessness, in anticipation of the day when they will have to move about unaided' (*GII*, 213). Most concise is the statement by the narrator of *From an Abandoned Work*: 'I have never in my life been on my way anywhere, but simply on my way', while Beckett's last prose work, *Stirrings Still*, contains this melancholic variation on the same idea: 'In the same place as when paced from wall to wall all places as the same' (*GIV*, 341; 488–89). These four lines attest to the imperative of movement for Beckett's characters throughout his writing, from the halting journeys of fictional protagonists to the free perambulations of poetic figures to barely mobile but restless characters onstage.

Conventionally, a prosthetic is a device to replace lost function.[2] The objects in this chapter supplement the decreasing physical capacity of

---

[1] Blaise Pascal, *Pascal's Pensées*, trans. W.F. Trotter (New York: E.P. Dutton, 1958), p. 37.
[2] *OED*.

Beckett's characters to keep moving, and in doing so, these objects prop up the narratives that are organised around this movement. These objects do not, however, either silently correct or seek to erase the underlying physical impediment to movement for Beckett's characters. On the contrary, Beckett's literary prosthetics assist the generation of his narratives precisely in their facility to make more visible and tangible the difficult motion of his characters. These objects follow the pattern of decreasing motility in Beckett's work: from the pleasurable speed of bicycles to the slower roll of wheelchairs, and from the swinging arc between crutches to the asymmetrical shuffle of sticks. As movement becomes ever more challenging for his characters, it is accompanied by a corresponding increase in the urgency with which they attempt to resist stasis, thereby preventing the fall into silence that would signal the cessation of their narratives. By foregrounding attention in this way on the anguished efforts through which his characters move and his texts are generated, Beckett's writing adopts a unique approach to the capacity and limitations of his characters' bodies. Physical disability is thus an essential element of Beckett's writing, while the literary prosthetics of this chapter signal Beckett's interest in disrupting the smooth progress of his characters' movement and narratives alike.

Beckett's idiosyncratic treatment of the kinetic struggles of his characters does not fit neatly within the literary models evoked in disability studies. In *Narrative Prosthesis* (2000), David T. Mitchell and Sharon L. Snyder set out what they see as the function of disability in literature: 'disability pervades literary narrative, first, as a stock feature of characterisation and, second, as an opportunistic metaphorical device.'[3] In this reading, the disability of a character is described in order to point out its deviation from the normality and bodily wholeness promoted as preferable elsewhere in the work of literature. This is evidently not the case in Beckett's writing, where conventional states, be they physical, social or moral, are only represented rarely and then in order to be decried and refused. A more useful conception of the function of physical disability in Beckett's work features in Ato Quayson's *Aesthetic Nervousness* (2007). Here, Quayson articulates what I believe to be the essence of Beckett's focus on the limping body and its efforts to complete impossible journeys: 'Disability has almost the character of an aesthetic repetition compulsion in Beckett, a return to the impaired human body as a means

---

[3] David T. Mitchell and Sharon L. Snyder, *Narrative Prosthesis: Disability and the Dependencies of Discourse* (Ann Arbor: University of Michigan Press, 2000), p. 47.

of framing a series of concerns of a creative and philosophical kind.'[4] Quayson proceeds, however, to take issue with the implausible physical aspects of Molloy's method of cycling while using his crutches. Quayson's frustration with the lack of strict verisimilitude in Beckett's description of Molloy astride his bicycle echoes similar criticism within disability studies of literary representations of disabled bodies that deviate from realistic portrayal.[5] This somewhat prescriptive demand within disability studies for conventionally realistic physical portraits has forcefully illustrated for me the unique quality of Beckett's treatment of the impeded and struggling body: his skewed realism rejects the socially valorized categories of family, work, love, sex and health; moreover, Beckett's broken bodies directly generate his texts.

This chapter builds on studies of the frustrated movement in Beckett's writing by Vivian Mercier, Pierre Chabert, Ulrika Maude and Steven Connor. In his 1956 *Irish Times* review, Vivian Mercier describes *Waiting for Godot* as 'a play in which nothing happens, twice', an aphorism which seems to damn Beckett with faint praise, and which has itself been praised and repeated ever since.[6] Mercier's bon mot was at one time referred to in order to underscore the argument that Beckett's work was centrally preoccupied with stasis and inertia, a perception no doubt encouraged by the prominence of the word 'waiting' in his most famous play. The critical shift of focus onto the phenomenological and material aspects of Beckett's writing has challenged this perception, however, and as early as 1982, Pierre Chabert emphasised the importance of the tension between movement and immobility in Beckett's dramatic works. Chabert describes the 'Beckettian body' as one typically 'deprived of the faculty of movement', and movement in Beckett's dramatic works as an attribute that is 'characteristically exposed or explored only in relationship to the difficulty or impossibility of moving', but he also proposes that in Beckett's theatre, 'Movement and immobility operate reciprocally and dynamically, each enhancing the dramatic effect of the other.'[7] In *Beckett,*

---

[4] Quayson, Ato, *Aesthetic Nervousness: Disability and the Crisis of Representation* (New York: Columbia University Press, 2007), p. 57.
[5] Quayson, *Aesthetic Nervousness*, pp. 82–83. See, for example, Lennard J. Davis, 'Constructing Normalcy', in *The Disability Studies Reader*, ed. Lennard J. Davis, 3rd edn (New York: Routledge, 2010), pp. 3–19, 13–14.
[6] Vivian Mercier, 'The Uneventful Event', *Irish Times*, 18 February 1956, p. 6. In context, Mercier's line was not a witheringly pithy put-down, but an expression of wonder that a writer who had had so little to do with the theatre had managed to create a work of 'consummate stagecraft', and a play that 'keeps audiences glued to their seats'.
[7] Pierre Chabert, 'The Body in Beckett's Theatre', *JOBS* 8 (1982), 23–28, p. 23.

Technology and the Body (2009), Ulrika Maude explores the voluntary and involuntary movement of characters in Beckett's trilogy of novels and *Waiting for Godot*. Maude notes the emphasis by Beckett on 'motility and its problems' in his writing, and argues that the body presented by Beckett is a 'grotesque' means of subverting the phenomenological conception of movement as an affirmative gesture.[8] While Maude's earlier studies in this area considered Beckett's treatment of movement in light of medical pathology and perceptual technology, in *Beckett, Technology and the Body*, she focuses upon the abject body and the impact of the grotesque tradition on Beckett's writing, and concludes that the 'body's weakness in Beckett turns out to be a form of strength'.[9] Such recuperation of a positive value is anathema to Beckett's work, I believe, but I agree with Maude that Beckett plays with the relationship between physical weakness and resilience in very interesting ways. However, my primary interest in this chapter is to examine how the difficult movement of Beckett's characters operates as a pivotal and constitutive element in the formation of his narratives. In this regard, Steven Connor's analysis of Beckett's kinetic corporeality in *Beckett, Modernism and the Material Imagination* (2014) helpfully identifies the attentiveness paid by Beckett's writing 'to questions of weight, balance, position, orientation and speed, whether in its precise notation of Watt's way of walking, or its composition of the constricted figures of *Ping* and *All Strange Away*, or the precise characterisations of stance, gesture and movement when Beckett directed his plays'. Connor is at pains to emphasise that this attentiveness does not reduce the body in Beckett's writing to 'an object of calculation or contemplation', but rather 'places the body in a field of action and reaction'.[10]

One of the advantages of tracing the recurrence of Beckett's poor materials across various media is that the insights offered by one medium-specific analysis of Beckett's use of an object may fruitfully be applied

---

[8] Ulrika Maude, *Beckett, Technology and the Body* (Cambridge: Cambridge University Press, 2009), p. 83.
[9] Maude, *Beckett, Technology and the Body*, p. 112. In a 2007 article, Maude identifies a number of objects as prosthetics, including telescopes, spectacles, crutches, a bicycle, stick and phial (Maude, '"whole body like gone": Beckett and Technology', *JOBS*, 16.1&2 (2007): 150–60). I have defined literary prosthetics as those objects used by a series of Beckett's characters to assist their movement while making their inability to do so unaided more visible, but Maude's prosthetic devices are 'instances of organ- or sensory extension, in a positive sense, or as a form of organ replacement, to make up for an individual deficiency or lack' (*Beckett, Technology and the Body*, p. 128).
[10] Steven Connor, *Beckett, Modernism and the Material Imagination*, p. 20.

when analysing appearances of the same object in other media. Recent developments in material studies of the theatre have yielded interesting ways of thinking about the function and meaning of dramatic objects. In *The Stage Life of Props* (2003), Andrew Sofer argues that 'motion is the prop's defining feature', and that any examination of a prop must therefore emphasise its dynamic, active nature, restoring to this object the meaning it accrues during a performance but is denied by a literary analysis that freezes it as a symbol.[11] Sofer's emphasis on the importance of animation and fluidity of meaning indicates the family resemblance between stage properties and Beckett's material canon. Both sets of objects carry with them a host of associational references and 'spring to imaginative life' in response to their manipulation by characters; yet while Sofer declares his intention to 'refocus the emerging critical dialogue on the stage property by locating the prop squarely in the theatrical event', I propose that as we follow the migration of the fourteen objects under study in this book throughout Beckett's oeuvre, these objects carry with them echoes of former appearances, thereby establishing a resonance that is not bound to their function in a single text, and which enables them to operate as recurring manifestations of Beckett's evolving literary imagination.[12]

When the objects in this chapter have attracted attention to date, they have most frequently been considered as ciphers for philosophical theories about the nature of selfhood, or the relationship between the mind and body.[13] Under its entry for 'stick', *The Grove Companion to Samuel Beckett* confidently declares that 'the problem of the stick is that of the body, the dilemma of self-extension' and asks 'If the body is known in immediate relation to the self, as Schopenhauer affirms, does the stick exist in the same way or in an intermediate relation, to either self or the body?' (*GC*, 542). This chapter proposes instead that Beckett transposed the ease or difficulty he was experiencing in moving the story onward onto his characters' ability, difficulty or inability to keep moving. Beckett's literary prosthetics play an integral role in translating the material challenges of writing into his characters' attempts to journey across page, stage and screen.

---

[11] Andrew Sofer, *The Stage Life of Props* (University of Michigan Press, 2003), vi.
[12] Sofer, *The Stage Life of Props*, p. 3; p. vii.
[13] See, for example, Tom Conley, 'Crutches', *Chicago Review*, 33.2 (1982), 84–92; Kathleen Woodward, 'Transitional Objects and the Isolate: Samuel Beckett's "Malone Dies"', *Contemporary Literature*, 26.2 (Summer 1985), 140–54; Hugh Kenner, 'The Cartesian Centaur' in *Samuel Beckett: A Critical Study*, pp. 117–32; Dan Gunn, 'La bicyclette irlandaise: Flann O'Brien et Samuel Beckett', *L'Errance. Tropismes No. 5* (1991), 143–71, 143, 162.

Props

The paucity of healthy, agile characters in Beckett's writing, and the profusion instead of weak, sick, suffering and deformed bodies, means that his characters often require aids to move around. The objects under study here are the most important of these props: bicycles, wheelchairs, crutches and sticks. These objects used by Beckett's weak or lame characters to keep themselves moving serve to emphasise the physical impediments to even minor progress for them, while simultaneously drawing attention to the hidden authorial effort behind such clumsily elaborate arrangements. Such objects are literary prosthetics because as they propel Beckett's lame characters forward and thus permit his halting narratives to advance, these objects reveal the degree to which Beckett's writing is dependent upon this deliberate hobbling of poetic, fictional or dramatic progress. Examination of the material aids used by his characters reveals Beckett's writing as a site where the integrity and power of the able body and the correspondingly linear narration of its movement within a literary work is rejected in favour of the more disruptive creative potential contained within the disabled body and frustrated progress.

Bicycles

In September 1967, Beckett sent a giddily courteous response to a query about bicycles he had received from Kenneth J.H. Reid, who is glossed rather tartly by the editors of the fourth and final volume of *The Letters of Samuel Beckett* as a 'resident of Toronto' who 'cultivated famous persons with Irish backgrounds'. (*LIV*, 88) Here is that letter:

Dear Mr Reid,

> Thank you for your letter.
> I am sorry to disappoint you, but I have nothing of interest to say on the subject of bikes and their place in the social life of Dublin at that time. They were used in a maniacal way by elderly persons desiring to keep young. I kicked many under me, from the age of 6 on, including a green one. I played childish bicycle polo with my brother in a field. Wisdom Healy had a bicycle-polo team of which my father was a member. When we punctured far from home we stuffed the tire with grass. I once knew one with rod-transmission. The smart way to mount was to spring into the saddle or via the projecting part of the back hub. A favourite term of abuse was 'cycling gouger.' There was a song:
> Daisy, Daisy, give me your answer, do,
> I'm half crazy all for the love of you,

> It won't be a stylish marriage,
> I can't afford a carriage,
> But you'll look sweet
> On the seat
> Of a bicycle built for two.
>
> Sincerely
> Sam. Beckett (*LIV*, 87–88)

Beckett's cheerful nostalgia for bicycles is on full display here, somewhat contradicting his opening claim that he had 'nothing of interest to say on the subject of bikes and their place in the social life of Dublin at that time.' The editors contextualise Beckett's points of reference in this letter: 'Wisdom Healy was a cycle agent, who in 1934 had a shop at 46a Rathmines Road, Dublin' and 'SB recollects (somewhat faultily) the refrain of a popular song … written by English composer Harry Dacre in 1892.' (*LIV*, 88) By the time he wrote this letter, the bicycle had disappeared from Beckett's writing, but his enthusiasm for this object is undimished. Characters wheel through Beckett's poetry and fiction on bicycles from the 1930s to the early 1960s. In her study of the twilight years of the Union of Great Britain and Ireland, Mary Jones has noted that 'by 1910, the bicycle has become ubiquitous' in Ireland.[14] Its continuing popularity in the following decades is indicated by Figure 7.

It is not true to claim, as Ackerley and Gontarski do in *The Grove Companion to Samuel Beckett*, echoing Clov, that 'there are no more bicycles' after *Endgame*, for bicycles feature in *All That Fall* in the late 1950s and *Film* in the early 1960s (*GC*, 55). Many of the narratives related to bicycles are taken up with descriptions of characters' motion on a bicycle, whether the euphoric speed of his competent cyclists or the jerking comic discomfort of his cripples. In addition to descriptions of bicycles, these narratives incorporate the formal experience of cycling. Recalling his discussions with Beckett about adapting *Mercier and Camier* for the stage, the theatre director Frederick Neumann relates their agreement that the novel was amenable to such adaptation because it was already generically like a 'road play'. He proceeds to identify this looseness of structure with the centrality of the bicycle in the novel:

> *Mercier and Camier* is a kind of road play. 'It's a picaresque work, therefore you can move the text around, as you will', Beckett said. I must say, I was just amazed. And it seemed to walk through time, not just down a road, but through time, and through different spaces. Or time spaces. That of the

---

[14] Mary Jones, *The Other Ireland: Changing Times 1870–1920* (Dublin: Macmillan, 2011), p. 224.

Figure 7 Independent Collection, 'Crowds on College Green, cyclists and tram' (c. 1940–50). Courtesy of the National Library of Ireland.

First World War: a time of bicycles. In fact, I once used that as a kind of subtitle for it: 'A Time of Bicycles'. And there was a kind of slow, wheeling movement by human beings that seemed to allow for conversation and gaff between two buddies. (*BR*, 243)

Like Neumann, W.H. Auden used bicycles to characterise this time: 'already it is millions of heartbeats ago / back to the Bicycle Age'.[15] Beckett's bicycles, in common with the rest of his poor materials, date from the very early twentieth century when they were commonplace, popular and culturally symbolic of romance and freedom.

In *Bicycle: The History* (2004), David Herlihy traces the evolution of its design from wooden draisine, velocipede or pedestrian curricle to the familiar machine with us since 'the end of the nineteenth century'.[16] These precursors to the bicycle fell under the generic term hobby-horse and were

---

[15] W.H. Auden, 'Thanksgiving for a Habitat: I Prologue: The Birth of Architecture', in *Selected Poems*, ed. Edward Mendelson (London: Faber and Faber, 1979), p. 252.
[16] David V. Herlihy, *Bicycle: The History* (New Haven and London: Yale University Press, 2004), p. 6.

all subject to ridicule. Herlihy notes that despite the original context of the hobby-horse as 'a substitute for a horse', it ended up a 'mere toy'.[17] The elaborately cumbersome progress of Molloy cycling on crutches, with its demented magnification of the physical work required to propel him forward, points up his infirmities and the difficulty for him of covering ground, but it also forcefully establishes Molloy's portrait, by emphasising the singular nature of the manic game he is playing. Beckett's strategy here echoes Laurence Sterne's celebrated literary hobby-horse in his 1759 novel *Tristram Shandy*. In a parenthetical aside, the manner in which most things are explained in the novel, Sterne's narrator describes the hobby-horse of his work as 'a secondary figure, and a kind of back-ground to the whole', and this is how it has hitherto been considered.[18] Critics have tended to reiterate Sterne's joke about how each character's preoccupation with his or her individual obsessions to the exclusion of any other points of view causes communication to collapse into slapstick confusion. No study has yet examined the type of motion implied by the hobby-horse and the possible relation of this wildly veering and jumpy movement to the narrative of *Tristram Shandy*. It is no coincidence that almost every page of Sterne's temperamental, jerking, weaving, gallivanting novel is peppered with references to the hobby-horse, and that the sudden halts or canters of the text are deliberately designed to unseat the rider or reader at any moment. I suggest that Beckett uses the bicycle as Sterne does the hobby-horse: in the works of both authors, the machines are used to determine the structure, theme, rhythm and speed of the narrative.

Many of Beckett's characters and narrators make toys of ostensibly useful things by introducing unnecessary complications and undermining their practical function. Indeed, this deliberate clumsiness is often their favourite form of play. The passionately childlike affection for and attachment to bicycles displayed by Beckett's characters contributes much to their curmudgeonly yet strangely innocent appeal. This explains the surprising similarity between several of Beckett's old men and the child narrator of L.P. Hartley's *The Go-Between*. Published in 1953, but set largely in 1900, the narrator Leo recalls being told by Marcus, his friend and host, that the surprise gift he is to receive for his thirteenth birthday is a bicycle.

> To a child of today this might have seemed an anti-climax, to me it opened the gates of heaven. A bicycle was the thing I wanted most in the world,

---

[17] Herlihy, *Bicycle: The History*, p. 30.
[18] Laurence Sterne, *The Life and Opinions of Tristram Shandy, Gentleman*, ed. Ian Campbell Ross (Oxford: Oxford University Press, 2009), p. 15.

> and had least hope of getting, for it was, I knew by inquiry, beyond my mother's purse. I plied Marcus with questions about it – its make, its size, its tyres, its lamp, its brakes.[19]

This perfect gift is somewhat soured for Leo when he is told that it is green to reflect his own naivety.[20] Without, one presumes, the same symbolic implications, Beckett also owned a green bicycle 'in his salad days' (*GC*, 55). Ackerley and Gontarski make this observation in parenthesis after describing Molloy's bicycle, implying that Beckett wrote his own bicycle into the narrative. This is indeed likely, for Molloy declares his affection for this 'dear bicycle' in terms worthy of Hartley's child narrator.

> Dear bicycle, I shall not call you bike, you were green, like so many of your generation, I don't know why. It is a pleasure to meet it again. To describe it at length would be a pleasure. It had a little red horn instead of the bell fashionable in your days. To blow this horn was for me a real pleasure, almost a vice. I will go further and declare that if I were obliged to record, in a roll of honour, those activities which in the course of my interminable existence have given me only a mild pain in the balls, the blowing of a rubber horn – toot! – would figure among the first. And when I had to part from my bicycle I took off the horn and kept it about me. (*GII*, 12)

On the opening page of the novel, Molloy is portrayed as a bedridden invalid who has taken the place of his ancient mother; immediately before the above excerpt, it is revealed that he is a cripple on crutches, so one purpose of this exuberant passage is to mark another phase along the dramatic trajectory of mobility central to his narrative and that of the trilogy. From a position of near-terminal immobility, the action of the novel allows for a series of receding retrospects on times of greater mobility, much of it, as we will see, characterised by a manic and ludic energy. Later, having been released by the police and reunited with his bicycle, Molloy plays with the contented focus of a child, watching the shadows thrown by his bicycle against the glaring white wall of the barracks in the sun:

> A confused shadow was cast. It was I and my bicycle. I began to play, gesticulating, waving my hat, moving my bicycle to and fro before me, blowing the horn, watching the wall. They were watching me through the bars, I felt their eyes upon me. The policeman on guard at the door told me to go away. He needn't have, I was calm again. (*GII*, 21)

---

[19] L.P. Hartley, *The Go-Between* (London: Penguin, 1958), p. 189.
[20] Hartley, *The Go-Between*, pp. 189–90.

Molloy's infantile fondness and enthusiasm for his bicycle is shared by several of Beckett's other characters. No explanation is given for Belacqua's abrupt decision to abandon his date and escape on a bicycle in the short story 'Fingal', because none is presumed necessary. He is simply referred to as 'Belacqua, who could on no account resist a bicycle' (*GIV*, 92). This description of Belacqua is a later, abbreviated version of the introduction to his namesake in *Dream of Fair to Middling Women*, the opening chapter of which is almost entirely taken up with a description of his pleasure astride a bicycle: 'Behold Belacqua an overfed child pedalling, faster and faster, his mouth ajar and his nostrils dilated, down a frieze of hawthorn after Findlater's van, faster and faster till he cruise alongside of the hoss, the black fat wet rump of the hoss.'[21] Like Hartley's Leo, who declares his imagined bicycle 'already dearer to me than anything I possessed' long before he sees it, or the narrator of Flann O'Brien's *The Third Policeman*, who decides to steal the Sergeant's bicycle upon realising that he 'liked this bicycle more than … any other bicycle, better even than … some people with two legs', it is implicit throughout most of Beckett's works that a bicycle is a thing to be desired with the ardent and unwavering will typical of a child.[22]

Moran's physical deterioration means the boon for his son of a bicycle. Faced with his son's lukewarm reaction to this good news, Moran perseveres for some pages in attempting to impress upon him the enormity of this turn of events, 'decidedly set on hearing him say he was pleased', until he gives up, exasperated and disappointed by the unnatural composure of the boy. 'I asked him if he was pleased. He did not look pleased. I repeated these instructions and asked him again if he was pleased. He looked if anything stupefied. A consequence perhaps of the great joy he felt. Perhaps he could not believe his ears' (*GII*, 138, 135). The converse situation is presented in *Endgame*, where it is recalled that the child Clov displayed all the passion absent in Moran's son, but to no avail, for Clov never received the bicycle he so vehemently desired.

> HAMM Go and get two bicycle-wheels.
> CLOV There are no more bicycle-wheels.
> HAMM What have you done with your bicycle?
> CLOV I never had a bicycle.

---

[21] Beckett, *Dream of Fair to Middling Women*, p. 1. In this illustration of pleasure derived from the motion of a bicycle, it is noteworthy that Beckett named his hero after the representative of indolence and stasis in Dante's *Divine Comedy*.
[22] Hartley, *The Go-Between*, p. 194; O'Brien, *Third Policeman*, p. 170.

> HAMM The thing is impossible.
> CLOV When there were still bicycles I wept to have one. I crawled at your feet. You told me to go to hell. Now there are none. (*GIII*, 97)

To add further insult to injury, and in an indication of his either perfect indifference or sadistic pleasure in needling Clov, Hamm returns to the topic soon after this exchange while Clov is taking him on a 'turn' of the room, declaring, 'We'd need a proper wheel-chair. With big wheels. Bicycle-wheels!' (*GIII*, 109).

Unlike Leo's bicycle, which was intended to ferry romantic messages between lovers, one of the main function of bicycles in Beckett's work is the achievement of freedom and escape from romantic encounters with women, elegantly realised as a result of the smooth and easy motion of the bicycle. This graceful union between man and machine in Beckett's writing was observed by Hugh Kenner in his 1962 *Samuel Beckett*, which offers the most thorough and influential study of bicycles in Beckett's work to date. Kenner's 'Cartesian Centaur' is man become machine. He identifies the strange cyclist of *The Calmative* as the most perfect example of contentedness in Beckett's writing, since the mind of the cyclist is preoccupied with the newspaper he holds in front of him, while his body maintains its posture and course on the bicycle: 'Across the entire Beckett landscape there passes no more self-sufficient image of felicity.'[23] The passage in question in Beckett's novella is part of a sequence of dreamlike scenes, all observed by the narrator with the same blithe, detached equanimity.

> I only saw one cyclist! He was going the same way as I was. All were going the same way as I was, vehicles too, I have only just realised it. He was pedalling slowly in the middle of the street, reading a newspaper which he held with both hands spread open before his eyes. Every now and then he rang his bell without interrupting his reading. I watched him recede till he was no more than a dot on the horizon. (*GIV*, 269)

Kenner accurately describes the strange figure as a 'phantom', as it rolls through the scene like a ghost who has returned to the town after the war that permeates the atmosphere of this story, but is nowhere mentioned directly.[24] The smooth, eerily silent progress of the cyclist in *The Calmative* is, however, atypical of bicycles in Beckett, and can be compared only with the two bicycles that pass in the background of *Film*. In both works, bicycles evoke a vividly otherworldly atmosphere, largely

---

[23] Kenner, *Samuel Beckett: A Critical Study*, pp. 121–22.
[24] Kenner, *Samuel Beckett: A Critical Study*, pp. 121–22.

due to the curious detachment from the action of the observing narrator or character. These two dispassionately described bicycles contrast starkly with the engrossed absorption in the variously pleasurable or painful motion of the many cyclist-narrators and characters elsewhere in Beckett. Kenner's influential study has determined the critical response to date of bicycles in Beckett's work, with the result that Beckett's keen attention to the embodied experience of his characters' movement has been largely ignored.[25] Given the uncritical acceptance of Kenner's suggestion that Beckett's fiction most often takes the shape of a journey and involves extended play with objects, while his theatre is objectless and static, it has also contributed to a larger discourse within Beckett studies where the prose is considered apart from the drama, a convention which this book seeks to challenge, following in the footsteps of scholars like Ulrika Maude.[26] Indeed, as the section on crutches will show, Beckett is at pains to undermine the narrative trope of the journey in the trilogy and later works of fiction.

In several works of poetry and fiction, Beckett matches the rhythm to a bicycle's motion. His first poetry collection, *Echo's Bones and Other Precipitates*, published in 1935, is particularly exemplary in this regard. The poems are dominated by great bursts of energy succeeded by calm that match the intermittent furious pedalling and gliding speed of the recurring cycling figure. In 'Sanies I', the dynamic throttle of the poem's opening is established by conjuring the physical effort and rhythm of pedalling: 'pounding along in three ratios like a sonata', 'pestling the transmission', 'potwalloping now through the promenaders', 'belting along in the meantime clutching the bike'. The frequent references of the poem to the cyclist's seat suggest a very particular form of pleasure: 'pommelled scrotum atra cura on the step', 'all heaven in the sphincter / the sphincter' (*GIV*, 18). In 'Enueg I', three very different types of movements are described. First, the effort required to climb a hill: 'toil to the crest of the surge of the steep perilous bridge'; next, the thrilling descent: 'lapse down blankly under the scream of the hoarding'; and last, the sustained but flagging momentum that carries the figure into a darkening evening: 'throttled with clouds' (*GIV*, 11). By the third stanza this speed has been spent

---

[25] Studies that follow Kenner's interpretation include John Fletcher, 'Samuel Beckett and the Philosophers', *Comparative Literature*, 17.1 (Winter, 1965), 43–56, p. 51; Daniel Gunn, 'La bicyclette irlandaise: Flann O'Brien et Samuel Beckett', *L'Errance. Tropismes No. 5* (1991), 143–71, 162; Janet Menzies, 'Beckett's Bicycles', *JOBS*, 6 (Autumn 1980), 97–105, 105.
[26] See Maude, *Beckett, Technology and the Body*, p. 83.

and the figure is on foot. The shift from bicycle to foot also features in 'Serena III':

> whereas dart away through the cavorting scapes
> bucket o'er Victoria Bridge that's the idea
> slow down slink down the Ringsend Road
> Irishtown Sandymount puzzle ...
> hide yourself not in the Rock keep on the move
> keep on the move. (*GIV*, 27–28)

In this sequence, Beckett realises in poetry the shifts in speed and different types of motion involved in walking and cycling, and the open-mouthed contentment of the speeding figure. Indeed, when this figure dismounts from the bicycle that carried him as far as the sand, the tenor of the poem shifts so that it no longer records a visceral sensation of speed, but descends into literary pastiche. At the end of 'Serena III', Beckett's figure breaks wind and makes water on the beach, placing him in the footsteps of Stephen Dedalus on Sandymount strand, undoing in this evocation the agency and individuality of his poetic figure and undermining the earlier vividly realised motion on the bicycle.

According to Knowlson, the bicycle scene in 'Fingal' has its origins in an exchange Beckett had with an old man in 1932 after cycling to Donabate. '"That's where Dean Swift came to his motte," said the old man. "What motte?" asked Beckett, not recognising the unusual word for mistress. "Stella" was the reply' (*DF*, 167). Beckett was not familiar with the word 'motte', the colloquial Dublin term for girlfriend, and used it in the story, where his own protagonist escapes from his mistress on a Swift bicycle at the same tower used for romantic assignations by Jonathan Swift.[27] As in Beckett's poetry, 'Fingal' translates the pleasurable speed of Belacqua's stolen bicycle into language that strains to incorporate sensual experience into its rhythm. The scene presents Belacqua at his most contented.

> It was a fine light machine, with red tires and wooden rims. He ran down the margin to the road and it bounded alongside under his hand. He mounted and they flew down the hill and round the corner till they came at length to the stile that led into the field where the church was. The machine was a treat to ride on, on his right hand the sea was foaming among the rocks, the sands ahead were another yellow again, beyond them

---

[27] Molloy also attempts to escape a woman hounding him on a bicycle. These two flagrantly unromantic cyclists find their opposite numbers in the nostalgic image of two bicycles passing by in the background of *Film*, each cycled by a man with his date sitting side-saddle on the crossbar.

in the distance the cottages of Rush were bright white, Belacqua's sadness fell from him like a shift. (*GIV*, 96)

Like several of Beckett's other bicycle scenes, this passage is characterised by a strangely sexual suggestiveness: man and bicycle are referred to as 'they' and after their shared ecstatic experience, conveyed with an emphasis on rushing movement and momentum, Belacqua's sadness drops from him. Significantly, it falls like a 'shift', that sexually charged word that provoked the *Playboy* riots in the Abbey Theatre in 1907. This implicit eroticism is all the more noteworthy given Beckett's marked antipathy to the more usual forms of human congress. Cycling is a considerably more arousing experience for Belacqua than his voyeurism in the later episode 'Walking Out'. He finds so 'little zest in the performance' that instead of watching the copulating couple he stares 'vacantly into the shadows, alive to nothing but the weight and darkness and silence of the wood bearing down on top of him' (*GIV*, 160–61). In 1931, the year before writing *Dream of Fair to Middling Women*, Beckett wrote a letter to Tom McGreevy full of the self-conscious circumlocutions of this period for him, in which he mocked the academic aspirations held on his behalf by Professor Rudmose-Brown in Trinity College. In a satiric self-portrait of professional contentment, Beckett imagines himself astride a bicycle: 'That'll be the real pig's back. I'll feel like a fricatrix on her bicycle, the sabreflat fricatrix, for dear death pedalling faster and faster, her mouth ajar and her nostrils dilated' (*LI*, 84). 'Fricatrix' here is a fricatrice, a 'lewd woman'. Beckett drew on the anachronistically misogynistic term when naming the Frica in *Dream of Fair to Middling Women*, and in the letter to McGreevy he taps into concerns expressed at the dawn of 'the bicycle age' that lady cyclists would derive sexual pleasure from the energetic activity of pumping their legs up and down, a fear that masked another, deeper concern about the dramatic increase in independence and freedom for women possessed of a bicycle.[28]

Fintan O'Toole has noted a similar identification of bicycles and eroticism in Flann O'Brien's writing:

> There is, in *The Third Policeman*, a parody of the kind of trashy sex scene that would undoubtedly have fallen foul of the censors, were it not for the fact that the object of desire is not a woman but a bicycle. The narrator slavers over 'the perfect proportion of its parts … How desirable her seat

---

[28] See Sidney H. Aronson, 'The Sociology of the Bicycle', *Social Forces*, 30.3 (March 1952), 305–312, especially p. 308.

was, how charming the invitation of her slim encircling handle-arms, how unaccountably competent and reassuring her pump resting warmly against her rear thigh!'[29]

The Third Policeman was written in the late 1930s. O'Toole has argued persuasively that the censorship and repression of Ireland in this period forced O'Brien to direct this expression of admiration for the female form at the Sergeant's bicycle. There are also, however, modern European antecedents for the trope of sexy bicycles. In an essay for the *London Review of Books*, Iain Sinclair examined the 'conceit promoted by the Surrealists: velocipede as sex aid'.

> The intimate contact with a hard leather saddle. The steady pumping rhythms. The gasping for breath on a steep ascent. The ecstatic, effortless, downhill swoop, hair blowing free – aaahhhh! – as a streaming landscape rushes deliriously past. The pataphysician Alfred Jarry was so excited by the close-fitting kit that, before the First War, he took to dressing in the uniform of a cycle racer. He caused a scandal by following Mallarmé's funeral cortège on his bicycle.[30]

The evident sexual pleasure of Beckett's early cyclists, and the characteristically freewheeling passages devoted to such scenes, vanishes during the Second World War. In *Watt* and Beckett's post-war fiction, the description of motion on a bicycle shifts in perspective from character to the narrator, and pleasure becomes discomfort as large spaces of text are devoted to describing challenging bicycle rides by characters that are physically impeded from enjoying the sort of uncomplicated speed of Belacqua and the cyclists of Beckett's early poetry. This is another example of the trope where a character's affection for a useful object not only undermines its usefulness, but makes it an impediment. The newsagent features only briefly in the train station scene of *Watt*, but Beckett devotes a paragraph to the attachment of this limping man to his bicycle: so fond of it that he never takes off his bicycle clips and carries the machine up and down stairs every day.

> He was short and limped dreadfully. When he got started he moved rapidly, in a series of aborted genuflexions ... Now at the end of the platform the newsagent came out of a door, wheeling his bicycle. He would carry it down the winding stone stairs and then ride home ... The next morning he would carry his bicycle up the stairs again. It was heavy, being a very good bicycle. It would have been simpler to leave it below, but he preferred to have it near him. (*GI*, 188)

---

[29] Fintan O'Toole, 'The Fantastic Flann O'Brien', *Irish Times*, 1 October 2011.
[30] Iain Sinclair, 'The Raging Peloton', *LRB*, 33.2 (20 January 2011), 3–8, p. 3.

In a letter written from Germany in 1936, Beckett declares in exasperation, but not without a certain bemused pride that 'I have just had a small fine (1 RM) imposed on me for walking in a dangerous fashion. As a result, I am leaving, for Braunschweig, in golden silence' (*LI*, 395). The terseness of this phrase shares its wry humour with Beckett's descriptions of the wayward gait of certain characters, particularly Watt, but it also echoes in the reprimand given by a policeman to Molloy who is resting from the exertion of managing his bicycle and crutches:

> What are you doing there? he said. I'm used to that question, I understood it immediately. Resting, I said. Resting, he said. Resting, I said. Will you answer my question? he cried … It ended in my understanding that my way of resting, my attitude when at rest, astride my bicycle, my arms on the handlebars, my head on my arms, was a violation of I don't know what, public order, public decency. Modestly I pointed to my crutches and ventured one or two noises regarding my infirmity, which obliged me to rest as I could, rather than as I should. But there are not two laws, that was the next thing I thought I understood, not two laws, one for the healthy, another for the sick, but one only to which all must bow, rich and poor, young and old, happy and sad. (*GII*, 16)

At several points in *Molloy*, Beckett devotes lengthy passages to descriptions of Molloy and Moran attempting to cycle while impeded by their lame legs and crutches. Characteristically, Molloy describes his impediments and means of overcoming them with a mad mechanical pedantry, undercut by frequent references to his degenerating physical and mental condition. He does so in a deadpan prose that translates the more sadistic elements of slapstick into narrative description, and in doing so, revels in sardonic literalness:

> So I got up, adjusted my crutches and went down to the road, where I found my bicycle (I didn't know I had one) in the same place I must have left it. Which enables me to remark that, crippled though I was, I was no mean cyclist, at that period. This is how I went about it. I fastened my crutches to the cross-bar, one on either side, I propped the foot of my stiff leg (I forget which, now they're both stiff) on the projecting front axle, and I pedalled with the other. (*GII*, 11–12)

Literal though it may be, this method of negotiating a bicycle on crutches is also scarcely credible. This sustained description by Beckett of physical difficulties magnified to manic implausibility indicates, I believe, that his primary interest is the generation of narrative from the slapstick challenges faced by his characters, rather than any sense of verisimilitude. In Molloy's description of cycling with crutches, as in his method of coordinating the distribution of his sucking stones among his pockets, what is at stake is not logical or physical credibility, but the demented comedy that results from taking a physical challenge to its logical but darkly absurd conclusion. Molloy, like Moran, is confronted with a world of objects that make little sense to him. His response is to play along.

Moran, in contrast to Molloy, seeks to overwhelm and control this mysterious and ill-ordered material world. Moran's analogous description of negotiating the limitations imposed by his bad leg and the demands of the bicycle is related in a markedly different register. The contrast illustrates the gulf between Moran's driven instrumentalism and Molloy's free playfulness, and hints at the unremittingly grim use of crutches to come in *The Unnamable*:

> Here then in a few words is the solution I arrived at. First the bags, then my son's raincoat folded in four, all lashed to the carrier and the saddle with my son's bits of string. As for the umbrella, I hooked it round my neck, so as to have both hands free to hold on to my son by the waist, under the armpits rather, for by this time my seat was higher than his ... I let myself slide to one side till the foot of my good leg touched the ground. The only weight now on the back wheel was that of my sick leg, cocked up rigid at an excruciating angle ... The wheels began to turn. I followed, half dragged, half hopping ... I bounded up to my place. The bicycle swayed, righted itself, gained speed. Bravo! I cried, beside myself with joy. Hurrah! cried my son. How I loathe that exclamation! I can hardly set it down. He was as pleased as I, I do believe. (*GII*, 150–51)

Although Moran is still possessed of his almost diabolical resolve, he repeats the breezy phrase 'happily' five times once he and his son are in full flight on the bicycle. The sensation of swift and easy movement provides such relief for the crippled cyclist that even the irascible and sarcastic Moran is moved to expressions of joy.

Just as the greatcoat is decisively cast off in *From an Abandoned Work*, before being taken up again in *That Time*, the bicycle undergoes the same process of rejection, absence and reappearance with an altered function. Molloy searches for his bicycle while he is trying to escape from Lousse's garden, but when he finds it at last, he discards it with the same sudden and emphatic dislike as the hanging up of the greatcoat.

> In the end I found it, half buried in a soft bush. I threw aside my crutches and took it in my hands, by the saddle and the handlebars, intending to wheel it a little, back and forth, before getting on and leaving for ever this accursed place. But I pushed and pulled in vain, the wheels would not turn. It was as though the brakes were jammed, and heaven knows they

were not, for my bicycle had no brakes. And suddenly overcome by a great weariness, in spite of the dying day when I always felt most alive, I threw the bicycle back in the bush and lay down on the ground, on the grass, careless of the dew, I never feared the dew. (*GII*, 42)

Molloy does not pick up the bicycle again, but leaves it where it fell, later explaining his change of heart by punning on 'vehicle' as mode of transport and metaphor: 'I left her my bicycle which I had taken a dislike to, suspecting it to be the vehicle of some malignant agency and perhaps the cause of my recent misfortunes' (*GII*, 54). Molloy's phrase also echoes the note of caution about bicycles made in *Mercier and Camier*: 'The bicycle is a great good. But it can turn nasty, if ill employed' (*GI*, 436).

When Molloy abandons his bicycle in Lousse's garden in 1947, Beckett follows his example. By the time the bicycle reappears in the twelfth *Texts for Nothing*, a series of thirteen stories written in the 1950s, it has become a ghostly cipher of the prominent, well-defined bicycles in Beckett's earlier work, spectral as the abandoned bicycle and bowler in Figure 8.

In *Texts for Nothing* the bicycle is used to evoke the spirit of the curmudgeonly and appealing earlier incarnation of Beckett's characters.

> So, I'm supposed to say now, it's the moment, so that's the earth, these expiring vitals set aside for me which no sooner taken over would be set aside for another, many thanks, and here the laugh, the long silent guffaw of the knowing non-exister, at hearing ascribed to him such pregnant words, confess you're not the man you were, you'll end up riding a bicycle. (*GIV*, 336)

After this reappearance in *Texts for Nothing*, the bicycle never features again in Beckett's fiction, and does so on only two further occasions, in the radio play *All That Fall* and in *Film*.

These last bicycles are profoundly altered: once instrumental in establishing the personality of characters and rhythm of narratives, now they are relegated to the background, registering how far removed these later characters are from the positive qualities of this object, its promise of escape, smooth motion and speed. In *All That Fall*, the bicycle is contrasted with the noisy and exotic motor-car, indicating the twentieth-century inter-war setting of the play. The bicycles in *Film* fulfil a similar role: in both cases, bicycles designate the past.[31] In contrast with the bicycles that offer untrammelled freedom in Beckett's writing from the 1930s to 1950s,

---

[31] *Film* was written in 1963, but the stage directions specify that it is set in 1929, while *All That Fall* evokes the 1930s. See Joseph S. O'Leary, 'Beckett and Radio', *Journal of Irish Studies*, 23 (2008), 3–11.

Figure 8 Eason Photographic Collection, 'Ranelagh Road from Canal Bridge, Dublin' (*c.* 1900–39).
Courtesy of the National Library of Ireland.

Mr Tyler's bicycle in *All That Fall* is a broken machine that greatly increases the efforts necessary for movement, prompting his exclamations of frustration and despair that supply great sound effects for this radio play. Mr Tyler's angry litany of complaints may have been particularly appealing to Beckett because one of the defining qualities of a properly working bicycle is its silence. It was, after all, invented for the military and conceived as an improvement on the horse, which made all sorts of noises, required nourishment and was subject to fatigue and death, so could not be relied upon to convey men or heavy equipment for the duration of a military campaign.[32] The incandescent and inventive curse of Mr Tyler upon his puncture more closely recalls the many debates on the various merits and dangers of the bicycle in *The Third Policeman* than anything else in Beckett: 'Nothing, Mrs Rooney, nothing, I was merely cursing, under my breath, God and man, under my breath, and the wet Saturday afternoon of my conception. My back tyre has gone down again. I pumped it hard as iron before I set out. And now I am on the rim' (*GIII*, 161). Mr Tyler's bicycle is a cross to be carried, rather than the mode of escape it has been for earlier

[32] See Jim Fitzpatrick, *The Bicycle in Wartime: An Illustrated History* (Washington: Brassey's, 1998), p. 3, 20, 112, 114, 189.

characters in Beckett, and the humour of this scene derives from precisely this disparity. The last appearance of a bicycle in Beckett's work is in *Film*, where its function is to pinpoint the early date and highlight the isolation of the hero. The two bicycles that briefly and silently cruise by in the background are cycled by men and used to ferry their dates on the crossbars. This shorthand for romance and belonging exaggerates the isolation of Buster Keaton's wretched, dark figure as he hugs the walls and shrinks away from such conviviality. Jettisoning the bicycle after *Film*, Beckett also abandons the freewheeling, episodic and roguish elements of his early and middle periods.

Wheelchairs

The history of the wheelchair charts a progression from the ancient litter to the twelfth-century wheelbarrow, the late eighteenth-century wood and wicker 'invalid chair', and the 1930s metal, four-wheeled model, to the powerful mobility aids of the later twentieth century.[33] True to this history, where wheelchairs were often ad hoc objects created by modifying an existing bath or garden chair, Beckett's most famous wheelchair in *Endgame* has been created by adding castors to an armchair. Makeshift wheelchairs offer limited movement or independence for their users. Beckett's work also features examples of more mobile and ludic wheelchairs, but these do not recall the motion of the bicycle so much as mark a progression in literary prosthetics: the manipulation of the relationship between his characters' desire to move and the frustrations they face in attempting to do so.

Murphy, Beckett's first novel, features his sole fictional character in a wheelchair, although Mr Kelly is bedridden until the last chapter. No wheelchairs feature in Beckett's poetry, and his theatre contains only two largely fixed wheelchairs for a pair of despotic characters: Hamm in *Endgame* and B in *Rough for Theatre I*, both written twenty years after *Murphy*. The theatrical chair-bound figure naturally lends itself to tableaux, thoroughly explored by Beckett in *Endgame*, and enhanced by concealing Hamm under a sheet at the start of the play. In *Rough for Theatre I*, Beckett turns instead to the dramatic potential of an entrance made by a figure in a wheelchair: 'Enter B right, in a wheelchair which he propels by means of a pole' (*GIII*, 233). B is guaranteed all eyes upon him,

---

[33] See Herman Kamenetz, 'A Brief History of the Wheelchair', *Journal of the History of Medicine and Allied Sciences*, 24.2 (April 1969), 205–10.

except those of the blind character A, his counterpart onstage, making his entrance at once attention-grabbing and invisible. This use of the wheelchair as a stage property creates a visual echo of one of the painter Francis Bacon's less individuated popes. Bacon is an apt reference point for the three weak but opinionated wheelchair-bound old men in Beckett's writing: by placing them in large, eye-catching chairs, the three figures evidently command authority, but are also trapped within the material signifier of their status.

It is this simultaneity of weakness and strength that Beckett so forcibly conveys with his characters' wheelchairs. Each man has the capacity and tendency to hector and bully those around him, but such assertions of power often wildly recoil as their throne-like chairs become cages, transforming these characters from monarchs or dictators to dribbling old invalids who are utterly dependent on their subservient fellow characters. The opening stage directions establish Hamm as the undisputed locus of *Endgame*: 'Centre, in an armchair on castors, covered with an old sheet, Hamm' (*GIII*, 91). Hamm registers his displeasure with the stiff, difficult movement of his chair by insisting that they would be better off with bicycle wheels, indicating his view of the wheelchair as a poor relation of the bicycle. Indeed, if bicycles promise escape and offer the thrill of speed and satisfaction of independence, the wheelchair guarantees the cramped horizons of the characters sitting in them, whose rancour and pathos is framed, if not determined, by the dependent status foisted upon them by their wheelchairs.

Beckett's two dramatic wheelchairs are radical transformations of the bicycle for the stage. The onstage wheelchair is a clumsy, slow and monumental thing, a hindrance to movement for the character immobilised in the chair, and a throne that indicates the symbolic power of the seated character. Beckett consistently emphasises how imperfect his dramatic wheelchairs are as vehicles: in *Endgame*, Hamm clamours for Clov to get the oilcan for the stiff wheels of his chair, even though Clov insists 'I oiled them yesterday', and in *Rough for Theatre I*, B demonstrates his mastery of propelling himself to and fro along a straight line, illustrating the rather constrained range of motion offered by the wheelchair (*GIII*, 122). The discovery by B that this line may be traversed backwards as well as forwards so radically improves the machine for his purposes that he puts on an enthusiastic display of his innovation to his blind companion:

> B Only one problem: the about-turn. I often felt, as I struggled, that it would be quicker to go on, right around the world. Till the day I realised

I could go home backwards. [*Pause.*] For example, I am at A. [*He pushes himself forward a little, halts.*] I push on to B. [*He pushes himself back a little, halts.*] And I return to A. [*With élan.*] The straight line! The vacant space! [*Pause.*] Do I begin to move you? (*GIII*, 235)

The double meaning of 'move' here is striking because the impassive A has been static throughout this scene, and only B has moved. Although B's satisfaction is an attenuated version of the pleasure other characters experience on their bicycles when lame or on crutches, he is celebrating his transcendence of the machine's limitations rather than deriving pleasure from its facilities. Characters in wheelchairs on Beckett's stage never attain the unalloyed physical and quasi-sexual gratification of cyclists in Beckett's early fiction and poetry. Nor, it must be noted, can their short-lived contentment be compared to the evident gleefulness of the single wheelchair-bound character in Beckett's fiction.

Murphy is a tale of two chairs: its titular hero's frustrated efforts to lull himself into a state of abnegation in his rocking chair, and Mr Kelly's propulsion of himself round a park in his wheelchair to partake in the raptures of kite flying. Murphy's rocker allows him to escape the clamour of life, while Mr Kelly's wheelchair takes him from repose into active engagement with life, but we are assured by the narrator that Mr Kelly 'was as fond of his chair in his own way as Murphy had been of his' (*GI*, 165). Mr Kelly's chair achieves a contented, ludic, easy motion that contrasts starkly with the stiff, jolting, bad-tempered movement of Hamm and B onstage. Beckett's only fictional wheelchair has significantly more in common with his contemporaneous poetic and fictional bicycles than the two later dramatic wheelchairs. This is evident in a description of the movement of Mr Kelly's chair. Narrative rhythm follows the motion of the machine once again, and although this passage is consequently disjointed and ungainly, it has a similar verve to several bicycle scenes.

> At the top of the incline he laid the winch and kite in his lap and seized the pulls. It was the signal for Celia to let go. His arms flashed back and forth, faster and faster as the chair gathered speed, until he was rocking crazily along at a good 12 m.p.h., a danger to himself and to others. Then resisting with one hand the pull, with the other the thrust of the levers, he brought himself smoothly to rest level with the statue of Queen Victoria, whom he greatly admired, as a woman and as a queen.
> It was only in the legs and face that Mr. Kelly was badly gone, he still had plenty of vigour in his arms and torso. (*GI*, 165)

Beckett's focus on the wild rocking motion of Mr Kelly's wheelchair as it hurtles along is clearly intended to prompt the reader to contrast it with the steady rock of Murphy's chair.

The emphasis on mechanical flamboyance here recalls the motorised chair in D.H. Lawrence's *Lady Chatterley's Lover* (1928). Like Lawrence, Beckett devotes considerable space to the machine-like qualities of the wheelchair, but it is difficult to accurately picture either Mr Kelly or Sir Clifford, or to imagine the physical experience of occupying either wheelchair, beyond a general impression of the mad bursts of energy required to propel them forward. Beckett tells us that Mr Kelly 'enjoyed the sensation of plying the levers, he said it was like working the pulls of a beer-engine' (*GI*, 93). The mysterious operation of Mr Kelly's chair, its pulleys and the reference to beer, suggests a toy-like machine. Charles Dickens presents a comparable display of amiable virtuosity by a wheelchair-bound character in *David Copperfield* (1850), where the genial and unflappable Mr Omer demonstrates the material advantages offered by the design of his chair to the wonderment of David Copperfield: 'He was as radiant as if his chair, his asthma, and the failure of his limbs were the various branches of a great invention for enhancing the luxury of a pipe.'[34]

The pleasure which attends Mr Kelly's overcoming of the mechanical limitations of his chair contrasts starkly with Hamm's strained and short-lived amiability as he recalls Clov's early, ramshackle efforts at pushing his chair.

> HAMM Do you remember, in the beginning, when you took me for a turn? You used to hold the chair too high. At every step you nearly tipped me out.
> [*With senile quaver.*]
> Ah great fun, we had, the two of us, great fun.
> [*Gloomily.*]
> And then we got into the way of it. (*GIII*, 137)

In both plays that feature wheelchairs, Beckett emphasises his characters' cramped horizons. Hamm is utterly dependent on Clov to move him or bring things to him, to describe the scene to him, and to administer the painkiller that we discover, in the course of the play, has run out. In

---

[34] Dickens, *David Copperfield* (London: Penguin, 2004), p. 738.

Rough for Theatre I, it is suggested that B once had a 'woman' to render similar service to him: 'I [had] mine to get me out of the chair in the evening and back into it again in the morning and to push me as far as the corner when I went out of my mind.' It is evident, however, that this female companion has either left or died, leaving him in a considerable state of privation (*GIII*, 234). Beckett inverts the disabilities of *Endgame* in *Rough for Theatre I*, and with it the power dynamic between the couples. Hamm is blind and chair-bound, therefore utterly dependent on Clov for information about his environment, but holds onto the key to the larder and whistle to summon Clov; by contrast, A is blind and largely immobile, for fear he get lost or lose his things, and it is the chair-bound B who has the facility of movement. In *Endgame* the blind lead the maimed, with Hamm directing Clov as he pushes and places his chair, while in *Rough for Theatre I*, the maimed character is pushed by the blind. As B is demonstrating his straight line, he wonders if the 'about-turn' costs more effort and takes longer than it would to continue on instead, 'right around the world' (*GIII*, 235). This is echoed by Hamm when he orders Clov to take him for 'a little turn', the confines of his room being, for him, 'Right around the world' (*GIII*, 109).

Hamm's vehement demand to be placed in the centre of the room is further expression of the tyrannical control he exerts on Clov and his parents, but this trope also indicates his vulnerability: because Hamm is sightless and confined to a wheelchair that also serves as a bed when he is covered with the sheet, the space of the room represents the ends of his earth, poles that are known to him exclusively through tactile means. This is why he is so insistent on touching the walls when Clov takes him on a tour of the room. Rather than simply emphasising his despotism, Hamm's insistence on his chair being at the dead centre of the room highlights his dependence on Clov, who could place him anywhere or tell him anything about his surroundings. As a result, Hamm has developed an obsessive need for Clov to describe them to him.

> HAMM Back to my place!
> [*Clov pushes chair back to centre.*]
> Is that my place?
> CLOV Yes, that's your place.
> HAMM Am I right in the centre?
> CLOV I'll measure it.
> HAMM More or less! More or less!
> CLOV [*moving chair slightly*] There!

HAMM I'm more or less in the centre?
CLOV I'd say so.
HAMM You'd say so! Put me right in the centre!
CLOV I'll go and get the tape.
HAMM Roughly! Roughly!
[*Clov moves chair slightly.*]
Bang in the centre! (*GIII*, 110–11)

The limitations and malfunctions of the wheelchairs in both *Endgame* and *Rough for Theatre I* leave the figures sitting in them in need of assistance, establishing the sour dependence that characterises the relationships between wheelchair-bound and mobile characters in each play. The dynamic of Hamm and Clov's relationship is that of a controlling, darkly enigmatic invalid and biddable yet uncommitted servant. In this, it bears strong similarities to that of Miss Havisham and Pip in Dickens's *Great Expectations* (1860), where it becomes evident on his first visit that Pip must offer himself as a crutch for Miss Havisham to lean on: 'She looked all round the room in a glaring manner, and then said, leaning on me while her hand twitched my shoulder, "Come, come, come! Walk me, walk me!"'[35] Later, Miss Havisham discards the stick in favour of 'a garden-chair – a light chair on wheels' that Pip must push between her mausoleum-like rooms, and around the decomposing wedding feast and bride's dusty dressing table. Pip's description emphasises the monotony and mindlessness of this activity: 'Over and over and over again, we would make these journeys, and sometimes they would last for three hours at a stretch.'[36]

Even when concealed by a sheet at the start of the play, Hamm is centre stage. Clov's laboured and deliberate movements all around him, when looking out of the window and removing the sheets from Nagg and Nell, generate the impression of an ungainly moon orbiting the centre of this particular universe. The delicacy which Clov reserves for removing the final sheet and revealing Hamm to the audience confirms, ever before Hamm has woken up, the unequivocal importance of this figure, monarch of all he cannot survey. That his chair is intended to be conflated with a throne is established through Hamm's echoing of Hamlet and through the perfect, if sullen, obedience offered to him by the other characters. In his survey of the relationship between the seated figure in Beckett's theatre and earlier seated figures onstage, Enoch Brater speaks enthusiastically of

---

[35] Dickens, *Great Expectations*, ed. Angus Calder (London: Penguin, 1985), p. 113.
[36] Dickens, *Great Expectations*, pp. 122–23.

the 'dramatic potential of restricted and limited mobility', and notes that when Suzanne encouraged Beckett to see Roger Blin's 1949 production of the Swedish playwright August Strindberg's *Ghost Sonata*, the 'image of an old man confined to a wheelchair had a profound effect' on Beckett.[37] Brater suggests that Beckett's use of the sitting figure 'involves nothing less than a reconsideration of how this device might be used within the entire dramatic enterprise itself'.[38] Brater does not explain how Beckett achieves this. I propose that in Beckett's work, the seated character onstage is a singular figure, removed from the normal hierarchy established by the implicit demarcations of occupied theatrical space.

The semiotic elasticity by which a wheelchair can gesture to regal authority at the same time as physical dependence and vulnerability is largely contingent on the various distinct and seemingly contradictory implications of the seated posture onstage. A character may demonstrate the degree of his authority over all others by refusing to stand, but conversely, sitting diminishes one's physical stature and dramatic potency: possession of an erect posture and the ability to pace while enunciating signal a dynamism absent in the lethargic, passive pose of sitting. Indeed, the seated posture so thoroughly undermines a character's dignity that it might be considered inappropriate for a tragic protagonist. However, to subordinate another character to the office of propelling a seated figure around, or to organise a scene around the seated figure's request that a character kneel to tuck a blanket into place around his legs, or leg in B's case, is to exert a very regal sort of authority. In *Rough for Theatre I*, the stage directions indicate that the blind beggar responds to B's crippled condition 'without emotion', calling him a 'Poor wretch', which is precisely how B himself assessed the blind beggar when he first propelled himself onstage in his wheelchair (*GIII*, 235, 233). Such subdued or absent sympathy is typical of Beckett's dramatic characters in wheelchairs, who are petty and bad-tempered but lacking in authority and gravitas, leading to outbursts of despotic behaviour intended to assert their contested power. Even the most benign of Beckett's wheelchair-bound characters, Mr Kelly, objects to Celia's declaration of love for Murphy with a short-lived but intense fit of pique. 'Mr. Kelly saw no reason why he should contain himself any longer. He started up in the

---

[37] Enoch Brater, 'The Seated Figure on Beckett's Stage', in *A Companion to Samuel Beckett*, pp. 346–57, p. 347.
[38] Brater, 'The Seated Figure on Beckett's Stage', p. 350.

bed, which opened his eyes, as he knew perfectly it would, and wanted to know the who, what, where, by what means, why, in what way and when' (*GI*, 13).

Mr Kelly's peevishness in this scene recalls the feelings of a once-favoured doll or plaything that has been replaced in the affections of a child. Beckett directly and repeatedly compares Mr Kelly to a doll when describing the curious coincidence of his posture and gaze: upright, his eyes open fully, but automatically shut tight when he reclines: 'Mr. Kelly fell back in the bed, which closed his eyes, as though he were a doll' (*GI*, 10). Beckett's identification of the bed-bound Mr Kelly with a doll serves to emphasise his withered and insubstantial physique, as it does his pettiness when Celia transfers her affections from him to Murphy. Mr Kelly is most explicitly presented as a doll-like plaything towards the end of the novel, when he appears in his kite-flying costume. Beckett plays here, as he does with many of his male characters, with the comedy of mismatched and disproportionate items of dress:

> Celia wheeled Mr. Willoughby Kelly south along the Broad Walk. He wore his kiting costume, a glistening slicker many sizes too large for him and a yachting-cap many sizes too small, though the smallest and largest of their kind obtainable. He sat bolt upright, with one gloved hand clutching the winch, with the other the kite furled and in its sheath, and his blue eyes blazed in the depths of their sockets. (*GI*, 165)

The asymmetry of the oversized jacket and undersized hat satisfies the same silent comedy logic as the outfits of Vladimir and Estragon, but also seems to have had its basis in real kite flyers that Beckett enjoyed watching as a young man in London. Duncan Scott was the lighting engineer in the Royal Court Theatre in London when Beckett directed several plays there in the 1970s, and the two men became friendly. Scott recalls a walk with Beckett, during which he became nostalgic about the old men who served as models for Mr Kelly.

> We were crossing Hyde Park, he naming the various locations as we came to them. He spoke of *Murphy* as if he [Murphy] had been of flesh and blood. 'It's Murphy's old haunt.' He said. 'He used to walk about here a lot. They used to fly kites, but I was here the other day and they don't do it any more.' There was disappointment in his voice. A few minutes later, we crossed the Broad Walk. A solitary kite soared in the sky. Sam beamed with pleasure. (*BR*, 70)

Each of Beckett's portraits of characters in wheelchairs ends on a pathetic note. Mr Kelly's kite escapes his hand while he is dozing. Having 'tottered' out of the chair to his feet and staggered, 'a ghastly, lamentable figure', after the vanishing kite, the novel closes with a final image of him collapsed in the chair while Celia pushes it home, her hair across her face and her eyes shut, as Mr Kelly's yachting cap clings 'like a clam to the skull' (*GI*, 168). A, the erstwhile victim of *Rough for Theatre I*, like the unnamed protagonist of *Catastrophe*, reaches a tipping point at the end of the play, and retaliates by snatching the pole with which B punts his chair along and throwing it away. Hamm similarly loses the means of punting his chair by the conclusion of *Endgame*. The final stage directions of the play describe the lowering of Hamm's arms to lie on the armrests: '*Pause. He covers his face with handkerchief, lowers his arms to armrests, remains motionless. / Brief tableau. / Curtain*' (*GIII*, 154). The semiotic implications of this passive seated posture are more thoroughly explored in *Rockaby*, where the importance of the armrests of the rocking chair are reiterated, both by the unchanging position of W, whose arms lie on them throughout, and in several textual echoes that conflate the armrests of the 'mother rocker' with an embrace from W's mother, who died in this same chair. W's perfectly still body is not even responsible for the rocking motion of the chair, which constitutes the sole physical action onstage. With her bleached, heavily made-up, mask-like and impassive face and her elaborate, old fashioned costume, W is rather like an old porcelain doll trapped in a sad game not of her own invention.

Questions of passivity and stillness bring us to the conception of Beckett's dramatic writing as a theatre of stasis. I hope that my examination of wheelchairs challenges the idea, advanced by Hugh Kenner and often repeated, that Beckett switches from a preoccupation with the failed journey in his fiction to stasis onstage. On the contrary, the difficult movement of his characters onstage registers a continuation and development of this focus in Beckett's poetry and fiction, where characters are faced with the cruel paradox of a host of impediments to mobility and the simultaneous imperative of keeping on the move. The wheelchair, in this respect, may be considered a middle term between the bicycle and bed, for it is an object that allows Beckett to consider variations on the theme of wheeled movement for incapacitated figures who would be reduced to bedridden immobility were it not for their wheelchairs. For Hamm and Mr Kelly, when the body is so thoroughly impeded, it swells to fill their imaginative space. This is evident in Mr Kelly's habitual dispersion of thought: 'Part was with his caecum, which was wagging its tail again; part with his extremities, which were dragging anchor; part with his boyhood; and so on. All this would have to be called in' (*GI*, 14). Hamm, similarly, describes this predicament as drifting in vast, undifferentiated darkness when he warns Clov that he too will lose the use of his legs: 'Infinite emptiness will be all around you, all the resurrected dead of all the ages wouldn't fill it, and there you'll be like a little bit of grit in the middle of the steppe' (*GIII*, 117). In an earlier soliloquy that is overheard and mocked by his parents, Hamm fantasises about flying and floating, achieving union with nature by being suspended in it: 'If I could sleep I might make love. I'd go into the woods. My eyes would see ... the sky, the earth. I'd run, run, they wouldn't catch me' (*GIII*, 104). Hamm's fantasy is part of a recurring trope in Beckett's drama, where the inertia of a largely immobile figure is dramatically contrasted with their dreams of movement across vast horizons. Impeded or impossible motion is a spur to the imagination for the blind and lame Hamm, as it is for Winnie in *Happy Days*, whose birdlike sensation of floating away follows the same logic: the more chthonic or sluggish in reality, the more airy in imagination. It is this tendency, more than any other, which indicates how Beckett uses bicycles and wheelchairs for opposing purposes: the former to convey the sheer buoyant delight or tentative discomfort of motion; the latter to trace the deleterious effects on a character denied the pleasure and autonomy of movement. The wheelchair, in marked contrast to the bicycle, serves finally to illustrate the effects of stasis in Beckett's work: where movement is practically impossible, the mind dilates to create it.

Crutches

It should come as no surprise that the sentimental pity associated by Dickens with crutches and so well exploited in *A Christmas Carol* is inverted by Beckett so that crutches register instead socially antagonistic, bloody-minded perseverance. Beckett's characters use crutches to escape other people or to attack them, and, it has to be said, derive considerable pleasure from both these uses. As we have seen, the function of literary prosthetics in Beckett's work is determined not by a linear trajectory of ever-increasing physical deterioration, but according to the particular characterological or semiotic set of effects generated by each material aid to movement. The type of crutch used in Beckett's work is wooden, with a fork and tucking in under the armpits, in line with its definition as a 'staff for a lame or infirm person to lean upon in walking'.[39] Beckett uses

---

[39] The *OED* definition continues: 'the symbol of old age'; 'A prop, a support.'

crutches promiscuously, pairing them with sticks and bicycles in his trilogy of novels, and in one poem.

Beckett twice refers to a crutch and stick in the same breath. In the first case, the crutch and stick are used simultaneously, pathetically amplifying the degree of assistance needed by a character in order to walk, and in the second, the props are invoked as an index of incremental decrepitude and loss of mobility. In 'Enueg I', written in the early 1930s, the narrator, who from the momentum of this part of the poem is likely on a bicycle, splashes past a wizened character 'scuttling along between a crutch and a stick' (*GIV*, 12). The second appearance of a crutch and stick together is in *Malone Dies*, when Malone recalls a time when his physical condition and mobility were much better. He observes that at this time he was still able to walk without the assistance of a stick. It follows, with pedantic logic, that he did not require crutches either:

> And I loved, as I remember, as I walked along, with my hands deep in my pockets, for I am trying to speak of the time when I could still walk without a stick and a fortiori without crutches, I loved to finger and caress the hard shapely objects that were there in my deep pockets, it was my way of talking to them and reassuring them. (*GII*, 241)

Here Malone invokes a logical order of deterioration, a progression from sticks to crutches as aids to movement. This logic is not strictly followed by Beckett's fiction, however, and the metamorphosis of sticklike objects, where sticks are replaced by crutches in the trilogy and then reappear afterwards alongside gaffs, poles and goads, is telling. This pattern indicates an authorial shift in interest from the fictional structure of the frustrated journey, in which sticks propel the characters forward, to that of a less conventional narrative in the trilogy, where crutches signal a degree of incapacity that renders the journey impossible from the outset. Characters in the trilogy are therefore faced with the task of generating the narrative through storytelling rather than being encompassed within and described by the structure of the novel. In later works of fiction, finally, stick-like props are used against characters, compelling them to they know not what confession in order to drag out more material from which to create the later narratives.

Although the trilogy features sticks and crutches, the latter play a far more central role, and are often used to add a cumbersome impediment to progress by bicycle, or a pleasurable spring to travel on foot. Crutches in the trilogy also produce pleasurable movement absent from Beckett's work since the cyclists of his early poetry and fiction. Molloy first alludes to his crutches immediately before registering surprise at the existence of his bicycle: 'So I got up, adjusted my crutches and went down to the road, where I found my bicycle (I didn't know I had one) in the same place I must have left it' (*GII*, 11–12). Molloy's distinctive practice of cycling with his crutches has already been noted. His use of crutches while wheeling his bicycle is similarly remarkable. Upon entering a town, he gets off his bicycle 'in compliance with the regulations' where 'cyclists entering and leaving town are required by the police to dismount, cars to go into bottom gear and horsedrawn vehicles to slow down to a walk' (*GII*, 15–16). Molloy states his approval for this rule and remarks that he observes it 'religiously ... in spite of the difficulty I have in advancing on my crutches pushing my bicycle at the same time.' This extraordinary feat is described thus: 'I managed somehow. Being ingenious.' Having cleared 'these difficult straits', his method of resting creates a dispiriting spectacle for the townspeople, prompting investigation by the police. Molloy's satisfaction on his crutches is such, however, that even as he is being escorted to the station, he describes their progress in an idyllic register: 'We took the little side streets, quiet, sunlit, I springing along between my crutches, he pushing my bicycle, with the tips of his white-gloved fingers' (*GII*, 16). Later, when Molloy leaves his bicycle in Lousse's garden, he reverts to playing with his crutches: 'I didn't feel I missed my bicycle, no, not really, I didn't mind going on my way the way I said, swinging low in the dark over the earth, along the little empty country roads' (*GII*, 61). He is eloquent about the graceful swinging movement of crutches:

> There is rapture, or there should be, in the motion crutches give. It is a series of little flights, skimming the ground. You take off, you land, through the thronging sound in wind and limb, who have to fasten one foot to the ground before they dare lift up the other. And even their most joyous hastening is less aerial than my hobble. (*GII*, 59)

By contrast, the grim and thorough use of the returning hero's crutches signals a distinctly mirthless progress in *The Unnamable*. Having returned from his travels, the prodigal son discovers that his extended family has been poisoned by botulism in corned beef. Their roars of pain and smells of decomposition keep him at a distance for some time, and when he does make his way into the house, it is on crutches:

> Finally I found myself, without surprise, within the building, circular in form as already stated, its ground floor consisting of a single room flush with the arena, and there completed my rounds, stamping under foot the unrecognisable remains of my family, here a face, there a stomach, as the

case might be, and sinking into them with the ends of my crutches, both coming and going. To say I did so with satisfaction would be stretching the truth. For my feeling was rather one of annoyance at having to flounder in such muck just at the moment when my closing contortions called for a firm and level surface. (*GII*, 317)

In this sequence, Beckett assiduously denies the welcome conventionally afforded to the prodigal son, or the pity granted the returning wounded hero. The injury suffered by the son that has left him on crutches has not made him more sensitive to the sufferings of others, and on the contrary has inured him to anything but the task at hand. While the family within the house comment on his progress as they watch his movement towards them, casting his efforts in terms of a bedtime story and epic narrative or fairy tale, the narrator is absorbed by his unfaltering determination to return to the family home, regardless of whether this involves wading through his family's remains: 'After each thrust of my crutches I stopped, to devour a narcotic and measure the distance gone, the distance yet to go' (*GII*, 310). This unflinching portrait is another of the ways in which Beckett undermines the trope of the narrative compulsion to complete a journey in the trilogy, here by aligning it with its damaging impact of sickness and pain, elsewhere by making it physically impossible.

In Lousse's house, Molloy briefly uses his crutches to push over items of furniture, striking them 'just hard enough to overturn them, without breaking them'. He soon gives up on thrusting and lunging at the furniture, however, stops 'pretending to be angry', and helps to right the items of furniture he has toppled (*GII*, 38). Later in his narrative, this mild and short-lived anger is expressed in a very different way, as he puts the pleasure-giving qualities of 'flight' on crutches to destructive use, in a disarmingly choreographed assault on the charcoal burner in the forest.[40] The nature of this attack is determined by the range and type of movement allowed by his crutches. Molloy first uses his crutch to give the man 'a good dint on the skull', and moves on, but he returns to examine the man on the ground and to deal him 'a few warm kicks in the ribs' (*GII*, 78).

---

[40] Molloy's difficult progress through the countryside and woods in poor weather may have been influenced by Schubert's *Winterreise (Winter Journey)*, a song cycle that was a great favourite of Beckett's. While Molloy is transfixed with desire to find his mother, Schubert's lied describes a broken-hearted poet leaving the lover who has lost interest in him. On his journey, the poet finds refuge in the hut of a charcoal-burner, and takes a well-needed rest. Molloy's sudden violence in dispatching the charcoal-burner may have been included by Beckett not only as a means of keeping his character moving and his narrative on track, but also as a way of disrupting the parallels between his novel and Schubert's melancholic work.

> I carefully chose the most favourable position, a few paces from the body, with my back of course turned to it. Then, nicely balanced on my crutches, I began to swing, backwards, forwards, feet pressed together, or rather legs pressed together, for how could I press my feet together, with my legs in the state they were? But how could I press my legs together, in the state they were? I pressed them together, that's all I can tell you. Take it or leave it. Or I didn't press them together. What can that possibly matter? I swung, that's all that matters, in an ever-widening arc, until I decided the moment had come and launched myself forward with all my strength and consequently, a moment later, backward, which gave the desired result. (*GII*, 78–79)

Molloy notes that, having knocked himself over with the force of his exertions on one side, he 'rested a moment, then got up, picked up my crutches, took up my position on the other side of the body and applied myself with method to the same exercise' (*GII*, 79). The scene provides a startling illustration of how the pleasurable arc of swinging between crutches can be misappropriated and used to inflict injury instead of propelling a character forward. When crutches are wielded as weapons, the destruction is done with the same mindless, rhythmic momentum that characterises pleasurable progress while balanced between them. That this scene is designed around the range of motion of crutches is evident in the jaunty line with which Molloy concludes his account of the attack: 'I always had a mania for symmetry' (*GII*, 79).

Extended descriptions are given in the trilogy of the two alternate functions of the crutch: a commonplace and utilitarian object with violent potential, and a toy that promises escapism as well as escape. These contradictory modes of usage explain why crutches feature so prominently here but nowhere else in Beckett's work. This prop may have been exhausted after *The Unnamable* because the type of character that makes such good use of crutches in the trilogy – a decrepit old man swinging with solipsistic contentment on his crutches along an empty road, occasionally channelling this momentum into unexpected violence – does not recur in Beckett's later writing. This relationship between painfully generated momentum and play or violence is central to the trilogy. Fintan O'Toole has astutely noted the capacity of Beckett and Flann O'Brien to convert inertia into manic comedy: 'Flann O'Brien was born into a culture of lingering, post-revolutionary dissolution. As with Beckett, his genius was to find energy, both comic and grotesque, in that entropy.'[41] This is clearly in evidence in the physical and material conditions of many of Beckett's characters,

---

[41] Fintan O'Toole, 'The Fantastic Flann O'Brien', *Irish Times*, 1 October, 2011.

particularly those in the trilogy, where they persevere with their journeys and stories despite the impediments stacked against them, as the famous last lines of *The Unnamable* attest.

Central to descriptions of crutches in the trilogy are accounts of the exertion required to achieve motion, whether the forward momentum necessary to generate the euphoric flight of swinging between the crutches, or the rather more grim details of the strain placed on the arms when dragging the body painfully forward. This latter attention to the effort required to move on crutches is nowhere more evident than at the end of Molloy's narrative:

> Flat on my belly, using my crutches like grapnels, I plunged them ahead of me into the undergrowth, and when I felt they had a hold, I pulled myself forward, with an effort of the wrists. For my wrists were still quite strong, fortunately, in spite of my decrepitude, though all swollen and racked by it … And in this way I moved onward in the forest, slowly, but with a certain regularity, and I covered my fifteen paces, day in, day out, without killing myself. And I even crawled on my back, plunging my crutches blindly behind me into the thickets, and with the black boughs for sky to my closing eyes. (*GII*, 84)

This passage is a clear precursor for the figures crawling in mud in the novel *How It Is*:

> push pull the leg straightens the arm bends all these joints are working the head arrives alongside the hand flat on the face and rest

> the other side left leg left arm push pull the head and upper trunk rise clear reducing friction correspondingly fall back I crawl in an amble ten yards fifteen yards halt (*GII*, 421)

The manic preoccupation of the figures of *How It Is* with the imperative of movement is attested to in the lines 'when the great needs fail the need to move on the need to shit and vomit and the other great needs all my great categories of being' (*GII*, 417). In keeping with the stripped back savagery of the piece, however, they must struggle forward without the support to motion and potential for play offered by the prop of crutches.

Sticks

Sticks feature in Beckett's poetry in the early 1930s and in his fiction and drama from 1941 to the early 1960s. They function, as the gallery director John Hutchinson puts it in his analysis of the tradition of walking sticks, as 'elementary extensions of the arm', 'simple tools' or 'forms of support'.[42] Sticks are used by Beckett's characters who can no longer walk unassisted, but do not yet require crutches, or, as in the case of Woburn in the 1960s radio play *Cascando*, who badly need more support and stability, but must make do with that provided by a stick: 'he goes on ... hugging the bank ... same old stick ... he goes down ... falls' (*GIII*, 344). Several sticks in Beckett's work have paternal origins or are associated with fathers. Such sticks have a particular resonance because like greatcoats they are evocative of the walks that characterised Beckett's fondest memories of his father. Sticks inherited from fathers present a belated opportunity to imaginatively recreate the hand-holding that characterised Beckett's boyhood walks with his father, providing a substitute for the father's hand and, in clasping it, an opportunity to mimic the shape made by the father and child walking with a hand outstretched towards each other. Unlike greatcoats, however, there are few sticks inherited from fathers in Beckett's work.

Towards the end of *Mercier and Camier*, Watt smashes Camier's stick onto a table in a fit of passion, breaking it in two. This prompts Camier's observations: 'I miss my stick', and 'it was my father's', and the immediate retort from Mercier: 'I never heard you speak of it' (*GI*, 475). In this way, many sticks are simply taken for granted by Beckett's host of dedicated, ancient walkers. Such is the case with the narrator of *From an Abandoned Work*, who pauses for the following brief aside in the middle of his narrative: 'My stick of course, by a merciful providence, I shall not say this again, when not mentioned my stick is in my hand, as I go along' (*GIV*, 346). A stick is also an essential prop in *Fizzles 3: Afar a bird*, where we meet a figure so hunched over that he crosses the 'ruinstrewn land' of the narrative 'clutching the stick in the middle', stumbling 'bowed over the fields' (*GIV*, 409). The stick in this story serves as an index of time and graphically illustrates this character's accelerated deterioration or shrinking since his appearance a page earlier, when he was 'hunched over his stick ..., one on top of the other the hands weigh on the stick, the head weighs on the hands' (*GIV*, 408). Mr Hackett is a character that not only draws solace from his stick, but is largely characterised by it. We meet Mr Hackett only briefly, at the beginning of *Watt*, when he is deriving satisfaction from the repetitive motion of his stick against the ground: 'Stretching out his left hand, he fastened it round a rail. This permitted him to strike

---

[42] John Hutchinson, *Seanie Barron: Sticks* (Dublin: Douglas Hyde Gallery, 2015), p. 8.

his stick against the pavement. The feel, in his palm, of the thudding rubber appeased him, slightly' (*GI*, 172).

More often than not, it is the great utility of sticks, rather than their paternal associations, which prompts the tone of affection or gratitude in which they are described. In the opening pages of *Molloy*, the narrator relates the usefulness of a stick for an old man walking alone: 'It was a stout stick, he used it to thrust himself onward, or as a defence, when the time came, against dogs and marauders' (*GII*, 6). The particular appeal of a stick to an old man as a compensation for weakness has been noted by Seanie Barron, a contemporary stick-maker from West Limerick. Describing the continued demand for hazel sticks to protect against spirits while walking the roads, he observes: 'It could be all lies too but when you have an auld stick in your hand you feel safe anyway. I sold a stick to Jim Hayes and he's over eighty-three years of age. The wind would knock him but once he has the stick in the hand he'd knock forty fellas. He gets the confidence.'[43] Barron creates hip-height and taller staff-like sticks that bridge the gap between craft and art and recall several of the sticks in Beckett's work, such as the stick photographed by Sean Lynch in Figure 9.

Sticks feature most prominently in the trilogy as weapons or projectiles, or, in a memorable incident in *Molloy*, as the means of initiating a sexual encounter. This scene occurs in the pointedly unromantic setting of a rubbish dump, where Molloy encounters 'an eminently flat woman' who supports herself with 'an ebony stick' (*GII*, 52). Molloy is introduced to the experience of love by this woman, or more accurately, by her stick:

> We met in a rubbish dump, unlike any other, and yet they are all alike, rubbish dumps. I don't know what she was doing there. I was limply poking about in the garbage saying probably, for at that age I must still have been capable of general ideas, This is life. She had no time to lose, I had nothing to lose, I would have made love with a goat, to know what love was … Anyway it was she who started, in the rubbish dump, when she laid her hand upon my fly. More precisely, I was bent double over a heap of muck, in the hope of finding something to disgust me for ever with eating, when she, undertaking me from behind, thrust her stick between my legs and began to titillate my privates. (*GII*, 52)

It is striking that so many of Beckett's sex scenes, characterised as they are by a relentlessly misanthropic disdain or disgust for physical desire, feature touchingly affectionate descriptions of objects. As Molloy recalls the

---

[43] Interview with Michele Horrigan, *The Root of the Matter* (Limerick: Askeaton Contemporary Arts, 2014), p. 3.

Figure 9 Seanie Barron, 'Blackthorn stick with a blackthorn root as handle' (2014). Courtesy of Seanie Barron and the Askeaton Arts Centre.

ensuing sexual encounter with the woman he meets in the rubbish dump, he cannot remember whether her name was Ruth or Edith and thoroughly disparages the act of physical congress, but his account is not without tenderness when describing the billows of fabric of her petticoats that 'welled up all frothing and swishing and then, congress achieved, broke over us in slow cascades', or indeed the dainty furniture in the flat, that he goes so far as saying that he 'liked', the look of which 'made you want to lie down in a corner and never get up again' (*GII*, 52). Such examples recall the keen rush of sexual pleasure experienced by Beckett's fictional and poetic narrators astride their bicycles and demonstrates once again his tendency to displace erotic fascination onto objects. The overwhelming impression is that this is a prudent decision on the part of Beckett's characters: there is a chance that desire will find fulfilment if it is directed at an object, in contrast with the inevitable failure of lavishing such hopes or attention onto people, who are fickle and may withdraw their affection, depart, grow ill or die. Objects threaten no such inconstancy.

Beckett's darkly satiric use of the stick as a love object in *Molloy* strikes a similar yet more emphatic blow against romance as the flourish of a stick in Laurence Sterne's *Tristram Shandy*. In attempting to divert his friend and master Toby Shandy from thoughts of marriage with the Widow Wadman, Corporal Trim uses his stick to describe a movement in the air that is expressive of the pleasures of freedom from love. An illustration of the movement of Trim's stick is recorded in the middle of the text as a wandering curve that fills a generous third of the page. This squiggle is illustrative of the shrugs and gestures made by Sterne's men when they find themselves at a loss for words. While Sterne is amiably foregrounding the inadequacies of language when it comes to passionate expression, the provocative stick in *Molloy* registers a rather less genial assessment of love and life. The setting of Molloy's amorous encounter in a pile of rubbish that he identifies with the simple, bleak comment, 'This is life', anticipates Beckett's stage directions for *Breath*. In his choice of environment for both works, Beckett telescopes the gamut of existence into brief writhings, romantic or not, amidst the 'miscellaneous rubbish' encountered in life.

Molloy is atypical in his discovery of love through a stick. For most other characters, sticks are used to help them navigate the spaces in which they find themselves. In the murky yet luminous opacity of the mysterious air about him, the narrator of *The Unnamable* wishes for a stick with which to identify the walls of his enclosure. He considers several alternative approaches: to 'dart' the stick 'like a javelin' in front of him, thereby establishing the shape of his world by the sound of the stick striking another surface. He revisits this plan for another that would not involve letting go of the stick, and imagines how he might 'wield it like a sword and thrust it through empty air, or against the barrier'. These fine plans come to nothing, however, and he abandons them with the phrase 'But the days of sticks are over, here I can count on my body alone' (*GII*, 294). Adapting his stick for his needs, Malone rummages in his heap of possessions with it, then uses it to draw objects towards him and send them back to the corner. He also uses the stick to hook the table on castors and drag it 'squeaking and lurching towards' him, or 'send it back to its place by the door', and inserts the stick into the 'two handles or ears, projecting above the rim and facing each other' of his pots, the stick his means of moving all these objects about at will.[44] Malone even wonders if he could use his stick to move his bed, 'wielding [it] like a punt-pole' (*GII*, 246). Like the wheelchair-bound characters that compensate for their immobility with fantasies of floating, as do the later iterations of this motif in the immobile figures of Winnie and Krapp, Malone's imagination takes flight at the prospect of this plan working:

> I might even succeed in steering it, it is so narrow, through the door, and even down the stairs, if there is a stairs that goes down. To be off and away. The dark is against me, in a sense. But I can always try and see if the bed will move. I have only to set the stick against the wall and push. And I can see myself already, if successful, taking a little turn in the room, until it is light enough for me to set forth. (*GII*, 246–47)

This eagerly anticipated movement remains pure fantasy for Malone, however, for this vivid passage is followed by Malone's declaration: 'I have lost my stick. That is the outstanding event of the day, for it is day again. The bed has not stirred' (*GII*, 247).

In an indication of the particularly intimate relationship he has with his stick, Malone keeps it under the blankets in his bed, and tells us 'there was a time I used to rub myself against it saying, It's a little woman' (*GII*, 240). Like Molloy, Malone briefly associates his stick with sex, but the great fondness he has for this object is due to its utility, which explains his distress when he loses it.

> It is a disaster. I suppose the wisest thing now is to live it over again, meditate upon it and be edified. It is thus that man distinguishes himself from the ape and rises, from discovery to discovery, ever higher, towards the light.

---

[44] *Malone Dies*, *GII*, 178–79, 245. These various functions of the stick seem to anticipate the succour provided by the mysterious hands in Beckett's 1982 play *Nacht und Träume*.

> Now that I have lost my stick I realise what it is I have lost and all it meant to me. And thence ascend, painfully, to an understanding of the Stick, shorn of all its accidents, such as I had never dreamt of. What a broadening of the mind. So that I half discern, in the veritable catastrophe that has befallen me, a blessing in disguise. How comforting that is. (*GII*, 247–48)[45]

The gaff is an 'iron hook; a staff or stick armed with this'.[46] Among Beckett's sticks, there are two gaffs, differentiated from all the other, ordinary sticks by the hook they sport at one end. The gaffs wielded by Hamm and Malone are therefore not primarily intended to be used as an aid to movement or as a prop, but rather as an implement to rake or gather things in. In both its appearances in Beckett's writing, however, the gaff is used in an abortive attempt to move the chair or bed in which each character is confined. Halfway through *Endgame*, Hamm orders Clov to get the gaff. Later stage directions indicate that Hamm, 'wielding it like a punt-pole, tries to move his chair' (*GIII*, 122). Like Malone in his bed, Hamm gets nowhere when he attempts to punt his chair with the gaff. The failed technique employed by both characters is to support the inert weight of their bed and chair on the stick or gaff, and leaning on the gaff, propel themselves forward upon it, seeking, perhaps, the pleasurable swoop of movement they faintly remembered enjoying on their crutches before they found themselves bed- or chair-ridden. Such depictions of debility may seem uniquely Beckettian, but these mirror the theatrical imagery of W.B. Yeats. Just as the physical restriction and attempted movement of characters in *Endgame* and *Malone Dies* recalls the actors Yeats imagined forcing to rehearse in barrels on castors that he would shove into position with a pole, the blind and lame beggars in *Rough for Theatre I* echo their counterparts in Yeats's 1926 play, *The Cat and the Moon*.[47] Beckett sets out a bleakly comic scenario in *Rough for Theatre I* where the maimed try to lead the blind, to pair together in order to compensate for each other's weaknesses, but who in so doing make things much harder for each other.

From their first appearance in *The Cat and the Moon*, it is clear that Yeats's couple are united by their physical afflictions: 'a blind man with a lame man on his back'.[48] This pair similarly forms an alliance involving

---

[45] The echo here, particularly in the closing lines, with Jonathan Swift's 'A Meditation Upon a Broomstick' (1711), is surely not accidental.
[46] *OED*.
[47] W.B. Yeats, *Explorations* (London: Macmillan, 1989), pp. 86–87.
[48] Yeats, *The Cat and the Moon*, in *W.B. Yeats: The Major Works*, ed. Edward Larrissy (Oxford: Oxford University Press, 1997), pp. 289–96, p. 289. Yeats's Blind Beggar also obsessively counts his paces like several of Beckett's later figures.

mutual physical dependence, before their arrangement is disrupted by the Blind Beggar swinging irascibly with his stick at the Lame Beggar, accusing him of having contradicted him.[49] This same sudden wild lurching with a stick features in *Rough for Theatre I*, which ends with B prodding A with his stick, while taunting him that he will be without his fiddle in future, and will be reduced to 'croaking to the winter wind'.[50] B punctuates each poke with an 'Eh Billy', a series of hectoring demands that have the same effect on A as the repeated 'Eh Joe?' that tortures the protagonist of Beckett's 1965 play of the same name. B makes the mistake of poking A with his stick once too often. Exasperated beyond self-control, the final stage directions of *Rough for Theatre I* indicate that 'A whirls round, seizes the end of the pole and wrenches it from B's grasp' (*GIII*, 239). Beckett does not specify if the stick is to be flung beyond the reach of B, or returned, or traded for information about the whereabouts of his fiddle, stool and bowl, but the decision to conclude the play with the seizure of this single prop well indicates its importance. Without the stick, B cannot propel his chair back to his room; without the benefit of B's eyesight and guidance, A will not be able to find his things. Since A has said that he cannot leave without them, the loss of the stick condemns these two figures to each other's company.

Just as Molloy speaks of his weakness and vulnerability immediately before launching himself into an assault of the charcoal burner, many of Beckett's characters that walk with sticks turn them to violent ends. In her assessment of the history of sticks, Catherine Dike suggests that the first stick was most likely fashioned from a branch of a tree by somebody who had difficulty standing up straight, and this same 'branch became his first weapon'.[51] This trope recurs often in Beckett's writing: a stick is first presented as a walking aid for an ostensibly weak or lame character, but is later wielded by them as a weapon. The stick is an ideal prop for frail characters that are capable of sudden violence, including the narrator of *From an Abandoned Work*, who finds himself cursing and 'lashing about with the stick', despite being 'mild and weak' and lacking any reason for such an outburst (*GIV*, 348). The eccentric Mr Madden, whom Mercier and Camier encounter on a train, emphasises his point by brandishing his

---

[49] Yeats, *The Cat and the Moon*, p. 292.
[50] *Rough for Theatre I*, *GIII*, 239. A note is appended to this line, where Beckett indicates that 'wind' is to be rhymed with '*unkind*', in another echo, perhaps, of Yeats, who insisted upon a distinctly idiosyncratic pronunciation and intonation of his own work.
[51] Catherine Dike, *Walking Sticks* (Buckinghamshire: Shire Publications, 1990), p. 5.

stick and bringing it down with a bellow and 'a thump on the seat which emitted instantaneously a cloud of fine ephemeral dust'. Soon after this, he descends from the carriage and stands still on the platform. In the final image of Mr Madden, the old man has adopted a posture of weakness and resignation, having bowed 'down his head till it lay on his hands at rest on the knob of his stick', a posture that will recur in several of Beckett's last prose pieces that are dominated by an ancient walking figure (*GI*, 410, 411). Sticks are quite frequently used to administer beatings in Beckett. When enthusing about the stick with which he rummages through his possessions and draws them to him, Malone exclaims, 'How great is my debt to sticks! So great that I almost forget the blows they have transferred to me' (*GII*, 179). The narrator of *The Expelled* expresses his relief and surprise that, having been ejected from his father's house and thrown into the street, 'they' decided not to pursue him 'down into the street, with a stick, to beat me in full view of the passers-by' (*GIV*, 248), while among his possessions, Malone discovers the ominous item of a club 'stained with blood, but insufficiently, insufficiently. I have defended myself, ill, but I have defended myself' (*GII*, 242).

Several sticks form part of the costume of a menacing background character, often a policeman, but also on occasion a mysterious stranger. Used to signal authority, these sticks are just as likely to be misused as those of Beckett's indigent characters. The 'ranger' is one of several powerful or violent characters in *Mercier and Camier* in possession of a stick. It is described as 'at once elegant and massive', and he uses it, with his boot, to drive a pair of rutting dogs from a shelter during the rain (*GI*, 388). Amongst the other mysterious figures in the novel wielding massive sticks or clubs, almost as though they have stepped out of a Grimm's fairy tale, there is the man encountered by Mercier and Camier in the 'saloon'. They watch him enter, dressed for the outdoors in an outfit as exaggerated as Clov's travelling suit: 'He wore a cap, a trench-coat all tabs, flaps, pockets and leather buttons, riding-breeches and mountaineering boots. His still brawny back was bowed beneath a knapsack filled to bursting and he held a huge stick in his hand' (*GI*, 419). The stranger Moran meets towards the end of his narrative is also described as having a stick of vast proportions. He first sees him 'leaning on a stick so massive, and so much thicker at the bottom than at the top, that it seemed more like a club'. Moran is so fascinated by this stick that he asks to hold it while stretching out his hand for it. 'He did not move. I put my hand on the stick, just under his. I could feel his fingers gradually letting go. Now it was I who held the stick. Its lightness astounded me. I put it back in his hand' (*GII*, 141).

Moran's description has a surface naivety, but this exchange takes place mere pages before he murders a man in an ugly blue suit who comes to his camp and offers no more insult than resembling Moran and stretching out a hand towards him, just as Moran himself did to hold the stranger's stick. The description of his assault of the blue-suited man is cavalier, even jaunty:

> I can still see the hand coming towards me, pallid, opening and closing. As if self-propelled. I do not know what happened then. But a little later, perhaps a long time later, I found him stretched on the ground, his head in a pulp. I am sorry I cannot indicate more clearly how this result was obtained, it would have been something worth reading. (*GII*, 145)

The register of this passage recalls Molloy's attack on the charcoal burner. Molloy's crutches enable him to make a game of killing the man who threatens to interrupt his journey. Moran does not have crutches, but since the man in the suit seems to be interfering in his quest to find Molloy, he dispatches him without regret.

These parallel scenes of assault help to balance the two halves of the novel, and are used by Beckett to indicate the relationship between physical weakness and access to an unnatural, prosthetic power that comes in the form of a stick or crutch, thereby granting vulnerable characters the capacity to dominate other, more physically capable characters. This juxtaposition of physical frailty and violence offers a striking example of Beckett's refusal to valorize illness and debility by associating it with moral wisdom. His sick and suffering characters are more often seen to be corrupted than purified by their experience, and if they are the victims of more powerful and physically stronger characters, it is simply because they lack the means to humiliate and subdue their assailants. These acts of aggression operate, however, under a strict logic of literary hierarchy: no central character in Beckett is subject to mindless, annihilating violence. It is precisely because the victims of these scenes in *Molloy* are background characters that attempt to halt the narrative that they can be killed off in such a perfunctory, even playful fashion. In this respect, the parallel killings in *Molloy* illustrate Beckett's interest in the manic, even diabolic imperative fuelling the narratives of the trilogy, to the point that the narrating voice of the Unnamable cannot relinquish this galloping need to keep going, even in its last, gasping words.

Literary Prosthetics and Ethics

Belacqua appropriates a bicycle to flee his date, and like several other characters, experiences a sexual gratification in the saddle that is more erotic than any encounter between human characters in Beckett. Sticks, similarly, are misappropriated as sex aids, while crutches become murder weapons. The multiple uses and misuses of these objects signal their utility to Beckett, as he draws on bicycles, wheelchairs, crutches and sticks to explore various ways of moving his characters along, and to describe the pleasure or pain they experience as a result of these different methods of progress. Literary prosthetics in this way highlight Beckett's preoccupation with the ethics of compelling his characters to follow the arc of his poetic, narrative and dramatic narratives. There is no other writer who so thoroughly interrogated the flawed ethics of authorial procedure. The closest point of comparison is Franz Kafka. 'In the Penal Colony', his short story written in 1914, is organised around the display and operation of a torture machine that inscribes the judicial sentence directly onto the body of the guilty as punishment. In the course of his narrative, the eager caretaker of the 'remarkable piece of apparatus', appalled by the idea that the days of administering justice in this way could be coming to an end, releases the prisoner and takes his place on the rack instead, in the hope of experiencing what he has described in awed tones as the miraculous epiphany granted the prisoner whose body comes to understand the sentence as it is carved into his flesh and kills him. Kafka's officer is amply rewarded for his celebration of this brutal machine, and his body is broken and cast into the pit without ceremony.[52] The story is animated by a fierce sense of outraged justice. Beckett's *How It Is* also describes the inscription of punishing words onto characters' bodies. The novel consists of a series of encounters between old men crawling in the mud. In each encounter, one man seeks to provoke a reply from the other by force, pinning him down and thumping, clawing or stabbing words into his body until the desired response has been achieved. Beckett gains the narrative framework of the story from this horrific procedure itself. *How It Is* provides an extreme illustration of a frequent scenario in Beckett's work, where characters are unwillingly conscripted into the service of a plot and are then punished by the narrative.

The process by which this occurs is most clearly indicated by the link drawn by Beckett between a number of sticks and pencils. In *Rough for Theatre II*, the authoritative A and easily startled B discover a bird cage. A asks B for a pencil and '*pokes it between the bars of the cage*' to confirm his suspicion that the bird is dead (*GIII*, 254). The contemporaneous *Act Without*

---

[52] Franz Kafka, 'In the Penal Colony' in *The Complete Short Stories of Franz Kafka*, ed. Nahum N. Glatzer (London: Vintage, 2005), pp. 140–167.

Words II features two similarly nameless characters, distinguished from one another with the same letters, who find themselves prompted into action by a goad that appears from the wings and intrudes onstage, much as the pencil is poked through the bars of the birdcage in *Rough for Theatre II*. Like a pencil, the goad is described as a long stick with a point at one end, and is it seems also used to check if an unmoving figure is alive or dead:

> Enter goad right, strictly horizontal. The point stops a foot short of sack A. Pause. The point draws back, pauses, darts forward into sack, withdraws, recoils to a foot short of sack. Pause. The sack does not move. The point draws back again, a little further than before, pauses, darts forward again into sack, withdraws, recoils to a foot short of sack. Pause. The sack moves. Exit goad. (*GIII*, 215)

Both pencils and sticks in these works are used to signal authority, and are wielded in the same way an author, working with pencil and paper, attempts to prod inert characters into activity.

The most striking example of a pencil used as a weapon to coerce characters into participation in a narrative occurs in the disintegrating closing lines of *Malone Dies*, where the hatchet Lemuel has used to kill off a number of characters mutates into his hammer, another weapon, and then into the stick and pencil Malone has used to tell his own stories, part of which activity has involved creating or killing off characters.

> Lemuel is in charge, he raises his hatchet on which the blood will never dry, but not to hit anyone, he will not hit anyone, he will not hit anyone anymore, he will not touch anyone anymore, either with it or with it or with it or with or
>
> or with it or with his hammer or with his stick or with his fist or in thought in dream I mean never he will never
>
> or with his pencil or with his stick or (*GII*, 280–81).

I suggest that the affinities between pencils and sticks above constitute authorial self-portraits of a similar nature to the Director in *Catastrophe* and Bam in *What Where*. All these figures proceed by subjugating and interrogating their fellow characters, controlling their movement, coercing them into providing a story.[53]

---

[53] *Catastrophe* consists of the same cast of characters as 'In the Penal Colony'. Both works feature an observer whose approval is sought and a victim whose body is manipulated and placed in position for torture and display. Both works also feature an overseeing controlling force who understands the mechanisms of the 'performance'. Crucially, both works also feature a reversal of the dynamic suggested by this cast of characters, with the victim reprieved and the overseeing controlling figure undone by the apparatus of torture and display they have set in place.

Beckett relied upon the same four objects to tease out different ways of keeping his characters mobile, and to fuel the dynamic of imperative and impediment in his writing, where the characters of his poems, novels and plays are compelled, as the Unnamable memorably put it, to 'go on', even though their ability to do so is under threat from their steadily increasing decrepitude. Literary prosthetics keep Beckett's characters – and therefore the story – moving. Beckett's treatment of movement offers a useful indication of how he thought about the writing process. The form of salvage in this chapter is the means by which Beckett translates authorial impetus and impediment into his characters' vexed but determined movement: the bodies of his characters must limp and creep along in order to generate his narratives, organised as they are around this movement. It is evident that Beckett was troubled by the ethics of authorship, and one of the ways he conveyed his sense of the debt of responsibility he owed to his literary creations was to foreground the suffering of characters that are prodded into motion, limping their way on impossible journeys to satisfy the demands of movement in narrative, and their creator's need to set such narratives in motion.

CHAPTER 4

Treasure

Pockets, Bags, Last Remaining Possessions

Storytelling Objects

In the opening paragraph of his narrative, Malone declares that before his death, he intends to pass the time by telling himself stories: 'I look forward to their giving me great satisfaction, some satisfaction' (*GII*, 174). It is only in the starkness of its execution that this scenario differs from much of the rest of Beckett's oeuvre, since the most pressing concern for many of his characters is precisely this imperative to tell stories, before deaths that are keenly imagined and often imminently anticipated. For Beckett's characters, as Salman Rushdie puts it, 'Words are essential and so a few words remain, and stories cannot entirely be disposed with, they are begun and changed and discarded but never entirely disposed of, because in stories resides life, while it resides, until the last eviction' (*GII*, xiii).

In *Malone Dies* and *Happy Days*, Beckett identifies the protagonists' need to tell themselves stories with the materials that allow this to happen. This emphasises the differing generic demands of storytelling in fiction and drama: while Malone hesitates and dithers about how to organise the stories that comprise the novel, Winnie is jolted into her routine with the opening bell and must improvise as best she can. They each have three stories that form the centrepiece of their narratives. Malone tells the stories of Saposcat, Macmann and Lemuel, and Winnie those of Charlie Hunter, Mildred and the Shower-Cooker couple. They turn to their stories to steady and fortify themselves in uncertain and hesitant moments when they have lost their voice or direction, and it is around the ballast of these stories that they organise their narratives. To date, critical evaluations of storytelling in Beckett have focused on the failure of narration rather than its purpose, on storytelling as habit or as a stain on silence, on stories as sources of psychological symbolism and revelation for the characters who tell them, or finally, as a means of pointing up the tension between the time of narration and the time of dying.[1] This chapter has a different focus. Through examination of the pencil and paper with which Malone records his narrative, and the toothbrush, parasol, handkerchief and nail file that Winnie uses to keep her poorly assisted monologue unsteadily reeling along, this chapter demonstrates how their storytelling objects allow these two characters to continue speaking about their worlds and themselves.

Malone explains his dependence on pencil and paper in the line 'At first I did not want to write, I just said the thing. Then I forgot what I had said' (*GII*, 201). The record of Malone's written word is essential for the same reason Winnie needs the rather inadequate audience of Willie for her stories, and Estragon and Vladimir depend on their routines: to be given the impression that they exist. So physically diminished and constrained as to be largely immobile, their fictional and dramatic environments so drastically emptied of people that they are effectively reduced to their own company, Malone and Winnie can do little other than narrate and describe their conditions. As Winnie observes, 'There is so little one can say, one says it all' (*GIII*, 300). Since this is all either character can do, they are at pains to draw attention to those stories that particularly merit attention. At several points in the first act, Winnie interrupts herself to address Willie and express her hope that he had not missed a particularly perceptive observation of hers: 'I hope you caught some of that, Willie, I should be sorry to think you had caught nothing of all that, it is not every day I rise to such heights' (*GIII*, 292). In the second act, when her shattered faculties have made such storytelling heights inaccessible, she makes no comment along these lines. Similarly, Malone spends a great deal of the start of his narrative talking about the type, subject matter and order of the stories he proposes to tell. He fusses over this in the dark when he cannot write and returns to the topic during the day: 'I must have thought about my time-table during the night. I think I shall be able to tell myself four stories, each one on a different theme. One about a man,

---

[1] See Andrew Gibson, *Reading Narrative Discourse: Studies in the Novel from Cervantes to Beckett* (London: Macmillan, 1990), esp. pp. 140–65; Kristin Morrison, *Canters and Chronicles: The Use of Narrative in the Plays of Samuel Beckett and Harold Pinter* (Chicago and London, University of Chicago Press, 1983), esp. pp. 1–51, pp. 214–20; Catharina Wulf, *The Imperative of Narration: Beckett, Bernhard, Schopenhauer, Lacan* (Brighton: Sussex Academic Press, 1997), esp. pp. 1–31, pp. 57–95; Simon Critchley, 'Who Speaks in the Work of Samuel Beckett?', *Yale French Studies*, 93 (1998), 114–30.

another about a woman, a third about a thing and finally one about an animal, a bird probably' (*GII*, 175). He revises this several times until he finds himself in the middle of a series of stories almost by accident, and without enough time left before the end of his narrative to make a new start.

Malone drafts his stories in an exercise book with two pencils, one a mere stub.[2] In keeping with the spirit of this exercise book, Malone makes use of a school-boyish pun to explain the strange ciphers and symbols at the start of the book: 'Calculations, I reckon' (*GII*, 203). Later, he gives a lengthy, gritty description of how hungrily his fingers grasp the remaining stub of this pencil, how his mouth and nails trim its point, and how gently he must press it against the face of the paper, so as to conserve it.

> My pencil. It is a little Venus, still green no doubt, with five or six facets, pointed at both ends and so short there is just room, between them, for my thumb and the two adjacent fingers, gathered together in a little vice. I use the two points turn and turn about, sucking them frequently, I love to suck. And when they go quite blunt I strip them with my nails which are long, yellow, sharp and brittle for want of chalk or is it phosphate. So little by little my little pencil dwindles, inevitably, and the day is fast approaching when nothing will remain but a fragment too tiny to hold. So I write as lightly as I can. But the lead is hard and would leave no trace if I wrote too lightly. (*GII*, 216)

After all this, he comically undermines this degree of care for his pencil, noting 'The strange thing is I have another pencil, made in France, a long cylinder hardly broached, in the bed with me somewhere I think. So I have nothing to worry about, on this score' (*GII*, 216).

Beckett's preference for the pencil rather than the pen is due perhaps to the greater sensuousness of the pencil in mark-making. In his descriptions of Malone's efforts to write, there is an emphasis on the tactile relation between hand and word: the requisite degree of pressure that must be applied for the pencil to make an impression without unnecessary wearing away of the lead, and the relation between his finger which guides ahead of the sentence and the pencil that follows its path to leave its trace of ciphers: 'My little finger glides before my pencil across the page and gives warning, falling over the edge, that the end of the line is near.' We are also, once again, directed to consider the scene with minute sensual

---

[2] Malone's 'thick exercise-book ruled in squares' corresponds with the notebook used by Beckett for the composition of this work. See the Harry Ransom Beckett Centenary Exhibition, 'Fathoms from Anywhere'.

attentiveness when Malone speaks of the sound of the paper's surface receiving these marks: 'I hear the noise of my little finger as it glides over the paper and then that so different of the pencil following after' (*GII*, 201, 202).

Malone's tenderly proprietorial attitude to his pencils also extends to his exercise book. On several occasions, he declares how much his writing materials mean to him and how they are, in the final reckoning of his inventory, his only remaining possessions, according them a status afforded to no other objects (*GII*, 248, 263). Later in his narrative, he explains the significance of the exercise book that he is holding, in terms that tell us much about the purpose of his storytelling.

> With my distant hand I count the pages that remain. They will do. This exercise-book is my life, this big child's exercise-book, it has taken me a long time to resign myself to that. And yet I shall not throw it away. For I want to put down in it, for the last time, those I have called to my help, but ill, so that they did not understand, so that they may cease with me. (*GII*, 267)

The evocation in these lines of an authorial debt of responsibility to his literary creations is something that will be explored more fully in the conclusion to this book. Here, I wish only to note that Beckett passes on this sense of authorial duty to Malone. We see Beckett playing with Malone's dependence on his writing materials when he becomes panic-stricken about losing his pencils or exercise book, something that happens with cruel frequency in the text. The first incidence of this distressing loss is described in under three lines, but is set apart as a paragraph in its own right, to indicate its importance:

> I fear I must have fallen asleep again. In vain I grope, I cannot find my exercise-book. But I still have the pencil in my hand. I shall have to wait for day to break. God knows what I am going to do till then. (*GII*, 202)

This passage conveys the extent to which the fragmentary and disorganised narrative that Malone records in his exercise book is identical to *Malone Dies* and has the effect of transporting the reader to the site of composition of the novel. Similarly, the sentence 'What a misfortune, the pencil must have slipped from my fingers, for I have only just succeeded in recovering it after forty-eight hours (see above) of intermittent efforts' opens a new section after a page break, marked by an ellipsis in the middle of the page (*GII*, 216).

The final unravelled passage of the novel, which seems to record Malone's death, is similarly typographically distinct. His consciousness slipping away, words come in confused eddies: as the previous chapter noted, Malone's pencil is conflated with Lemuel's stick, the weapon that has discharged two characters in his story, and then with 'light', twice voiced, as if Malone is moving towards the light, welcoming or perhaps bidding it farewell. The novel ends on the word 'anymore', and in the jumbling together of pencil, stick and light, Beckett gathers together in the last lines the means of creating, recording and killing characters, and a symbol conventionally associated with the moments of both life and death (*GII*, 281). If Malone is unable to continue with his stories, he cannot maintain the continuous reinvention that his fictional world seems to require. Indeed, it is suggested at several points in the novel that Malone's storytelling calls into existence not only his own room, bed and possessions, but is also responsible for the creation of many of Beckett's other characters. Dismissing further consideration of his stories, Malone says: 'But let us leave these morbid matters and get on with that of my demise, in two or three days if I remember rightly. Then it will be all over with the Murphys, Merciers, Molloys, Morans and Malones, unless it goes on beyond the grave' (*GII*, 229).

While Malone's writing materials are fundamental to the very existence of his narrative, the printed word powerfully impedes Winnie's ability to sustain her monologue and unfolding dramatic narrative. For much of *Happy Days*, all we glimpse of Willie is the upper edges of the newspaper that absorbs him to the degree that he barely acknowledges Winnie's presence. If Willie can be imagined as a model of the inattentive audience member, scarcely aware of the main theatrical event taking place on top of the mound, he might also be thought of as a realisation of the reader of fiction onstage, absorbed in the words of his newspaper while Winnie's drama runs its course. Winnie's hunger for any crumb of conversation suggests that her isolation is more keenly felt with a poor listener that it would be if she was alone. Towards the end of the second act, when Willie makes his dramatic appearance after a long absence, Winnie refers to his newspaper-reading habits in an acid, single sentence summary of their relationship: 'I worship you Winnie be mine and then nothing from that day forth only titbits from Reynolds' News' (*GIII*, 306).

The titbits that Willie reads aloud from his newspaper during the course of the play prompt one of Winnie's stories, and cause her to fall silent on three occasions. Without preamble, Willie reads the death notice for Charlie Hunter: 'His Grace and most Reverend Father in God Dr. Carolus Hunter dead in tub.' Stirred to 'fervent reminiscence', Winnie swoons in recollection of her youth, of a leafy garden, of the first and second balls she attended as a young woman and of her first kiss (*GIII*, 279). When Willie reads out the job notices, by contrast, Winnie visibly wilts. She loses the thread of her conversation and stares ahead in silence. Once Winnie is interrupted or loses her way with the routines anchored in her material resources, she is unable to pick up the pieces of her story, and must wait in silence before she can generate the momentum to move on to something else. When she does so, she proceeds with gusto. Malone's storytelling, by contrast, is broken up by hesitations, improvisation and interjections such as 'What tedium' and 'Mortal tedium' (*GII*, 210, 211). Such comments disrupt the surface of Malone's narrative invention and return the reader to the image of an old, withered, naked man in a bed trying to sustain himself with objects and stories.

Both Malone and Winnie vehemently express their need to record and be heard, but the nature of their storytelling differs because it is rooted in their use of the storytelling objects allotted them: Malone's pencils and exercise book allow him to compose and record his stories, while Winnie uses her parasol, handkerchief and nail-file to inspire the tangential comments that compose her monologue. Winnie's objects provoke speech, in the form of the improvisatory arabesques of discourse that are used to fill her day, but they do not trigger stories in the same way as Malone's objects. This difference in their modes of storytelling is rooted in the demands of their respective media. Winnie's need to narrate her day and to feel certain that she has an audience is the defining condition of a theatrical monologue. The importance of an audience or witness even if they do not overtly contribute to the play is indicated by Beckett's initial provision of an androgynous Auditor to indicate mutely their 'helpless compassion' for Mouth in *Not I* (*GIII*, 405). Winnie uses certain objects to initiate Willie and herself into the old round of stories and fragments of stories they have both heard many times already. She relies on her parasol to jolt Willie awake, and in the opening moments of the play, holding it by the butt, uses it to assault him into wakefulness so he can provide a witness for her, if not quite a conversation partner. Winnie's parasol is yet another sticklike object in Beckett's writing used to poke, prod or goad another character, to force them to behave as desired.

In his *Happy Days* production notebook for the 1979 Royal Court production, Beckett organised the play around blocks of action framed by Winnie's use of objects. The notebook consists of detailed descriptions of the sequences in which Winnie turns to the bag, removing or replacing its contents. There are long lists of movements, detailing, for example, which hand is to be used to move objects and when objects are to be transferred between hands. Beckett also indicates the consequences of handling certain objects in a particular way, noting the importance of Winnie's handkerchief and nail-file, which, when they are used to wipe other objects or file Winnie's nails, lead to a dramatic change in emotional register. Throughout the play, there are frequent, desperate moments when Winnie loses her way and what Beckett describes in the notebook as 'défaillance', a fainting spell or moment of weakness, takes over, where she is overcome by her situation and slips into despondency. Winnie is handless in the second act of the play, when she can enumerate all the things outside the bag and on the mound beside her, but has lost everything hidden within the bag. In the second act, Winnie must use her eyes in the same way she used her hands in the first, to play with and engage the objects. That she can no longer draw upon the resources within the bag is doubtless part of the reason why in the second act she cannot connect her thoughts, or recover from the moments of défaillance that, like sorrow, keep knocking her off balance.

Each time défaillance happens while Winnie is wiping, polishing or filing; however, these repetitive, mindless and rhythmic gestures encourage a certain dreamy kind of monologue, where her attention wanders and fragments and remnants of anecdotes and quotations, once learned by rote, return to her, floating or drifting up out of the dark. Winnie's imperfectly remembered 'classics', her assorted fragments of verse or prose, resemble the objects she takes from the bag. She fondles and fetishises them in the same way, and they are also evidently falling apart. After sporadic attempts during the first act, Winnie finally deciphers the words on her toothbrush handle as the enigmatic phrase 'hog's setae'. Winnie's slow retrieval of these words from the toothbrush handle enacts the close relationship between her material and imaginative resources. The physical gestures of repeatedly polishing the handle and scrutinising it through an array of visual aids mirror her mental exertions when trying to access the hazy fragments of her 'classics'. The set piece with the toothbrush handle also articulates many of the key elements of the first act of the play. The illegibility of the writing on the handle gives Winnie a purpose, while pointing up Willie's reticence and ability to give information and support at will, suggesting that his silence at other times is capricious.

During the first act, Winnie reminds herself at several points that she must be careful not to use up her store of words and must hoard them for the future. To do so, she turns to her possessions. The link between the action of filing her nails and recollection of one of her stories is indicated by the following passage:

Something says, Stop talking now, Winnie, for a minute, don't squander all your words for the day, stop talking and do something for a change, will you? [*She raises hands and holds them open before her eyes. Apostrophic.*] Do something! [*She closes hands.*] What claws! [*She turns to bag, rummages in it, brings out finally a nailfile, turns back front and begins to file nails. Files for a time in silence, then the following punctuated by filing.*] (*GIII*, 293)

The story that floats into Winnie's thoughts while filing her nails is that of the Shower–Cooker couple, who pass by and comment on her predicament with the sort of impatient literalness that Beckett scorned in his audiences. Winnie's anecdote lasts as long as her filing, and she punctuates the story with changes of fingers or hand and inspections of her handiwork. She concludes her telling of the story by repeating her gratitude for the memory of it: 'Thankful for it in any case. [*Voice breaks.*] Most thankful' (*GIII*, 294). The Shower–Cooker story is not therefore habitual, like Hamm's narrative in *Endgame* or, for that matter, her own story of Mildred, recounted towards the end of the second act, but directly prompted by the action of filing her nails.

Towards the ends of their narratives, Winnie and Malone disintegrate under the force of their isolation, because they no longer have access to the possessions that had enabled them to ward off the damaging impact of being stuck in a strange environment for a long period, of struggling against the insidious effects of loneliness and tedium, and of attempting to make sense of their predicament. These possessions were so precious because they enabled them to convert the experience of confinement and prolonged discomfort into some form of storytelling. This brings us to the question: why should objects, in Beckett's idiosyncratic mode of literary progress, fuel stories? The fourteen objects in this book are sources of comfort for Beckett's characters and narrators; never more so than for the figures *in extremis* of Winnie and Malone, whose isolation and imprisonment means that they can draw their narratives neither from exchanges with others, nor from their own movement. Later in this chapter, I will consider how *Happy Days* and *Malone Dies* operate as turning points in Beckett's drama and fiction. Both texts feature characters whose most acute wish is not to escape their predicaments, but to keep themselves going by engaging in storytelling, something that becomes increasingly difficult as Beckett removes the objects that prompt these stories. Unlike later characters, Winnie and Malone are not subject to the imposition of narrative from an outside authorial agency: their storytelling is sustaining rather than compulsive, and it depends on objects. The steady disappearance or removal of the material resources required for storytelling signals the imminent fall of both characters into silence, and the disintegration of their narratives as they can no longer articulate or hope to understand their predicaments.

Treasure

This last chapter examines those objects that Malone in *Malone Dies* and Winnie in *Happy Days* simply cannot do without. Winnie and Malone's treasure takes several forms, most tangibly the heap of objects cherished by both characters. These material resources are housed in the receptacles of pockets and bags and used by both characters to prompt and sustain the stories that keep them going. For Malone and Winnie, treasure is a succour and resource, but having it renders them vulnerable. The potentially devastating impact on these characters of using up or being without their treasure is a central tension in both works, with the heightened dependence of Malone and Winnie on their treasure the most succinct illustration of the particular relation between people and things in Beckett's writing. The strategic restriction of material elements in *Malone Dies* and *Happy Days* recalls Jerzy Grotowski's poor theatre: 'The acceptance of the poverty of theatre, stripped of all that is not essential to it, revealed to us not only the backbone of the medium, but also the deep riches which lie in the very nature of the art-form.'[3] In similar fashion, Beckett's deliberate impoverishment of Malone and Winnie functions as a creative strategy: the limited resources granted in this novel and play starkly reduce his inventive potential, throwing him back on the rudimentary purpose of both media: that of storytelling.

Fictional Pockets and Dramatic Bags

When Malone reaches into his pocket and Winnie explores the recesses of her bag, they produce the resources that keep their narratives unsteadily in motion. The receptacles that hold their possessions moreover determine the shape of their narratives. Malone's narrative unfolds as though it were produced from a pocket: he guards his treasure jealously, turning it over in his hand and head, and derives great pleasure from secretly fondling his objects and stories, hiding them from any visitor to his room

---

[3] Jerzy Grotowski, T.K. Wiewiorowski and Kelly Morris, 'Towards the Poor Theatre', *The Tulane Drama Review*, 11.3 (Spring 1967), 60–65, p. 63.

and wary of revealing too much to the reader. He is playing to amuse himself alone, an exemplary personification of the fictional narrator. Winnie, by contrast, swoops on and presents her objects and stories as though she were pulling them out of such a bag. The misremembered, misplaced, disorganised fragments of memory and anecdotes that float up to the surface of her narrative resemble a penny or hairpin discovered by chance at the bottom of a capacious bag. She puts her treasure on display in the hope of eliciting some response and initiating a conversation with her sole, almost mute companion, but when she applies herself too emphatically to this game, runs the risk of emptying her bag of resources completely. We see the consequences of this in the deterioration in number and quality of her remaining stock of objects, anecdotes and memories in the second act.

In terms of their practical function, pockets and bags are similar: both store and transport possessions. There are, however, clear phenomenological differences between them. Pockets are intimate spaces that hold their contents against the body, while bags are carried at a slight remove, containing objects that are more cumbersome or less personal than those housed in pockets. Objects in pockets are held out of sight of other characters and hoarded for private use while objects are drawn out of bags for display. Barbara Burman has described how pockets 'offer one of the few permissible breaches of the clothed space between the private body and the public world'.[4] This phenomenological distinction has implications for the literary form in which each receptacle works best. In her memoir *How It Was*, Anne Atik relates Beckett's original concept for *Happy Days*: 'At some point in the 1950s Sam showed A[vigdor Arikha] a text about a man and his pocket, which he referred to as *La poche*, then abandoned, but which later led to Winnie's bag in *Happy Days*.'[5] Beckett's decision to abandon his initial idea of a play organised around a man's pocket in favour of a woman's dependence on her bag may have been influenced by European cultural associations of men with trousers, and therefore pockets, and women with skirts or dresses, which are pocketless garments in the main, and therefore bags. However, Atik's account of this early draft of *Happy Days* seems to indicate that Beckett's preference for one rather than the other means of keeping small personal objects safe and close to a

---

[4] Barbara Burman, 'Pocketing the Difference: Gender and Pockets in Nineteenth-Century Britain', in *Material Strategies: Dress and Gender in Historical Perspective*, ed. Barbara Burman and Carole Turbin (Oxford: Blackwell, 2003), pp. 77–99, p. 90.
[5] Anne Atik, *How It Was*, p. 6.

character was determined by questions of medium, with theatrical necessity dictating that fictional pockets become dramatic bags.

Much of what I want to say about Beckett's use of pockets and bags in *Malone Dies* and *Happy Days* is condensed and distilled in the following curiously dreamlike comment by Malone: 'For this may well be my last journey, down the long familiar galleries, with my little suns and moons that I hang aloft and my pockets full of pebbles to stand for men and their seasons, my last, if I'm lucky' (*GII*, 229–30). This lyrical invocation of what he hopes will be his final journey conveys the mysterious telescoping of literary levels that animates the trilogy: Malone is imagined as a lamplighter moving through his narrative, lighting its way by hanging aloft the 'little suns and moons', the light and time that each story requires, with his pockets 'full of pebbles to stand for men and their seasons' to people each story. What this passage presents is not simply Malone as a poetically conceived authorial persona, but a rare glimpse of Beckett's creative procedure. If he can be supposed to be grumbling here because his characters are no more lifelike than pebbles, he is also engaged in an inventive collapsing of literary hierarchy. The process of writing is imagined as a dark corridor through which the figure of Malone stumbles, bringing light and colour and detail, the meagre space of his pockets containing all that his creator might invent. The impact of these lines, where we seem to witness Malone pulling Beckett's pages out of his pockets as a clown might lines of colourful scarves, is both a denigration of the act of writing and a demonstration, by fiat, of its potential: entire worlds are produced from the mean space of a fictional pocket. The equation of characters with objects, of men with pebbles, moreover, is closely bound up with Malone and Winnie's expressions of desire for their narratives to come to an end, something that will be considered more fully in the conclusion to this book.

The extraordinary potential of a pocket was celebrated by the English writer G.K. Chesterton in 1909, when one of his narrators declares his intention 'to write a book of poems entirely about things in my pockets. But I found it would be too long; and the age of the great epics is past'.[6] This keen attentiveness to pocketed objects is echoed by Malone, who takes great pleasure in the distinct phenomenological pleasure of blind sight granted by pockets:

> I loved, I remember, as I walked along, with my hands deep in my pockets ... to finger and caress the hard shapely objects that were there in

---

[6] G.K. Chesterton, *Tremendous Trifles* (New York: Dover, 2007), p. 9.

my deep pockets, it was my way of talking to them and reassuring them. And I loved to fall asleep holding in my hand a stone, a horse chestnut or a cone, and I would be still holding it when I woke, my fingers closed over it. (*GII*, 241)

This tender account of Malone fondling his objects is, however, followed by a lengthy consideration of the ways in which he may dispose of these loved objects:

> And those of which I wearied, or which were ousted by new loves, I threw away, that is to say I cast round for a place to lay them where they would be at peace for ever, and no one ever find them short of an extraordinary hazard, and such places are few and far between, and I laid them there. Or I buried them, or threw them into the sea, with all my strength as far as possible from the land, those I knew for certain would not float, even briefly. But many a wooden friend too I have sent to the bottom, weighted down with a stone. Until I realised it was wrong of me. For when the string is rotted they would rise to the surface, if they have not already done so, and return to the land, sooner or later. In this way I disposed of things I loved but could no longer keep, because of new loves. And often I missed them. But I had hidden them so well that even I could never find them again. (*GII*, 241)

This too recalls Chesterton, who observes in the story 'What I Found in My Pocket', 'I suppose that the things that I have dropped into my pockets are still there; the same presumption applies to the things that I have dropped into the sea.'[7] Beckett's juxtaposition of embrace and rejection here may signal his stringent refusal to allow sentimentality to creep into his work. More prosaically, it may be that Beckett was thinking of Molloy's system for distributing his stones between his pockets, and was anxious lest his reader overestimate the number or degree of capaciousness of Malone's pockets.[8]

Pockets in Beckett's fiction serve as hidden spaces, miniature stages upon which events of reduced proportion but great importance take place. Because the pocket is an intimate, secretive space, it may be thought of as housing those private, precious resources that shore up a character against the many threats of the outside world. In a striking passage, Malone considers the origins of the bowl of a pipe he comes across on the road and pockets, a meditation that leads him to describe other objects also discovered and acquired in this way. He is moved, in the

---

[7] Chesterton, *Tremendous Trifles*, p. 75.
[8] Molloy's sucking stones are considered in the conclusion to this book.

course of this sustained recollection, to expressions of deep contentment, including even tears of happiness. Later in the passage, we are given to understand that the comfort provided by such objects as these 'little portable things in wood and stone' was great enough to palliate Malone's loneliness: 'but for the company of these little objects which I picked up here and there ... which sometimes gave me the impression that they too needed me, I might have been reduced to the society of nice people or to the consolations of some religion' (*GII*, 240–41). For an able-bodied, mobile character, a pocket is composed of a fold of fabric pressed close against the body, within which is held important and small possessions. Imagining that death is close at hand, as he does sporadically throughout his narrative, Malone fantasises about transforming his bed itself into a sort of pocket, and taking all his possessions into bed with him, surrounding himself on all sides with them, fortifying himself, and holding tightly on to them, like a down-at-heel Egyptian king: 'Then I shall have them all round me, on top of me, under me, in the corner there will be nothing left, all will be in the bed, with me ... Perhaps I shall have something in my mouth ..., and I shall be lying on other treasures still' (*GII*, 244).

While most bags in Beckett's work feature in his stage plays, a number of bags also appear in his prose and radio drama. Two fictional bags are celebrated in terms as rapturous as Winnie's. Mercier and Camier share a conviction that their sack is the 'crux of the whole matter' (*GI*, 425–26), while the sack in *How It Is* offers tangible proof of a potentially divine and certainly benevolent force in its otherwise cruel world. This nihilist parable is a blistering dramatisation of the confusion, misery and meaninglessness of life, where the inherent violence of human relationships is mercilessly staged in a series of encounters between characters blindly crawling towards or away from each other in the mud. Struggling face down through such a world, the narrator thinks of the sack he drags along with him.

> no the truth is this sack I always said so this sack for us here is something more than a larder than a pillow for the head than a friend to turn to a thing to embrace a surface to cover with kisses something far more we don't profit by it in any way any more and we cling to it I owed it this tribute (*GII*, 457)

Just as the bag in *Happy Days* contains a medicine bottle and revolver, those bags in the novellas *The Calmative* and *The End* and the radio play *Embers* hold drugs that offer sedation or suicide to Beckett's characters.

Embers features the story of Bolton, a distressed old man who pleads hysterically with his friend, the doctor Holloway, for something stronger than the injection he has offered, having called Holloway out to his house in the middle of the night and instructed him to bring his 'little black bag' (*GIII*, 199). The narrator in *The Calmative* exchanges a kiss for a phial that may contain a sedative or poison. The 'big black bag' that the stranger in *The Calmative* holds on his knees is said to resemble a midwife's, but the assistance offered by its contents is not to help one into the world, but rather to cope with, or perhaps leave it: the stranger displays his collection of 'glittering phials' to the narrator and asks 'What are you grinning and bearing?' (*GIV*, 271). This mysterious phial resurfaces in the final lines of *The End*, where the narrator, significantly, calls it his 'calmative'. Its effect upon him is dramatic: 'The sea, the sky, the mountains and the islands closed in and crushed me in a mighty systole, then scattered to the uttermost confines of space' (*GIV*, 293). This is infinitely preferable to the scenario described by Malone, who recalls 'among my possessions I once had a little phial, unlabelled, containing pills. Laxatives? Sedatives? I forget. To turn to them for calm and merely obtain a diarrhoea, my, that would be annoying' (*GII*, 248).

Bags, and Winnie's bag in particular, serve a similar function to pockets in Beckett's work, but are deployed with considerably more ostentation. Observing that 'not since *The Importance of Being Earnest* has a handbag played such an important role in advancing the dramatic action', Enoch Brater takes us to the heart of its function in *Happy Days*, since the contents of Winnie's bag directly determine the course of the play.[9] Marooned in an inhospitable and unforgiving environment, she can rely only on an ingenious, but increasingly desperate, use of the contents of her bag. The stage properties held within the bag have thus become life buoys. The various objects that Winnie withdraws from the bag are as essential to the production of her narrative as her similarly finite store of words, for Winnie uses both to initiate the routines that sustain her. In the first act of the play, Beckett demonstrates how dependent Winnie is on her words and objects by giving her striking turns of phrase and extended monologue sequences, and equally memorable and intricate sequences of play

---

[9] Enoch Brater, 'Beckett's Dramatic Forms, Considered and Reconsidered', lecture presented at the Samuel Beckett Summer School, Trinity College Dublin, 18 July 2012. There is a distinction to be made between the late Victorian and twentieth-century meanings of the term handbag. In Wilde's play, the handbag is large enough to accommodate a baby, and is therefore a capacious and sturdy shopping bag such as Winnie's.

with the contents of her bag, but in the second act, he places impediments between Winnie and her sources of succour, taking away her hands and making words fewer and more dearly earned. Winnie seems to anticipate this process, warning herself in the first act:

> Do not overdo the bag, Winnie, make use of it of course, let it help you … along, when stuck, by all means, but cast your mind forward, something tells me, cast your mind forward, Winnie, to the time when words must fail – [*she closes eyes, pause, opens eyes*] – and do not overdo the bag. (*GIII*, 288)

The degree to which the bag and its contents are essential for Winnie has been emphasised by many actresses who have performed the role. For Rosaleen Linehan, the entire performance grows out of the bag and Winnie's 'careful play' with its treasures.[10] The powerful function of the bag and Winnie's straitened circumstances when it is beyond her reach in the second act is well illustrated by John Haynes's photograph of Linehan in the role (Figure 10).

Beckett directed *Happy Days* at the Royal Court in London in June 1979, with Billie Whitelaw and Leonard Fenton. The production notebook he prepared for rehearsals offers an invaluable insight into the emphasis he placed on Winnie's possessions, particularly her bag. Knowlson describes the effect of Beckett's direction, centred as it was on a deliberate and expressive mode of engagement with the contents of Winnie's bag:

> Winnie flitted rapidly from topic to topic, fitfully inspired by objects to hand that recalled moments from an uncertain past, which hardly seemed any more discontinuous, however, than her fragmented present … Her hands fluttered, bird-like, before they settled on something to which she clung, a precious commodity that, given her capacity for verbalisation in the first act, would enable her to negotiate another phase of her lonely 'day'.[11]

Beckett explicitly directed that Winnie give the bag a look of 'special significance', registering the resources and support it provided for her.[12] Martha Fehsenfeld kept a diary at these rehearsals, and records that Beckett

---

[10] This is Linehan's phrase. During the course of an interview with Linehan at her home in February 2011, the actress insisted that any analysis of Winnie was impossible without an intimate understanding of her possessions, and generously assembled on the kitchen table a parasol, dainty hat, empty tube of toothpaste and old toothbrush, through which we explored the stage directions.
[11] *Happy Days: The Production Notebook of Samuel Beckett*, ed. James Knowlson (London: Faber, 1985), pp. 16–17.
[12] *Happy Days: The Production Notebook of Samuel Beckett*, p. 87.

Fictional Pockets and Dramatic Bags

Figure 10 John Haynes, 'Rosaleen Linehan, *Happy Days*' (1999).
Courtesy of John Haynes and Lebrecht Music & Arts.

instructed Whitelaw to 'look at her bag with affection before she dipped into it. "The bag is all she has. Look at it with affection. From the first you should know how she feels about it."'[13] As director, Beckett wanted to emphasise Winnie's relationship with the bag from the very start of the play. Fehsenfeld describes the time and 'infinite trouble' he spent assembling the opening tableau, where the audience discovers Winnie asleep on the mound: 'Whitelaw was placed with her left arm on the mound, her right arm over it and with her head down, resting on her right forearm, which in turn rested on the mound. To her left, her right hand cradled the front of the bag, which represented a constant source of comfort to her.'[14]

In *Paraphernalia*, Steven Connor describes Beckett as 'probably the great, hitherto uncelebrated dramatist of bags'.[15] Connor notes the various potential puns on 'wait' and 'weight' materially embedded in the bags of *Waiting for Godot*:

> 'Time', we say, 'hangs heavy'. To bear, to carry, means to endure, to last out; to carry and to carry on, to carry over, to endure: weight means time: so

---

[13] *Happy Days: The Production Notebook of Samuel Beckett*, p. 163.
[14] *Happy Days: The Production Notebook of Samuel Beckett*, p. 123.
[15] Steven Connor, *Paraphernalia*, p. 17.

weight means waiting. Samuel Beckett puns lengthily on the two different kinds of wait in his play *Waiting for Godot*, which contains a memorable bag-carrier in the person of Lucky, the slave of the tyrant Pozzo, who spends most of the play encumbered by his master's enormous bags.[16]

Connor is correct to suggest that Beckett was indeed punning here, because in the second act, Pozzo tells Vladimir that the bags that so weigh down Lucky are filled with sand. Significantly, this material is traditionally used in hourglasses, which is the material logic for Beckett's pun on the homonyms of 'wait' and 'weight.' A similar analysis of these bags features in Enoch Brater's *Ten Ways of Thinking about Samuel Beckett*, in which Brater suggests that 'no one before Beckett would have thought of putting bags and baggage into so much play'.[17] Like Connor, Brater does not specify that the bags carried by Lucky are filled with sand, but this fact is clearly integral to his argument that through the laborious efforts of carrying them across the stage so often in the play, the bags come to take the measure of time in *Waiting for Godot*.[18]

Connor clearly articulates the nature of Winnie's relationship with her bag, and the devastating impact on her of its withdrawal from use in the second act:

> In ... *Happy Days*, the first act of which is the monologue of a woman buried up to her waist in a mound of earth, the action is punctuated and parcelled out by Winnie's plunges and sallies into her bag for lipstick, toothpaste, mirror, medicine, and all the possibilities they embody of beguiling the vicious time of her existence – 'Perhaps just one quick dip', she says, as a boozer to his tipple. When, in the second act, she is inhumed up to her neck, the horror of her situation is signalled most of all by the bag which lies on the mound, tauntingly gaping just in sight and to hand, though for the handless Winnie now unreachable, as though all the resources of life and memory and history were held inaccessibly in it.[19]

Winnie's evident reliance upon her bag and its contents is matched by Malone's similarly dependent relationship with his salvaged possessions. Next, I want to consider how the inventories composed by each character allows them to take stock of all they have been given and permitted to

---

[16] Connor, *Paraphernalia*, p. 17.
[17] Enoch Brater, *Ten Ways of Thinking about Samuel Beckett: The Falsetto of Reason* (London: Methuen Drama, 2011), p. 157.
[18] Connor and Brater concentrate exclusively on Beckett's stage theatre, and neglect the bags in his fiction and radio plays that serve, like Winnie's, the crucial formal function of a prop-box from which the catalyst for the action may be withdrawn.
[19] Connor, *Paraphernalia*, pp. 17–18.

retain by life: a particularly pressing concern in narratives that involve the gradual withdrawal of these last mercies and resources.

Winnie and Malone's Inventories

In his account of translating Beckett's letters, George Craig speaks of his surprise upon encountering 'the sudden and pleasurable realisation of ownership, possession' in a comment of Beckett's about eating onions from his garden: 'I am already, do not miss this, eating my own onions. It is the first time that I've ever found myself in a position to have any.'[20] Indigence and deprivation loom large in Beckett's work, yet his characters exhibit a similar sense of satisfaction in declaring their possession of certain objects, as if the corollary of a decline or collapse in material circumstances is that any object salvaged and retained is automatically considered treasure and henceforth regarded with pride and delight. Isolated, their spirits and bodies failing them, Winnie and Malone fall back on their possessions and sustain themselves with talk of these objects, naming and listing them, emphasising their importance with frequent delight.

An inventory is a 'catalogue' or 'detailed account,' differentiated from a more general list by its concentration on 'goods and chattels'.[21] The composition of an inventory holds out the same pleasures of enumeration as the list, with the added satisfaction of taking stock and reminding oneself of one's property. This accounts for its being one of the very earliest forms of writing.[22] Patrick Murray has identified Beckett's use of the 'technique of exhaustive enumeration', and suggests that Beckett's novels are comparable to those of Rabelais, Swift, Fielding, Sterne and Joyce in their reliance upon 'long catalogues of oddly assorted objects for comic purposes'.[23] Many of Beckett's jumbled, heterogeneous and redundant lists clearly serve a comic function, heaping digression upon digression so that the original purpose of detailed description is more often than not abandoned in disgust, but this is not the function of the inventories in *Malone Dies* or *Happy Days*. Malone insists that only certain things may

---

[20] Craig, *Writing Beckett's Letters*, p. 35.
[21] OED.
[22] 'Many of the earliest palaeographic documents are inventories of objects and persons, stock itemisations of goods for trade, payments, rations, work requirements and so on.' See Florian Coulmas, *The Blackwell Encyclopaedia of Writing Systems* (Oxford: Blackwell, 1996), pp. 298–301.
[23] Patrick Murray, 'Samuel Beckett and Tradition', *Studies: An Irish Quarterly Review*, 58.230 (Summer, 1969), 166–178, p. 167.

be included in his inventory: 'only those things are mine the whereabouts of which I know well enough to be able to lay hold of them …, that is the definition I have adopted, to define my possessions. For otherwise there would be no end to it' (*GII*, 243). This chapter examines the function, complications and satisfactions of inventory-making for Malone and for Winnie, who does not attempt to write an inventory but provides a running commentary on the heterogeneous contents of her bag, as she takes them out in turn.

The French writer Georges Perec worked as a scientific archivist, and the compulsion to objectively sort material is evident in his preface to *Thoughts of Sorts*, where Perec identifies four 'modes of questioning' that have consistently informed all his writing: the sociological, autobiographical, ludic and novelistic.[24] Perec was concerned, throughout his writing life, with the irresistibility and pathos of classifying and inventorying: their resemblance of the activity of thinking and utter inadequacy in organising the material of life. This inadequacy explains why, for Perec, the attempt to create an exhaustive list was fraught with peril. In this, he resembles Malone. The seedy satisfaction that the younger, mobile Malone derives from secretly fondling the objects in his pocket is balanced by his passion for classifying and describing the contents of the inventory he is desperate to compose when bedridden. Very early on, Malone declares his intention to prepare such an account: 'then I shall speak of the things that remain in my possession, that is a thing I have always wanted to do. It will be a kind of inventory.' Although he spends a great deal of the start of the novel describing or using the objects in his room, he is loath to commence this inventory, lest he should leave something out through forgetfulness, or erroneously include another object in its place. This repeated oscillation between a firmly expressed determination to write and the prompt interjection of excuses for putting it off may have held a wry appeal for Beckett, who spoke of the difficulties of writing throughout his life and whose sustained and successful period of writing came late in life: 'All my life long I have put off this reckoning, saying, Too soon, too soon. Well it is still too soon' (*GII*, 175–76).

Malone and Winnie are both deeply preoccupied with the idea and ideal of an inventory, but lack the necessary discipline and mastery to realise such an exhaustive account. Instead, we see these characters

---

[24] Georges Perec, *Thoughts of Sorts*, trans. David Bellos (London: Notting Hill Editions, 2011), p. 2.

deriving comfort from both imagined and real handling of their possessions. In the first act of *Happy Days*, Winnie declares herself incapable of reciting an inventory of the contents of her bag:

> [*Turning towards bag.*] There is of course the bag. [*Looking at bag.*] The bag. [*Back front.*] Could I enumerate its contents? [*Pause.*] No. [*Pause.*] Could I, if some kind person were to come along and ask, What all have you got in that big black bag, Winnie? give an exhaustive answer? [*Pause.*] No. [*Pause.*] The depths in particular, who knows what treasures. [*Pause.*] What comforts. (*GIII*, 288)

Winnie summarily dismisses her ability to catalogue the contents of her bag because she cannot guarantee that she could give an 'exhaustive' description of them, particularly those objects in its 'depths'. Malone, too, considers abandoning his inventory for 'scrupulous' reasons: he cannot be certain that he is faithfully and fully composing a list of his possessions, being at best vaguely informed about where they came from, when they came to him, and, with an emphasis on the mysterious agency of these objects, whether they have left, are currently missing or have left and already returned to Malone's room.

The differing shape of Malone's and Winnie's inventories is largely determined by the formal demands of the two works. *Malone Dies* is organised around the rambling digressive thoughts of its central character. It is therefore amenable to the alternating passages of order and disarray implied in the attempted composition of an inventory, and a great amount of space can be given over to such an enterprise, whether or not it is successful. The balancing act of flaunting descriptive and imaginative failure at the same time as composing a narrative that is baggy and elegant enough to encompass such failure is a technique particularly in evidence in Beckett's trilogy. Such attempted inventory-making is fundamentally unsuited to the dramatic form. This is why *Happy Days* is not organised around inventories to anything like the same degree as *Malone Dies*. Moreover, Winnie's possessions are not the product of her imagination or memory like those objects Malone can no longer handle, but are rather pulled out of her bag and displayed to the audience in all their tangible, visible materiality. Unlike Malone, Winnie is not therefore obliged to describe the appearance or nature of her possessions. As she removes her toothbrush and toothpaste, lipstick and medicine from the bag, Winnie notes the degree of deterioration of each with the comment 'running out – ah well', a phrase that punctuates the first act. Objects that have not visibly depleted or fallen apart when she takes them out of the bag are given a thorough if peremptory assessment and preparation before use, such as Winnie's spectacles and magnifying glass, which both require a good wipe and polish with her handkerchief. A clowning sequence is conjured by the stage directions here, as Winnie cleans her spectacles in order to check if her magnifying glass needs to be cleaned, then uses both aids together in order to decipher the print on her toothbrush handle.

> *Winnie lays down glass and brush, takes handkerchief from bodice, takes off and polishes spectacles, puts on spectacles, looks for glass, takes up and polishes glass, lays down glass, looks for brush, takes up brush and wipes handle, lays down brush, puts handkerchief back in bodice, looks for glass, takes up glass, looks for brush, takes up brush and examines handle through glass.* (*GIII*, 280)

This compulsive cleaning and maintenance, we understand, is another of the routines with which she fills her day, and yet another degree of attentiveness that she brings to bear on her objects. In this way, Beckett indicates that the contents of her bag are subject to an ongoing process of dilapidation that Winnie attempts to delay with her system of quality control and preservation. The vulnerability of these objects to the deleterious effects of time and use is thereby flagged for the audience, and when Winnie returns them to their places in the bag after use, the audience has received the kind of detailed account achieved in prose by the composition of an inventory.

After considerable commentary and procrastination throughout the novel, Malone eventually delivers a rushed and imperfect inventory, in a slapdash account of nine pages that is riddled with pleasurable digressions, and summarised by the précis: 'all that is left to me of all I ever had, a good dozen objects at least' (*GII*, 241–42). The objects he claims and includes in his inventory answer to this number, and include two pencils, 'the one of which nothing remains between my huge fingers but the lead fallen from the wood', an exercise book, a stick, a needle held between corks with a 'wisp of black thread', the bowl of a pipe in which he stored tiny things, a club 'stained with blood, but insufficiently, insufficiently', a yellow boot, 'I forget for which foot', his hat that 'has lost its brim, it looks like a bell-glass to put over a melon', a 'scrap of newspaper', some buttons, a photograph of a donkey and three socks (*GII*, 239–44). Malone includes and describes his pots, although he is not entirely certain that they belong to him, while he regrets not speaking of 'the cap of my bicycle-bell, of my half-crutch, the top half, you'd think it was a baby's crutch' (*GII*, 245). The nine-page inventory is framed by the expressions, 'Quick quick my possessions', and 'I did well to stop my inventory, it was a happy thought.'

Upon the conclusion of this inventory, Malone immediately undermines the basis for its composition: 'In the meantime nothing is mine any more, according to my definition, if I remember rightly, except my exercise-book, my lead and the French pencil, assuming it really exists' (*GII*, 239, 248). Having abandoned the composition of his inventory, Malone anxiously turns to the 'resource' of his story about the man: 'But enough about me … Go and see how Macmann is getting on perhaps. I have always that resource' (*GII*, 248). Like his author, Macmann is discovered in bed and in a state of anxiety about his possessions, described as 'the trappings of his derelict days'. Macmann passionately and hysterically clamours for his clothes and the contents of his pockets, crying 'My things! My things!, over and over again, tossing about in the bed and beating the blanket with his palms.' When he is calmer, Moll, the old woman in charge of his care, tries to reason with him about the impossibility of having his possessions returned, explaining that his clothes had been destroyed and the objects in his pockets 'had been assessed as quite worthless and fit only to be thrown away with the exception of a little silver knife-rest which he could have back at any time' (*GII*, 251).

Beckett's inclusion of this knife-rest enacts a sly collapse in the distinctions between preceding characters in the trilogy, and constructs a hall of mirrors from those objects desirable enough to be stolen or claimed by these characters. We first encounter the knife-rest in *Molloy*, when the titular protagonist explains that he stole 'a little silver' from Lousse, including some 'massive teaspoons' and a strange object, the name or utility of which has remained a mystery to him. As he attempts to describe the appearance of this mysterious object, Molloy's matter of fact tone is overwhelmed by the accumulation of detail and becomes one of bewilderment and finally wonder:

> This strange instrument I think I still have somewhere, for I could never bring myself to sell it, even in my worst need, for I could never understand what possible purpose it could serve, nor even contrive the faintest hypothesis on the subject. And from time to time I took it from my pocket and gazed upon it, with an astonished and affectionate gaze, if I had not been incapable of affection. (*GII*, 58)

The knife-rest reappears in the second half of *Molloy*, in the house and hand of Moran, who declares his habit of playing with it before dinner is served: 'For as a rule I was at table, my napkin tucked into my collar, crumbling the bread, fiddling with the cover, playing with the knife-rest, waiting to be served, a few minutes before the appointed hour' (*GII*,

110–11). Finally, as we have seen, the knife-rest is included in Malone's inventory. The knife-rest, in this way, allows Beckett to create echoes in the trilogy.

In *Beckett's Happy Days: A Manuscript Study*, Gontarski goes through the production notebook Beckett prepared for his 1971 direction of the play at the Schiller theatre in Berlin. The notebook gives a more thorough description of Winnie's bag than the finished text of the play: 'The "known contents" of Winnie's bag are detailed, including items which are never shown (i.e., her comb and brush), and a cryptic "miscellaneous" category is included.'[25] In his notes for the Berlin production, Beckett indicated that he wanted Winnie's objects to have a specifically worn quality.

> Beckett's description of the props used in his production of *Happy Days* reinforces the decay and deterioration. The toothbrush has few hairs. Only fragments of a label remain on the toothpaste. The medicine bottle too has a damaged label. Winnie's handkerchief, Willie's boater and newspaper are all yellowed. Winnie's necklace has more thread than pearls.[26]

These are all visual markers of the decline and contraction that characterise the entire play and further emphasise the shift between the first and second acts of the play. According to this logic, all matter, living or not, is running out or tending to inertia, but never quite coming to an end. There seems no prospect of relief through death for Winnie, and if the play were to continue into a third act, she would be further incapacitated, perhaps incapable of seeing or recalling the possessions that will have fallen into disrepair from lack of use.

Given her decline in the second half of the play, the running oral account that Winnie makes of her possessions in the first act serves as a final catalogue of them, for she will certainly never open her bag again to consider them. Winnie's inventory is in this respect a means of cataloguing her legacy, a function that is explicitly attributed to Malone's inventory, too. Anticipating his death, Malone states his intention to mark 'the great day' by listing the objects he has acquired during his life, declaring that 'I should be sorry to let slip this unique occasion which seems to offer me the possibility of something suspiciously like a true statement at last.' No greater testimony is possible to the privileged importance granted to

---

[25] Gontarski, *Beckett's Happy Days*, p. 15.
[26] Gontarski, *Beckett's Happy Days*, p. 22.

his possessions than his vehement statement of intent: 'I want, when the great day comes, to be in a position to enounce clearly, without addition or omission, all that its interminable prelude had brought me and left me in the way of chattels personal' (*GII*, 190). Malone's compulsion to compose such an inventory is directly related to his occupation during the course of the novel: dying. His use of the phrase 'chattels personal' makes the purpose of his inventory clear: a legal distinction is made between chattel real, composed of 'leases and wards', and chattel personal, which comprise 'all moveable goods, as money, plate, cattle'.[27] Malone's inventory is characterised by the conflation of tiny detail and minute specifications with an expansive, if desperately haphazard, approximation of thoroughness and finality. In this, it resembles two important kinds of inventory: the last will and testament composed before death, and the list drawn up upon admitting a person to prison. Their isolation and the dramatic restriction of their physical means leave Malone and Winnie exposed. The powerlessness of their circumstances, and their extreme dependence on a limited number of objects that provide the substance of their narratives, is directly comparable with the situations of characters in prison and castaway narratives.

Winnie and Malone as Prisoners and Castaways

Brenda Bruce played Winnie in the British premiere of *Happy Days* at the Royal Court in 1962. Beckett exasperated Bruce during rehearsals by dismissing all her questions about the character with the line 'Tis of no consequence' (*BR*, 162–63, *DF*, 500). Eventually banned from the theatre for undermining her confidence, Beckett did, however, give Bruce valuable direction and insight into Winnie's character when he shared his concept of the play with her, over a meal:

> He said: 'Well I thought that the most dreadful thing that could happen to anybody, would be not to be allowed to sleep so that just as you're dropping off there'd be a "Dong" and you'd have to keep awake; you're sinking into the ground alive and it's full of ants; and the sun is shining endlessly day and night and there is not a tree … there'd be no shade, nothing, and that bell wakes you up all the time and all you've got is a little parcel of things to see you through life.' He was talking about a woman's life, let's face it. Then he said: 'And I thought who would cope with that and go down singing, only a woman.' (*DF*, 501)

[27] *OED*.

The phrase 'and all you've got is a little parcel of things to see you through life' is central to an understanding of Winnie and Malone. For characters that lack the possibility of escaping or altering their difficult circumstances, salvaged possessions offer the crucial possibility of routine and companionship.[28]

This scenario is also at the core of two related genres: prison and castaway literature. *Malone Dies* and *Happy Days* share the same central dynamic as Daniel Defoe's *Robinson Crusoe* (1719), Antonio Gramsci's *Letters from Prison* (1973) and Aleksandr Solzhenitsyn's *One Day in the Life of Ivan Denisovich* (1962): that of isolated and trapped characters relying on a few remaining objects. While Beckett has often been compared with Defoe, scholars have not thus far considered Beckett's work in the light of the writings of Solzhenitsyn or Gramsci. These writers shared an ideological motivation for exposing conditions in the gulag and prisons of the twentieth century that is evidently antithetical to Beckett's creative purpose, but the manner in which they relate the experience of imprisonment shares a marked similarity with Beckett.[29] Surprisingly little critical attention has been paid to the thematic and formal importance of incarceration in Beckett's work, while biographical accounts emphasise the impact on Beckett of experiences related to the Second World War, including the death of his friend Alfred Péron soon after release from a concentration camp.[30] Outside the extraordinary circumstances of wartime, Beckett was directly confronted with the spectacle of imprisonment on a daily basis when he moved into an apartment on Boulevard Saint-Jacques in 1960 that faced onto La Santé prison. According to Knowlson, 'It was from this window that, with a small pair of binoculars, Beckett used to scan the tiny, barred windows of the cells in the Santé prison, often feeling

---

[28] Jan Kott has similarly emphasised the importance of entrapment and a limited set of objects in *Happy Days* by comparing Winnie to a paralytic in a nursing home. See Jan Kott, 'A Note on Beckett's Realism', trans. Boleslaw Taborski, *The Tulane Drama Review*, 10.3 (Spring 1966), 156–159, p. 159.

[29] *The Grove Companion to Samuel Beckett* lists a number of references to Defoe in Beckett's work: from the early poem 'Serena I', to *Murphy*, 'What a Misfortune' and 'Yellow', in *More Pricks than Kicks*, *Malone Dies* and *Happy Days*. (GC, 130). See also Hugh Kenner, *Samuel Beckett: A Critical Study*, pp. 68–69; Robert Kiely, 'Samuel Beckett Harping', p. 82; Peyton Glass, III, 'Beckett: Axial Man', *Educational Theatre Journal*, 29.3 (October, 1977), 362–73, p. 364; Therese Fischer-Seidel, ' "The Ineluctable Modality of the Visible": Perception and Genre in Samuel Beckett's Later Drama', *Contemporary Literature*, 35.1 (Spring 1994), 66–82, p. 76.

[30] The only such examinations of this subject to date are Agnieszka Tworek, '*Endgame* Incarcerated: Prison Structures in Beckett's Play', *JOBS* 16.2 (2007), 247–58 and Victoria Swanson, 'Confining, Incapacitating, and Partitioning the Body: Carcerality and Surveillance in Samuel Beckett's *Endgame*, *Happy Days*, and *Play*', *Miranda*, 4 (June 2011), 2–15.

emotion for those who were imprisoned inside.'[31] André Bernold recounts a story told by Beckett's German translator, Elmar Tophoven, who was working on revisions besides Beckett in the apartment when Beckett in a 'distracted state' moved to the window: a prisoner was communicating by using a mirror to send light into the room. Tophoven watched as Beckett made 'sweeping semaphore gestures in return, which signified nothing save for: "Courage!"'[32] The first work he composed in his study on the Boulevard Saint-Jacques was centrally preoccupied with imprisonment, isolation and unhappiness. That work was *Happy Days*.

Beckett's 'natural sympathy for those who were incarcerated', in Knowlson's phrase, is evident in his encouragement of productions of *Waiting for Godot* by the inmates of the Lüttringhausen prison in 1953, and of *Waiting for Godot*, *Endgame* and *Krapp's Last Tape* by those of San Quentin prison from 1961 to 1963 (*DF*, 409–11, 611–12). Moreover, Beckett responded enthusiastically to a request for a play by the International Association for the Defence of Artists (AIDA) in 1982. He wrote and contributed *Catastrophe* to the event 'Une Nuit pour Václav Havel', at the Avignon Festival that July. Beckett's play was performed as part of a night of solidarity for Havel, the Czech playwright and dissident writer who was then imprisoned for subversion. Beckett dedicated *Catastrophe* to Havel. In his analysis of Beckett's motivation to support Havel in this way, Knowlson describes how Beckett was 'appalled to learn that, as part of the punishment for his courageous stand against abuses of human rights, Václav Havel had been forbidden to write. This seemed the ultimate oppression'.[33] Malone and Winnie are also prevented from writing, of course, Beckett having already articulated his horror of this scenario in these works. Upon his release, Havel wrote to Beckett, thanking him for his tribute. Knowlson quotes from Havel's letter: 'For a long time afterwards there accompanied me in the prison a great joy and emotion and helped to live on amid all the dirt and baseness', and notes that Beckett was 'deeply moved' by it (*DF*, 680).

Prison and castaway narratives are both constrained by the cramped horizons and reduced means of their characters. There are, however, several important differences between the genres. The castaway tends to have recourse to exotic raw materials, from which he may fashion makeshift

---

[31] Knowlson, 'A Writer's Homes – A Writer's Life', p. 15. See also *DF*, 476, 558–59, 662 and *LM*, 501, where Cronin describes how Beckett established 'a form of communication with one long-term prisoner, waving to him in salutation at certain hours of the day'.
[32] André Bernold, *Beckett's Friendship*, pp. 54–55.
[33] *DF*, 678, and see Jo Glanville, '"Godot is here": How Samuel Beckett and Vaclav Havel Changed History', *Guardian*, 15 September 2009.

versions of his possessions left at home or on the seabed after the shipwreck that stranded him. The titular protagonist of *Robinson Crusoe* mends and patches and makes do with a deteriorating stock of possessions, and much of the novel is taken up with descriptions of an imaginative resourcefulness, which is by definition denied to the prisoner. The prisoner, by contrast, is compensated for this material poverty by potential contact with the outside world through letter writing, a prospect denied to the castaway, access to whose thoughts tend instead to be related through the convention of composing a diary. Letters and diaries are the means of recording the experience of the prisoner or castaway, but they also serve to stave off disorder and insanity by organising this experience into some sort of narrative form. Such letters and diary entries are composed, almost exclusively, of descriptions of the prisoner or castaway's daily routine, where every detail is granted importance and recorded.

The affinities between this manic attention to detail and the practice of the novelist are obvious. James Wood has noted the appeal for novelists of reduced spaces such as the prison cell:

> All fictions are closed worlds, smaller than our own, and so it is not surprising that novelists are often drawn to represent very small worlds – boarding houses, hotels, a plague-sealed town, a single day in prison, a bare room. These reduced spaces intensify the fictionality that made them: they are as bound as a book. Depending on the intensity of the reduction, plot slows down to an agonising verisimilitude, because the writer needs both to entrap the reader and to persuade the reader that this entrapment is abnormally normal.[34]

The model for such closed fictional worlds, Wood observes, is 'prison literature, in which the smallest detail – a breadcrumb, a passing bird, a drop of rainwater – is tortured, from desperation, into a swollen effigy, many times its normal size'.[35] Both *Happy Days* and *Malone Dies* share this desperate attention to detail with prison and castaway narratives. It manifests itself in three common features: the tendency of characters to comment upon the strange environment in which they find themselves, the impact upon these characters of prolonged isolation and their need to keep going with few possessions.

In both works, the foreign and strange environment in which Beckett's central characters discover themselves is scrupulously recorded, with an emphasis on their dispiriting realisation that there is no hope of escape.

---

[34] James Wood, 'Rite of Corruption', *LRB*, 32.20 (21 October 2010), 13–14, p. 13.
[35] Wood, 'Rite of Corruption', p. 13.

Malone seems awkwardly at odds with the sequence of night and day, and impatiently and vainly wishes for one to replace the other: 'And yet how often I have implored night to fall, all the livelong day, with all my feeble strength, and how often day to break, all the livelong night' (*GII*, 214). Winnie, similarly, cannot read the changing signs of her environment well enough to say what time of day it is, and frets with an ironically clockwork regularity about how well advanced the day, and how imminent the bell for sleep, may be (*GIII*, 282, 288, 290, 295, 296, 302, 303, 305).

Malone follows his comments on the inadequacy of both day and night and his dissatisfaction with either half of the cycle with a sustained analysis of the curious light in his room during a twenty-four hour period:

> But before leaving this subject and entering upon another, I feel it is my duty to say that it is never light in this place, never really light. The light is there, outside, the air sparkles, the granite wall across the way glitters with its mica, the light is against my window, but it does not come through. So that here all bathes, I will not say in shadow, nor even in half-shadow, but in a kind of leaden light that makes no shadow, so that it is hard to say from what direction it comes, for it seems to come from all directions at once, and with equal force … And does not that simply amount to this, that there is really no colour in this place, except in so far as this kind of grey incandescence may be called a colour? Yes, no doubt one may speak of grey, personally I have no objection, in which case the issue here would lie between this grey and the black that it overlays more or less, I was going to say according to the time of day, but no, it does not always seem to depend on the time of day … In a word there seems to be the light of the outer world, of those who know the sun and moon emerge at such an hour and at such another plunge again below the surface, and who rely on this, and who know that clouds are always to be expected but sooner or later always pass away, and mine. (*GII*, 214–15)

Malone's curiosity about his environment and suspicion that there has been a disruption of time and therefore the natural order of things are preoccupations shared by Winnie.

Given her predicament, trapped in the ground under a blistering sun, Winnie's interest in the seeming derangement of nature is hardly surprising. The glaring physical fact of her being buried alive is never explained or discussed, although Winnie does refer to it at several points in the play. She prosaically observes in the first act: 'The earth is very tight today, can it be I have put on flesh, I trust not. [*Pause. Absently, eyes lowered.*] The great heat possibly. [*Starts to pat and stroke ground.*] All things expanding, some more than others' (*GIII*, 286). Later, Winnie wonders aloud about the 'earthball', asking Willie if he thinks 'the earth has lost its atmosphere'

(*GIII*, 300). At another point, as he crawls about with apparent freedom behind her, she asks if he finds that gravity has changed.

> Yes, the feeling more and more that if I were not held – [*gesture*] – in this way, I would simply float up into the blue. [*Pause.*] And perhaps some day the earth will yield and let me go, the pull is so great, yes, crack all round me and let me out. [*Pause.*] Don't you ever have that feeling, Willie, of being sucked up? [*Pause.*] Don't you have to cling on sometimes, Willie? (*GIII*, 289)

Beckett thus sets up a distinction between the intransigent solidity and weight of the earth, and the ephemeral, birdlike Winnie partially trapped within it.

Our attention is drawn to Winnie's concealed lower half in the second act by her story about the 'coarse fellow' Mr Shower or Cooker, who wanted to know if she had any feeling in her legs or was wearing anything on her invisible lower half and in the first act by an interjection of Willie's that feeds on the comedy and horror of her predicament. Seeing an ant or emmet carrying a 'little white ball', Winnie follows its progress over the mound with her magnifying-glass, until it disappears beneath the surface. Unsolicited, Willie offers the elliptical observations 'eggs', and 'formication'. Because Winnie does not hear or understand the first time, he repeats each observation twice. After a pause and murmur of 'God', Winnie joins him in laughter and observes, 'How can one better magnify the Almighty than by sniggering with him at his little jokes, particularly the poorer ones?', before wondering if they had each in fact been 'diverted by two quite different things'. There is no further discussion of the possible cause of Willie's amusement, or the implications for Winnie herself if ants are laying eggs in her mound, but the idea has evidently rattled her, for soon after Willie's laughter she gestures expansively about her and comments 'What a blessing nothing grows, imagine if all this stuff were to start growing' (*GIII*, 287, 289).

The most obvious feature of the environment of *Happy Days* that makes it unlikely to support life is, of course, the blazing sun, the ferocity of which causes Winnie's parasol to spontaneously combust. The parasol is described in the opening stage directions as '*a collapsible collapsed parasol, beak of handle emerging from sheath*', and in Winnie's fond reminiscence, as 'the sunshade you gave me … that day … [*pause*] … that day … the lake … the reeds' (*GIII*, 275, 301). These fragmented lines bear a striking similarity to the confusion about time that runs like a refrain through *That Time*, and to the more fully evoked romantic scenes of Nagg and

Nell rowing in *Endgame*, and Krapp's punt on the lake (*GIII*, 106, 108, 227, 229). It is notable that Winnie's more substantial possessions have all been given to her by Willie: the bag for her to bring to market, the parasol to shade her and the revolver to prevent him putting himself out of his misery. Winnie's use of her parasol drastically alters the tableau on stage and undermines the initial impression of her as a victim of torture. For those moments when the parasol shelters her from the sun, she instead resembles an ageing seaside belle, her legs buried while she slept by a playful companion. The widely held misapprehension that the mound in *Happy Days* is made of sand may be due to this brief but suggestive use of the parasol.[36] As a material, sand lacks the two most alarming qualities of the earth in which Winnie is buried: the pressure on her body exerted within the mound by the compressed soil that is tightly packed around her, and the chilling possibility that insects or animals might nest and breed around the submerged parts of her body. Willie's enjoyment of the ant carrying an egg into the mound contains the horrifically sly hint that such creatures might feed on Winnie to sustain themselves. The mound in *Happy Days* is a living grave.

Winnie's parasol provides the only means of shielding her from the 'hellish sun'. She tires holding it, so transfers it between hands, but once she seems to have become accustomed to holding it, the parasol bursts into flames and she must throw it from her. No matter that it reappears unscathed beside her in the next act, as she has predicted, for without hands she cannot use it. Beckett's decision to maintain Winnie's props in a constant and unchanging state, even when objects are discarded or broken, draws on the routine operation of stage hands who replace the incinerated parasol with a new one each performance, to emphasise the cruel inexorability and nightmare logic of Winnie's scenario. When Winnie protects herself from the sun with the parasol, we see how vulnerable she is without it. Her parasol thus recalls the ingenious if ungainly contraption invented by Robinson Crusoe to shield him from the sun and rain. Basing his design on the umbrellas he had seen in 'the Brasils', he 'spent a great deal of time and pains' fashioning his own.[37] Once he has

---

[36] See, for example, Reiko Inoue, 'The Mound of Sand in *Happy Days*: Tomb to Womb', *The Harp*, 14 (1999), 60–69; Uncredited, *Beckett on Film* souvenir programme (Blue Angel, 2001), p. 21; *The Reader's Encyclopedia of World Drama*, ed. John Gassner and Edward Quinn (New York: Dover, 2002), p. 410; *A History of English Laughter: Laughter from Beowulf to Beckett and Beyond*, ed. Manfred Pfister (Amsterdam: Rodopi, 2002), p. 179; Sara Keating, 'Happy Days Actress is Up to Her Neck in it,' *Irish Times*, 8 November 2010.

[37] Daniel Defoe, *Robinson Crusoe*, ed. Angus Ross (London: Penguin, 1999), p. 145.

eventually built it to his satisfaction, Crusoe covers it with skins, 'the hair upwards, so that it cast off the rains like a penthouse', and enthuses that this final attempt was so effective 'that I could walk out in the hottest of the weather with greater advantage than I could before in the coolest, and when I had no need of it, cou'd close it and carry it under my arm'.[38] In 'Crusoe in England', the American poet Elizabeth Bishop imagines what happened to the objects that Crusoe brought back as relics of his time on the island. She devotes particular attention in the last stanza of the poem to his parasol:

> The local museum's asked me to
> leave everything to them:
> the flute, the knife, the shrivelled shoes,
> my shedding goatskin trousers
> (moths have got in the fur),
> the parasol that took me such a time
> remembering the way the ribs should go.
> It still will work but, folded up,
> looks like a plucked and skinny fowl.
> How can anyone want such things?[39]

In both *Malone Dies* and *Happy Days*, Beckett evokes the hell imagined by Dante, particularly the lake of ice comprising its lowest circle.[40] Malone's comment about 'the fires and ice of hell' echoes Winnie's observation that instead of being ravaged by relentless heat and light, she might just as easily have found herself tormented by the cold: 'It might be the eternal cold. [*Pause.*] Everlasting perishing cold. [*Pause.*] Just chance, I take it, happy chance. [*Pause.*] Oh yes, great mercies, great mercies' (*GII*, 174; *GIII*, 301). Winnie's preoccupation with extremes of hot and cold constitutes Beckett's first attempt to illustrate the arbitrary, capricious control available to the author, who, omnipotent and unfeeling, can inflict any sort of punishment on his characters and can place them in any environment, as he explores more fully in the almost contemporaneous short fictions of *All Strange Away* (1964) and *The Lost Ones* (1965), both of which feature wide swings between intense heat and cold. Extremely isolated and without access to other means of distraction or

---

[38] Defoe, *Robinson Crusoe*, p. 146.
[39] Elizabeth Bishop, 'Crusoe in England', in *Complete Poems* (London: Chatto and Windus, 2004), pp. 162–66, p. 166.
[40] See Daniela Caselli, *Beckett's Dantes: Intertextuality in the Fiction and Criticism* (Manchester, Manchester University Press, 2005) and Julien Carrière, 'Beckett's *Happy Days* and Dante's *Inferno*, Canto 10', *Samuel Beckett Today/Aujourd'hui*, 25, (2013), 197–209.

stimulation, Winnie and Malone's limited possessions swell in importance. The unhealthy glare of their attention that causes this loss of proportion is also directed inwards. Loneliness breeds introspection, a pathological fascination with the most minute changes in their own persons or their environment, and engenders a mounting suspicion that they are the last remaining inhabitants of the world. This exacerbated isolation receives expression in Winnie's repeated reference to her dread of telling her stories to the wind, of existing in a 'wilderness' (*GIII*, 282, 286, 294). The same sense of isolation is expressed in Malone's comment that 'the earth seems uninhabited' (*GII*, 246). This phrase also features twice in *Krapp's Last Tape*, but it acquires particular potency in a work of fiction where there is no solacing recorded voice to listen to and scorn in the distorted comfort and companionship Krapp derives from the tapes of his younger self.

Defoe evokes a more desperately plangent loneliness when Crusoe, the sole survivor of the shipwreck, comments that he saw no sign of his drowned comrades, 'except three of their hats, one cap, and two shoes that were not fellows'.[41] The principle of synecdoche, by which the unfulfilled ambitions and suddenly eradicated vitality of a drowned man can be embedded in a single shoe, may also work in the prisoner or castaway's favour, as he or she seeks to keep going with the few possessions upon which they lavish attention and devotion. Malone's objects stand in for human company, while Gramsci speaks of the 'Byzantine work' of analysing his surroundings in minute detail: 'Everything that happens around me, everything that I'm able to see, becomes of exceptional interest'.[42] In 1926, in accordance with a series of emergency laws put in place by the Italian fascist regime, Gramsci was arrested. He was committed to solitary confinement and imprisoned until his death in 1937. At his trial, in 1928, the official prosecutor urged the judge, 'We must stop this brain working for twenty years!'[43] In prison, however, Gramsci produced thirty-three handwritten volumes of his *Prison Notebooks*, which form the bedrock of his thought on the role of intellectuals in education and politics. Through letters to various friends, in particular his sister-in-law, Tania, he also left a striking account of his experience in prison. His world reduced to a bare room, Gramsci sought to compensate for

---

[41] Defoe, *Robinson Crusoe*, p. 66.
[42] Gramsci, *Letters from Prison*, trans. Lynne Lawner (New York: Harper, 1973), 11 April 1927 to Tania, from Milan, p. 84.
[43] Attilio Monasta, 'Antonio Gramsci (1891–1937)', *Prospects: The Quarterly Review of Comparative Education*, 23.3–4 (1993), 597–612, p. 599.

its monotony and lack of stimulation with a rare intensity of focus and intellectual purpose.

Describing at length two sparrows with which he has shared his cramped surroundings, one such letter to Tania conveys the pride and satisfaction of ownership, and of how feeling oneself king of one's environment is almost compensation for being trapped in it.

> The first sparrow was much more likeable than the present one. He was very proud and extremely lively ... What I liked in this sparrow was his resistance to being handled ... My present sparrow, on the other hand, is quite nauseating in his domesticity. He likes to be fed, although he can eat perfectly well by himself; he hops onto my shoes and nestles in the cuffs of my trousers; if his wings were unclipped, he would fly onto my knee; this is obvious from the way he stretches up tall, quivers, and then hops onto my shoe. I think he will die, too, because he insists on eating burned match heads, quite apart from the fact that a constant diet of soggy bread must be fatal to these birds. At the moment, he is quite healthy but sluggish, runs about very little and sticks close to me, in fact has already been the accidental victim of several kicks. So now you know all about my sparrows.[44]

This perfunctory final line, undermining in a shrug the preceding descriptive flourish, is very like Beckett, as is the detailed and jaunty tone of the passage, with its unsqueamish attitude to sickness and death. Gramsci differs greatly from Beckett, however, in his direct, almost allegorical projection on to the birds. Implicit in his account of the sparrows is Gramsci's fear that captivity will corrupt his independence: a quality celebrated in the first sparrow, and will leave him a craven, wretched creature, like the second sparrow he clearly despises. Gramsci claims his sparrows as possessions, but Beckett's imprisoned characters never project themselves on to the objects that keep them company in this direct fashion. Their possessions remain irreducibly their material selves, never the emblems that Gramsci's sparrows become.

In captivity, the management of one's daily physical requirements can shrink to alarmingly reduced and simplified arrangements. This prospect of drastically restricted opportunities for description or fictive embellishment is capitalised on by Beckett in *Malone Dies*. In a comment that seems at first an act of self-sabotage by Beckett on the inventive capacities of the author, Malone observes 'What matters is to eat and excrete. Dish and pot, dish and pot, these are the poles' (*GII*, 179). This

---

[44] Gramsci, *Letters from Prison*, 8 August 1927, to Tania, pp. 91–92.

reduction of the world to the 'poles' of Malone's chamber pot and dish is preceded by a description of how these objects are used to regulate his physical needs:

> When I want to eat I hook the table with my stick and draw it to me. It is on castors, it comes squeaking and lurching towards me. When I need it no longer I send it back to its place by the door. It is soup. They must know I am toothless. I eat it one time out of two, out of three, on an average. When my chamber-pot is full I put it on the table, beside the dish. Then I go twenty-four hours without a pot. No, I have two pots. They have thought of everything. (*GII*, 178–79)

Malone's description of the system in place for dealing with his dietary and toilet requirements could conceivably exist in a hospital, nursing home, prison or camp. By identifying and focusing on the minimum material provision for managing the bare essentials of meals and waste, Beckett deliberately revels in the reduction of his character's bodily needs to the pair of objects – nearly identical in form, but so different in function – a soup and chamber pot.

In *One Day in the Life of Ivan Denisovich* (first published in the magazine *Novy Mir* in 1962), Aleksandr Solzhenitsyn gives similarly detailed accounts of scant material provisions for sleeping, working, dressing and eating in captivity. Solzhenitsyn's account is motivated by outrage at the degradation that follows a failure to attend adequately to these rudimentary human needs. While serving as an officer in the Soviet army, Solzhenitsyn criticised Stalin in letters to a friend, and in 1945 was sentenced to eight years hard labour in a prison camp. He served this sentence in a Moscow prison and then in the labour camp, on which *One Day in the Life of Ivan Denisovich* is based. On his release from the camp in 1953, he was sentenced to perpetual exile and was banished to southern Kazakhstan. Solzhenitsyn spent eleven years in prisons, in camps and in exile. His biographer Michael Scammell has spoken of how thoroughly Solzhenitsyn's experiences of imprisonment infiltrated the material conditions of his writing, with most of his novels set in 'closed institutions' as a result.[45] While serving his time in the labour camp, Solzhenitsyn became determined to write about the experience, to convey an exact impression of the camp to which he had been sent by describing a day of prison life in minute detail, thereby exposing the gulag system of imprisonment in the Stalin regime.

---

[45] Michael Scammell, 'In Pursuit of Solzhenitsyn', *The Wilson Quarterly (1976–)*, 10.3 (Summer 1986), 144–57, p. 156.

Ivan Denisovich, or Shukhov, as he is called in the novel, has scant material resources. Numbed by the brutalising regime of the camp, he seeks ways to pass the day a little more easily. Without confidants or comforts, his is a desperate, improvisational existence. He has, however, managed to salvage one object that bears comparison with the jealously hoarded possessions under examination in this chapter: his spoon. At meal times, he draws his spoon from his boot, where he keeps it hidden from the other prisoners, licking it clean and returning it to its hiding place once he has finished eating: 'That spoon was precious, it had travelled all over the north with him. He'd cast it himself from aluminium wire in a sand mould and scratched on it "Ust-Izhma, 1944." '[46] This is the sole description of ownership Solzhenitsyn's novel, and it recalls Malone's pot and dish, the treasure in Winnie's bag, Gramsci's proprietorial delight in his sparrows and Crusoe's relics, as imagined by Bishop. However, the different forms of comfort derived from their possessions by Solzhenitsyn and Gramsci on one hand, and Beckett's characters on the other, is revealing. Solzhenitsyn's spoon is a souvenir from an earlier camp and is treasured as a material reminder of the tenacity and capacity for survival of its owner. Merely by retaining it, as he is transferred from one camp to another, he signals to himself his refusal to be institutionalised. It is a discreet form of protest, comparable to Gramsci's determination to retain his analytical faculties in the absence of external mental stimulation.

The Grove Companion to Samuel Beckett notes that 'Winnie in the early drafts of *Happy Days* records the passing days by notches on a tally stick, in precisely the manner of Crusoe' (*GC*, 130). All the characters in this chapter share a sense of ignorance about the passage of time. Beckett explored the implications and effect of this ignorance when writing *Happy Days*, and steadily ratcheted it up in successive drafts of the play by removing Winnie's loss of agency, as he altered the prop used to mark time from tally stick to alarm clock and finally to prison bell. Winnie's initial arrangement allowed her a degree of control absent from the finished play. The tally stick was, moreover, her possession, and unlike its two subsequent replacements, it did not wake her up. In his manuscript study of *Happy Days*, Gontarski notes that the alarm clock allowed Winnie a degree of autonomy and control unthinkable with the bell: 'While she regulated her action with the alarm clock, she retained a certain freedom of choice; she could conceivably choose not

---

[46] Aleksandr Solzhenitsyn, *One Day in the Life of Ivan Denisovich*, trans. H.T. Willets (London: Vintage, 2003), p. 12.

to respond to the gentle summons of the alarm, or she might simply switch it off and return to sleep.' Gontarski proceeds to suggest that 'the relationship between Winnie and the clock is clearly less hostile than between Winnie and the bell' and concludes: 'Choice and what limited free will Winnie had were eliminated as the play developed', as Winnie became steadily more subject to the 'demands of the grotesque, absurd force' symbolised by the bell. Gontarski goes on to quote Jan Kott on the grotesque, where 'paltry man is pitted against the absolute, which "is not endowed with any ultimate reasons; it is stronger and that is all. The absolute is absurd".'[47] Or, Winnie's relationship with the bell is that of the prisoner.

In *One Day in the Life of Ivan Denisovich*, Solzhenitsyn explores this relationship. Prisoners, 'zeks' in the slang of forced labour camps, 'are not allowed clocks. The big boys tell the time for them'.[48] Later in the narrative, he returns to this question of time. Noting that 'No *zek* ever lays eyes on a clock or watch', he asks, 'What good would it do him anyway? All a *zek* needs to know is – how soon is reveille? How long till work parade? Till dinner-time? Till lights out?'[49] This corresponds with Winnie's regular anxiety about the bell for sleep. Indeed, *One Day in the Life of Ivan Denisovich* and *Happy Days* are very similarly organised around the bells that torment their central characters. Like the opening moments of *Happy Days*, the first words of Solzhenitsyn's novel present an aural assault to startle us into a visceral identification with the main character: 'The hammer banged reveille on the rail outside camp HQ at five o'clock as always. Time to get up. The ragged noise was muffled by ice two fingers thick on the windows and soon died away. Too cold for the warder to go on hammering.'[50] The bell is such a dominant structuring force in the labour camp, framing the beginning and ending of each day's work, that it is used as a synonym for the day: a unit of punishment. Shukhov scorns another prisoner's prayers, saying 'pray as much as you like, they won't knock anything off your sentence. You'll serve your time from bell to bell whatever happens.'[51]

The bell does not belong to Winnie. It is not one of her possessions, but rather a noxious external force compelling her to attentiveness. In this way it serves the same function as the light in *Play*, written two years

---

[47] Gontarski, *Beckett's Happy Days*, p. 38.
[48] Solzhenitsyn, *One Day in the Life of Ivan Denisovich*, p. 16.
[49] Solzhenitsyn, *One Day in the Life of Ivan Denisovich*, p. 141.
[50] Solzhenitsyn, *One Day in the Life of Ivan Denisovich*, p. 1.
[51] Solzhenitsyn, *One Day in the Life of Ivan Denisovich*, p. 146.

later from 1962 to 1963, which is itself an echo of the sweeping patrol light used in the surveillance of prisoners. Like the interrogating light in *Play*, the bell in *Happy Days* also serves as a stylised, nightmarish illustration of one of the key elements in theatrical performance. Just as light is required for the audience to see the onstage scene, the events of each play must be organised within a timeline, particularly if the natural order of day and night has been relegated to an antiquarian 'old style'. The bell opens the play, ringing 'piercingly' for ten seconds, then, after a pause, for another five seconds, startling both Winnie and the audience into alertness. The bell also disrupts the final tableau of the play, brutally shattering any impression of a happy ending.

Throughout the play, Winnie refers to the bell whenever she attempts to frame the order of her day, describing it as the period 'between the bell for waking and the bell for sleep' (*GIII*, 282), and reassuring herself, at a particularly fraught moment, 'Ah well, not long now, Winnie, can't be long now, until the bell for sleep. [*Pause.*] Then you may close your eyes, then you *must* close your eyes – and keep them closed' (*GIII*, 305). The bell becomes louder and more violent during the course of the play. As Winnie weakens, it punctuates her pauses and hesitations, and pitilessly rings however briefly she closes her eyes. Winnie comments most thoroughly on the bell in the second act:

> The bell. [*Pause.*] It hurts like a knife. [*Pause.*] A gouge. [*Pause.*] One cannot ignore it. [*Pause.*] How often … [*pause*] … I say how often have I said, Ignore it, Winnie, ignore the bell, pay no heed, just sleep and wake, sleep and wake, as you please, open and close the eyes, as you please, or in the way you find most helpful. [*Pause.*] But no. [*Smile.*] Not now. (*GIII*, 302)

This desperately accurate synaesthesia in the comparison of the aural assault of the bell with the sensation of a knife or gouge plunged into one's flesh recalls the phrase, in the thirteenth of the *Texts for Nothing*, of 'no's knife in yes's wound', and conveys, with alarming immediacy, the panic and suffering of such characters (*GIV*, 339). With her sharply circumscribed movements in response to the bell throughout the play, but particularly in the second act, Winnie resembles a panicking and trapped bird.[52]

Unlike Beckett's characters, Crusoe has the comforting provision of a benevolent God, however remote this benign force may seem. This sense

---

[52] See *Happy Days: The Production Notebook of Samuel Beckett*, pp. 16–17, where both the editor, James Knowlson, and Martha Fehsenfeld, who kept a diary of the rehearsals of the production at the Royal Court directed by Beckett, describe Winnie as 'bird-like'.

of a divine order inspires Crusoe's decision to battle his depression and organise the causes of his suffering through the composition of a table, with a reckoning of reasons to despair and hope in either column. Under the headings 'evil' and 'good', he lists related instances of his condition and 'the comforts I enjoyed against the miseries I suffered'.[53]

Evil	Good
I am cast upon a horrible desolate island, void of all hope of recovery.	*But I am alive, and not drowned as all my ship company was.*
...	
I have no soul to speak to, or relieve me.	*But God wonderfully sent the ship in near enough to the shore, that I have gotten out so many necessary things as will either supply my wants, or enable me to supply my self even as long as I live.*[54]

Crusoe concludes by describing this account as an 'an undoubted testimony, that there was scarce any condition in the world so miserable, but there was something negative or something positive to be thankful for in it'.[55]

Solzhenitsyn's novel similarly contains an account by the protagonist of the good and bad elements of his day that recalls Crusoe's table for counting his blessings:

> Shukhov felt pleased with life as he went to sleep. A lot of good things had happened that day. He hadn't been thrown in the hole. The gang hadn't been dragged off to Sotsgorodok. He'd swiped the extra gruel at dinner-time. The foreman had got a good rate for the job. He'd enjoyed working on the wall. He hadn't been caught with the blade at the search-point. He'd earned a bit from Tsezar that evening. And he'd bought his tobacco.
>
> The end of an unclouded day. Almost a happy one.
>
> Just one of the three thousand six hundred and fifty-three days of his sentence, from bell to bell.
>
> The extra three were for leap years.[56]

---

[53] Defoe, *Robinson Crusoe*, p. 83.
[54] Defoe, *Robinson Crusoe*, pp. 83–84.
[55] Defoe, *Robinson Crusoe*, p. 84.
[56] Solzhenitsyn, *One Day in the Life of Ivan Denisovich*, pp. 149–50.

This account forms the final page of the novel. By ending with a calculation of the total number of days in Ivan Denisovich's sentence, Solzhenitsyn moves the narrative from the particularity of a single day to the general experience of imprisonment and evokes the near-endlessness of this sentence. Ivan Denisovich's inventory of his day's satisfactions enables Solzhenitsyn to affirm the capacity of the human spirit to survive in the most desperate of circumstances. The ending of Solzhenitsyn's novel does not echo the entropy evoked by Beckett in similar passages, where his characters or narrators draw attention to the duration of their suffering. It more closely resembles the character studies and vignettes collected in Primo Levi's *Moments of Reprieve* (1986), his testimony to the flashes of humanity encountered within the Nazi concentration camp that enabled him to survive.[57]

At times, Beckett puts would-be moral observations in his characters' mouths that seem to recall Crusoe or Ivan Denisovich, but the effect of Malone's 'Men are like that', and Winnie's 'Another happy day' is, instead, deeply dispiriting, since these characters are more profoundly lost than Crusoe could ever be: without the consolations of faith or a rational world, Beckett's characters languish without understanding or the prospect of relief within the cramped surroundings of their illogical and unpredictable narrative arcs. In *Malone Dies* and *Happy Days*, Beckett thoroughly undermines the conventionally heroic characteristics of the prisoner, typified by the kind of piety and providentialism expressed by the castaway figure of Crusoe and in the defiant resistance of Solzhenitsyn and Gramsci's imprisoned characters. The subtle difference between Malone's and Winnie's comments on this matter reveals much about Beckett's altered approach in either work. This difference has often been interpreted by critics as predominantly one of gender: Winnie has been charged with lacking insight and self-awareness, and the cruel implausibility of her strained positivity has been taken as evidence of Beckett's intention to create a misogynist portrait in the play. Malone's scornful pessimism, by contrast, has been taken as the measure of his greater awareness of his predicament, an awareness that has been automatically identified as typically masculine.[58] As I have suggested in discussing the generic convention by which pockets feature most often in Beckett's fiction and bags in his theatre, the real difference between Malone and Winnie is not one of gender, but of medium.

---

[57] Primo Levi, *Moments of Reprieve*, trans. Ruth Feldman (London: Penguin, 2002).
[58] See, for example, Francesco Orlando, *Obsolete Objects in the Literary Imagination*, pp. 341–42.

Two years into his sentence, Gramsci expresses his anxiety of succumbing to this deadening force of lengthy imprisonment:

> When I observe men who have been in prison for five, eight, or ten years and observe how their minds have become warped, I shudder to think what will become of me ... Of course I intend to resist; but, you know, I'm not able to laugh at myself as I used to, and this is a bad sign.[59]

Beckett charts these devastating effects of imprisonment in the deterioration between the acts of *Happy Days*: what is lost by Winnie in the interval conveys the horror of unending routine by making it an immediate and tangible loss, a diminution of speed, light and volume, and unravelling of coherence. James Wood has described the use of 'reduction and rallentando' as 'the prison literature principle'.[60] Rallentando is a 'gradual decrease of speed; a passage performed or to be performed increasingly slowly'.[61] Gramsci's comment that he is no longer able to laugh at himself as readily as he used to do may be compared with the changes that happens by degrees to Winnie and Malone, as each character exhibits the principle of rallentando, a steady deterioration towards inertia.

Malone Dies and *Happy Days*: Twin Texts and Turning Points

Although written over a decade apart and in different media, *Malone Dies* and *Happy Days* are animated by the same dynamic of an exacerbated dependence on objects. Malone and Winnie rely on their material resources to a far greater degree than other characters in Beckett. They are both largely immobile and without interlocutors, and both experience during the course of their narrative and dramatic arcs a marked deterioration in their powers of recollection and concentration, and therefore their capacity for telling stories. Without recourse to their last remaining objects, they would be lost and silent. *Happy Days* and *Malone Dies* also constitute important turning points in Beckett's treatment of storytelling in his theatre and fiction respectively.

Their possessions sustain both Malone and Winnie, offering succour, companionship, distraction, and, crucially, shoring up their damaged memories and imaginations, providing the means for these extravagantly isolated characters to continue telling stories about their worlds and themselves.[62] Although

---

[59] Gramsci, *Letters*, November 19, 1928, to Giulia, from Turi, p. 137.
[60] James Wood, 'Rite of Corruption', p. 13.
[61] *OED*.
[62] For Beckett's sensitivity to the companionship offered by certain objects, see André Bernold's account of showing Beckett a quartz crystal he treasured: 'he examined it carefully and asked me

they do all they can to keep their possessions near them, in sight and in use, both characters mishandle these objects at times, or discover that they have been mysteriously put beyond their reach and use. This inability to get a hand to their things is foreshadowed by a series of earlier characters: Vladimir and Pozzo in *Waiting for Godot*, Krapp in *Krapp's Last Tape* and the girl in *Eh Joe* are all described as fumbling with buttons or rummaging in their pockets in moments that convey their incompetence or the pathos of their situation (*GIII*, 14, 28, 221, 227, 395). It is rather different with Malone and Winnie, whose difficulties making use of their possessions serve to highlight how desperately they need the objects in question. One of the curious consequences of this ostensible authorial cruelty in denying Winnie and Malone prompt and continued access to their possessions is to guarantee the endurance of their desires. With the figure of Tantalus in mind, Arsene in *Watt* notes the good fortune of those with strong desires who find themselves in circumstances where there is no hope of fulfilling, and therefore slaking, these desires:

> The glutton castaway, the drunkard in the desert, the lecher in prison, they are the happy ones. To hunger, thirst, lust, every day afresh and every day in vain, after the old prog, the old booze, the old whores, that's the nearest we'll ever get to felicity, the new porch and the very latest garden. (*GI*, 203–4)

This means of putting their treasure beyond the reach of Winnie and Malone also serves a function that is intimately allied with Beckett's larger creative project: in *Happy Days* and *Malone Dies*, Beckett conducts his most thorough exploration of the crucial function of salvaged objects for desperate characters who still struggle to make sense of their experience by organising it into narrative form. Both works are animated by the dynamic of a group of objects that are essential for the inspiration and recording of the central character's stories. These texts mark the most extreme exploration of this dynamic on Beckett's part, and his last.

The relation between *Malone Dies* and *Happy Days* and the works that immediately follow these texts in their respective media show that a shift in Beckett's creative practice has taken place. After *Malone Dies* Beckett's fiction no longer flows from the conceit of a fully realised central character putting together a story, inventing a host of supporting characters and details in sustained tangents that together comprise the wider story. Instead *The Unnamable*, the novel that follows *Malone Dies* in the trilogy, is preoccupied with a stillborn form of creativity, in which only

---

what it was to me: ' "Like a friend," I said to him. "Yes, a friend,' he murmured." ' See *Beckett's Friendship: 1979–1989*, pp. 40–41.

isolated moments of invention are accomplished, then quickly abandoned and shed like sediment in the text. Following *Happy Days*, rather than playing with the theatrical artifice of embellishment and exaggeration, Beckett's dramatic characters struggle to recall fragments of memory. The dramatic works that immediately follow *Happy Days* were written for the radio. *Rough for Radio I* and *II* (1977) both feature troubled characters straining to capture or record a particular musical or verbal phrase, more or less explicitly through means of torture (*GIII*, 312, 314). The characters in these works are compelled to speak and the practice of writing is imagined as an interrogation. They are forced to expiate the terms of a mysterious sentence by giving voice under duress, but without the ability, it seems, to invent. *Malone Dies* and *Happy Days* present an exacerbated version of the relation between earlier characters in Beckett and their possessions: Malone and Winnie find themselves in extreme conditions of isolation, but their predicaments are balanced by the comfort they derive from the sustaining treasure that fills Malone's pocket and Winnie's bag.[63] Their abilities to tell their stories are inextricably linked to their possessions, for their material resources grant them the capacity to invent. The characters that come after Malone and Winnie and are without possessions also lack the means of storytelling that animates these and earlier works, and their narratives are correspondingly attenuated.

In the dwindling series of paragraphs that close *Malone Dies*, the roving perspective shifts from the 'absurd lights, the stars, the beacons, the buoys, the lights of earth and in the hills the faint fires of the blazing gorse' outside and in the past to rest on the contents of Malone's room: 'Macmann, my last, my possessions, I remember, he is there too, perhaps he sleeps' (*GII*, 280). The inclusion of Macmann, Malone's last fictive invention, alongside Malone's possessions within the frame of the same sentence suggests that they occupy the same place in Malone's inventory. This jumbling of categories suggests that a character in one of Malone's stories might be identified with his inanimate if far from inert possessions. The same collapsing of hierarchies between character and object, where characteristics are attributed to an object and material qualities to a character, may also be seen in *Happy Days*. In what seems like an unfortunate slip and a result of Winnie's easily distracted running observations, she uses the

---

[63] This authorial gift of the bag and pocket containing sustaining objects to Winnie and Malone by Beckett creates a far livelier tone than might be expected from the scenarios and narratives of these works, which is clear from even a perfunctory comparison of them with other confined and isolated characters who lack recourse to objects in Beckett's theatre and fiction of the 1960s and 1970s, such as *Eh Joe*, *Not I*, *Footfalls* and *Ping*, *Lessness* and *Fizzles I*.

phrase 'running out' to describe Willie rather than the tube of toothpaste which she is handling: 'Poor Willie – [*examines the tube, smile off*] – running out – [*looks for cap*] – ah well – [*finds cap*] – can't be helped – [*screws on cap*] – just one of those old things – [*lays down tube*] – another of those old things – [*turns towards bag*] – just can't be cured' (*GIII*, 276). This implication recurs moments later, when she refers to herself as an object in the process of deterioration: '[*Takes off spectacles, lays them and brush down, gazes before her.*] Old things. [*Pause.*] Old eyes. [*Long pause.*] On, Winnie' (*GIII*, 278). The most explicit description by Winnie of herself as an object comes towards the end of the play, when she apologises to Willie about her neglected features, saying 'I haven't been able to look after it, you know' (*GIII*, 306).

Winnie speaks of herself in this way because, in *Happy Days* and *Malone Dies*, Beckett is concerned with the boundaries between animation and inertia, confinement and death, the solace of the imagination, and the wandering incoherence and emptying out that follows mental disintegration. He is, in short, engaged in an exploration of how the human approaches the condition of matter. If Malone and Winnie barely exhibit signs of life, particularly towards the conclusion of their respective narratives, their objects are most emphatically alive. Malone is prevented from compiling his inventory by all those objects that have left his room or changed since he last observed them. In Winnie's oddly moving phrase in the second act, 'Ah yes, things have their life, that is what I always say, *things* have a life. [*Pause.*] Take my looking-glass, it doesn't need me' (*GIII*, 302). The animate nature of Winnie and Malone's treasure serves to point up their relative lifelessness: their immobility and powerlessness and the hopelessness of change in their predicaments mean that in a very important sense, Winnie and Malone's things are more alive than they are themselves. Winnie and Malone can be seen, in this respect, to be approaching the condition of inert objects. Maddy Rooney's outburst 'What's wrong with me, what's wrong with me, never tranquil, seething out of my dirty old pelt' apostrophises the condition of all Beckett's characters up to the end of *Happy Days* and *Malone Dies* (*GIII*, 163). After these works, more and more characters are granted a reprieve from the frenzied imperative of movement discussed in the third chapter, and are released from the voracious, galloping need to tell stories, to narrate their condition.

In *Crowds and Power* (1981) Elias Canetti identifies the curious complex of power and vulnerability, pleasure and furtiveness that attend a pile of treasure:

> Treasure, like all other heaps, is something which has been collected … A hoard of treasure is a heap which should be left to grow undisturbed.

The man it belongs to may be powerful, but there are always others equally powerful to rob him. The prestige treasure gives its owner carries danger with it; fights and wars have arisen over treasure and many a man would have lived longer if his treasure had been smaller. Thus it is often of necessity kept secret. The peculiarity of treasure lies in the tension between the splendour it should radiate and the secrecy which is its protection. The lust of counting, of seeing numbers mount up, derives largely from treasure and is most comprehensible there.[64]

Canetti's warning that treasure 'should be left to grow undisturbed' is drastically illustrated by Beckett in *Happy Days* and *Malone Dies*. Winnie and Malone each pay assiduous attention to their objects and it is through enthusiastic over-handling that they disturb their hoards of treasure and cause them to deteriorate. Objects are less valuable once they are taken out of the pocket or bag or mind and fondled or spoken about. Because they fuel the stories, anecdotes and verbal routines of the characters, such objects can be drained by narration, hence Winnie's anxious reminders to herself to avoid turning to the bag whenever her monologue stalls. Once an object has been exhausted in this way, it ceases to be a treasure and is discarded, as in Malone's inexplicable and sudden decision to get rid of his formerly hoarded and loved treasures, and the many stories, anecdotes and memories of *Malone Dies* that are initiated, but then interrupted with a dismissive phrase, and allowed to collapse into silence. Winnie and Malone both exhaust their treasure according to the strange logic outlined by Malone himself, when he speaks of hooking objects with his stick and pulling them to him. Malone describes the progress of such objects across the floor as 'gliding, jogging, less and less dear' (*GII*, 243). This curious turn of phrase identifies the perverse dimension of need, where it is more precious the less it is satisfied. Conversely, the more access Winnie and Malone have to their heaps of treasured objects, the less such objects mean to them. This formulation of Winnie and Malone's relation to their treasure accords with Beckett's singularly cold-eyed vision of the obsessive, inherently destructive relationships his characters have with other people and with things, where characters seek to comfort and sustain themselves by using up whatever resources they have at their disposal. Those objects, fragments of memories and stories that have sustained Winnie and Malone so loyally, eventually cease to do so, for nothing is treasured forever in Beckett.

---

[64] Elias Canetti, *Crowds and Power*, trans. Carol Stewart (London: Penguin, 1981), pp. 103–4.

Conclusion: Beckett's Art of Salvage

Stones

Extinct Materials

This book has been thematically divided in half. Chapters 1 and 2 explored the means by which Beckett uses objects to house certain social forces and personal memory in his writing, profoundly changing its register as a result, while the Chapters 3 and 4 considered the means by which Beckett's writing is continually engaged in reflections upon its own method of procedure. This interrogation of the ethics of creativity and the duty that follows literary invention is, I believe, one of Beckett's most important legacies. Here, I want to outline how thinking about Beckett's writing as an art of salvage opens up a new approach to his work, restating his importance as a writer and addressing his continuing relevance today. Those objects explored in the earlier chapters of this book are worn-out, and it is their capacity to record and transmit the traces of that wearing out resonate for Beckett's characters. Indeed, as we saw in Chapter 4, characters who are imprisoned, immobile and all but struck dumb by their confusion, lack of stimulation or hope in any future can still extract stories from their diminished possessions. These storytelling objects are such because they hold within them the history of their previous use. In this way, Beckett's characters can draw upon the material elements that have passed through most of his earlier characters' hands to assemble narrative time and the possibility of new narratives.

This sustained and novel investigation into the traces of time, stories and narrative potential contained within objects is why Beckett's example of a literary imagination engaged with a restricted set of objects in a wide range of media over half a century can contribute a new perspective to material studies: because Beckett maintained a lifelong creative commitment to the objects under study in this book, his work can be read as a limit case for the potential of literature to engage with and shape itself around objects, and for the capacity of material elements to generate narrative. The archaeologist Nanouschka M. Burström has advocated a move towards the humanities within material studies, while the cultural critic William Viney has called for attentiveness to the characteristic treatment of objects in literary narratives:[1]

> And, rather than separate the ways that objects are described from the time that we perceive in them, we might demonstrate how narrative plays a crucial role in organising time, ascribing potential action and delineating the transition between use and waste. From cherished objects, places or people to the most ruinous and decrepit of structures, narratives affect, broker and maintain the divergent times we distribute to things.[2]

In this final section, I want to explore how Beckett's art of salvage not only stages a fifty-five-year-long exploration of the relationship between worn materials and time, but in its final expression sees him imagine the return of fictive characters to inert matter. Beckett's characters and narratives exist in a tenuous present tense that is in the process of winding down, of ceding to the past tense that is always threatening to devour it, most explicitly in his final works. 'To restore silence is the role of objects' (*GII*, 9), the strange aphorism at the beginning of *Molloy* that is proved wrong throughout Beckett's early and middle periods, is enacted at last in his final works. The past is weighty, substantial in Beckett, the present uncertain, the future non-existent. Beckett registers this on a material level throughout his early and mid-periods through his use of miscellaneous rubbish, and in his final works, does so through stone.

Because it is both an object and a common material element, stone has served important functions in the work of writers, artists, philosophers and scientists.[3] Figures as diverse as Carl Linnaeus and Martin Heidegger have used stone to denote a category apart from the living. For the eighteenth-century Swedish botanist and the twentieth-century German philosopher alike, stone represented the mineral or inert, as opposed to the categories of animal or vegetable.[4] A similar taxonomy features in

---

[1] See Nanouschka M. Burström, 'Things in the Eye of the Beholder: A Humanistic Perspective on Archaeological Object Biographies', *Norwegian Archaeological Review*, 47.1 (2014), 65–82.
[2] William Viney, *Waste: A Philosophy of Things* (Bloomsbury, 2014), p. 5.
[3] Freud and Jung, Rilke and Goethe take their place among the psychoanalysts and poets fascinated with stone.
[4] In his *Systema Naturae* (1768), Linnaeus divided life into three 'kingdoms': stones, plants and animals. Heidegger made a similar distinction between the categories of man, animal and stone in *The Fundamental Concepts of Metaphysics* (1983).

Malone Dies. Malone frets about the appropriate subject matter and order of his stories, anxious that they should leave nothing out. He resolves to tell himself only a limited number of stories that will cover the essential themes and categories: 'One about a man, another about a woman, a third about a thing and finally one about an animal, a bird probably.' This plan is revised several times until it matches Heidegger's distinction between the categories of man, animal and stone: 'There will therefore be only three stories after all, that one [about the man], then the one about the animal, then the one about the thing, a stone probably. That is all very clear' (*GII*, 175, 176). Malone, of course, does not follow this carefully devised schema. Despite his mockery of manias such as Malone's for organising forms of life into categories, stone serves a similarly central function for Beckett as it does for Linnaeus and Heidegger.[5]

Stone plays an exemplary role in Beckett's canon of objects. Indeed, Beckett's use of stone distils the trajectory of the other thirteen objects in his canon, such that examination of the various functions of stone in Beckett's work reveals much about his singular form of creativity. At the beginning of *Damned to Fame*, Knowlson relates a conversation between Beckett and Gottfried Büttner, a literary critic and friend of Beckett's, to whom Beckett expressed the peculiar relationship with stones he had as a child, and his 'love' for certain stones.

> He recounted how he used to take stones of which he was particularly fond home with him from the beach in order to protect them from the wearing away of the waves or the vagaries of the weather. He would lay them gently into the branches of trees in the garden to keep them safe from harm. (*DF*, 29)[6]

Beckett's preoccupation with stone was certainly long-lasting: the dinner during which he described his childhood habits took place in 1967. Knowlson observes that having told Büttner his story, Beckett went on to link this with 'Freud's view that human beings have a prebirth nostalgia to return to the mineral state' (*DF*, 29). Only one substantial essay has been written on Beckett's use of stone in his writing, and like the few other notes on the subject, it is organised around a psychoanalytic reading.[7] To

---

[5] Heidegger first outlined his three categories of life in his lecture series of 1929–30 at the University of Freiburg, which later became *The Fundamental Concepts of Metaphysics*. Beckett's friend Jean Beaufret was very interested in Heidegger, but the lectures were not published until 1995, so it is unlikely that Beckett was engaged in a direct swipe at Heidegger in *Malone Dies*. See Steven Connor, 'Beckett and the World', *Beckett, Modernism and the Material Imagination*, pp. 176–188.

[6] Curiously, Nevill Johnson, whose attitude to the bowler hat closely resembled Beckett's own, also saved stones as a child. See *The Other Side of Six*, p. 32.

[7] Under its entry for 'geology', *The Grove Companion* focuses on stone as a symbolic element of all that is underground and submerged, and concludes its account by suggesting that in the radio

date, stone has been interpreted as the manifestation of an underlying Freudian death drive or Jungian phallic obsession in Beckett's writing, but I want to propose instead that stone functions in Beckett's work as a coda to his other materials.

Many of Beckett's characters carry a stone in their pocket, reflecting their author's own tender impulse to salvage stones as a child. The narrator of *The Expelled* attracts the attention of the driver while sitting in the back of his horse-drawn cab by knocking on the partition between them with a stone he takes from his pocket (*GIV*, 255). Later, in *Malone Dies*, Malone claims that 'pretty' objects such as stones inspire in him an appropriately rhyming feeling of 'pity', prompting him to stoop and pocket them (*GII*, 240–41). For several characters, holding a stone in their pocket or hand is not intimate enough, and they comfort themselves by putting the stone in their mouths instead. This first occurs in one of Beckett's novellas. The narrator of *The Calmative* is given a boiled sweet by a boy in rags, which he takes 'eagerly and put it in my mouth, the old gesture came back to me'. He wishes for a penny to give the boy as thanks for this gift of a penny sweet, but does not have one. He does, however, have his stone, which he considers next: 'I suspect that I had nothing with me but my stone, that day, having gone out as it were without premeditation'(*GIV*, 266). It is not clear whether the narrator intends either to give his stone as a gift to the child, or to use it himself as a sucking stone, but the association between the sweet and stone is suggestive. *The Calmative* was written in the same year as *Mercier and Camier*, where stones are clearly designated as objects to suck, in lieu of something more nourishing: 'You'll spoil him' Mr Conaire tells Camier while he is buying Mercier sandwiches: 'Yesterday cakes, today sandwiches, tomorrow crusts and Thursday stones' (*GI*, 428).

---

play *Cascando*, having failed to achieve consciousness, Woburn is being returned to the mineral form, which includes stone, sand, mud and bilge. The littoral is the threshold he must cross to return to this mineral form, which presumably he will achieve if he can make it into the sea (*GC*, pp. 219–21). The longest and most sustained study of Beckett's use of stone is Benjamin Keatinge's 2007 essay, which identifies stone as the medium through which Beckett explores psychic processes relating to the Freudian death drive. See Keatinge, '"The Hammers of the Stone-Cutters": Samuel Beckett's Stone Imagery', *Irish University Review*, 37.2 (Autumn–Winter 2007), 322–39. A rival psychoanalyst is invoked by J.C.C. Mays in his 1991 introduction to Beckett for the *Field Day Anthology*. Mays quotes Robert Creeley's report of a conversation with Beckett: 'It was his dream to realise one word that was absolutely self-created. And he said it's about this big [indicating a height of about seven inches, both laughing] and it has the situation of stone.' Mays explains the joke by noting 'Creeley points out the connection with Jung's phallic stone.' See Mays, 'Samuel Beckett (1907–89)' [sic], in *Field Day Anthology of Irish Writing*, 3 (Derry: Field Day Publications, 1991), p. 237.

In *Molloy*, Beckett's narrator sings the praises of a sucking stone: 'I thought of the food I had refused. I took a pebble from my pocket and sucked it. It was smooth, from having been sucked so long, by me, and beaten by the storm. A little pebble in your mouth, round and smooth, appeases, soothes, makes you forget your hunger, forget your thirst' (*GII*, 21–22). James Wood has suggested that Beckett borrowed Molloy's sucking stones from the Norwegian author Knut Hamsun's *Hunger* (1890), whose starving protagonist, Tangen, puts stone to the same use before later in the novel sucking his finger, and then, in an idle and shocking gesture, biting and drawing blood from this finger in an absent-minded act of eating himself. Wood reads Tangen's starvation as a deliberate gesture that follows the 'logic of Christian perversion', and suggests that sucking stone is part of this process of abasement and martyrdom.[8] There is no such symbolism in Beckett's sucking stones. Rather, the passage where Molloy enumerates the charms of a sucking stone recalls Beckett's anecdote about salvaging stones from the beach and carefully storing them in the garden at home: as a child, Beckett wished to protect the stones from the erosive effects of the water, but Molloy derives comfort from putting stones in his mouth, continuing the erosion of sea and storm by the gentler means of sucking them. It is telling that Beckett here indicates the impact on both stone and the man: the latter is soothed from sucking the stone, which is itself diminished, little by little, by giving this satisfaction. As ever in Beckett's dramatisation of a dependent relationship, one half of the pair suffers to provide solace to the other. Obsessively sucking each of his stones in turn, Molloy performs an elegantly organised variation on the theme of the inevitable deterioration of all things through use. Given the extraordinarily slow dissolution of a stone in the mouth, Molloy is able to derive considerable pleasure from carefully managing the erosion of his stones. The journalist Bruce Arnold has noted the parallel between Molloy's coordination of his stones and the operations of a cricket umpire transferring pennies from one pocket to the other as each ball of an over is bowled.[9] Most critics, indeed, assert that Molloy's extended account of this process conveys his or Beckett's fascination with the mathematics of order.[10] I believe, however, that Molloy is utterly engrossed for six pages

---

[8] James Wood, 'Addicted to Unpredictability', *LRB*, 20.23, 26 November 1998, 16–19.
[9] Arnold's observation is cited by Alec Reid in 'Samuel Beckett: The Reluctant Prizeman', *Politico*, 1 November 1969, 1–5, p. 1.
[10] Hugh Kenner, for example, compares Molloy to Newton and concludes, 'No more desperate assault on the randomness of things has ever been chronicled'. *Samuel Beckett: A Critical Study*, p. 111. See also David Hesla, *The Shape of Chaos: An Interpretation of the Art of Samuel Beckett* (Oxford: Oxford

by this fantasy of a choreographed erosion of his stones as a result of the latent sensual charm and poignant farce of seeking comfort from the most inanimate of objects. After all, Molloy's painstaking efforts to control the order in which he sucks the stones fail utterly, with the sequence limping to a bathetic end: 'And the solution to which I rallied in the end was to throw away all the stones but one, which I kept now in one pocket, now in another, and which of course I soon lost, or threw away, or gave away, or swallowed' (*GII*, 69).

While some stones in Beckett's work are cherished for the comfort they give, others are used as projectiles. To the respectable Lady McCann, Watt's extraordinary walk represents a disturbance of the peace. She registers her objection by throwing a stone at him, which falls 'on Watt's hat and struck it from his head, to the ground' (*GI*, 193). The narrator of *The End*, astride his friend's donkey on their way to the sea, experiences a similarly emphatic welcome from a group of local boys, with the same result. 'The little boys jeered and threw stones, but their aim was poor, for they only hit me once, on the hat. A policeman stopped us and accused us of disturbing the peace' (*GIV*, 283). The narrator of *The Unnamable* wishes for 'a stick, an arm, fingers apt to grasp and then release, at the right moment, a stone, stones, or for the power to utter a cry and wait, counting the seconds, for it to come back to him', since without missile or voice he is reduced to the extreme deprivation of many of Beckett's characters, 'a head abandoned to its ancient solitary resources' (*GII*, 354–55). The pattern whereby an object that is affectionately fondled by one character is then used in an assault occurs elsewhere in Beckett's work.[11] Unlike other objects in his canon, however, stone is not limited to this double use where it can cause either pleasure or pain. Indeed, its further uses distinguish it from the other thirteen objects of Beckett's miscellaneous rubbish.

The stone, which appears in *Eh Joe*, serves as a severe and unyielding material against which to contrast the vulnerable fragility of the girl's broken heart and dying flesh. Here the imposing stone structures of the viaduct and 'the Rock' past which the girl wanders add a note of monumentality, suggesting that the girl is dwarfed by her sorrow, while evoking the headstones and sculptures used to mark final resting places.

University Press, 1971); Alan J. Howard, 'The Roots of Beckett's Aesthetic: Mathematical Allusions in "Watt"', *Papers On Language And Literature*, 30.4 (1994), 346–52; and Steven Connor, 'My Fortieth Year Had Come And Gone And I Still Throwing the Javelin', in *Beckett, Modernism and the Material Imagination*, pp. 15–26.

[11] This is a frequent dynamic in the function of sticks and can also be seen in Winnie's use of her parasol to strike Willie.

A memorial function is also performed by the stones in the shallow waters. The following passage seems to describe her last moments, and is preceded by a stage direction: '*Voice drops to whisper, almost inaudible except words in italics.*'

> Lips on a *stone* ... Taking Joe with her ... Light gone ... *'Joe Joe.'* ... No sound ... To the *stones* ... ... *Imagine* the hands ... The *solitaire* ... Against a *stone* ... Imagine the eyes ... Spiritlight ... ... Breasts in the stones ... And the hands ... Before they go ... Imagine the hands ... What are they at? ... In the stones ... (*GIII*, 396–97)

These brief, breathy phrases evoke the noises of shallow water washing and lapping round the girl's head and hands, upon which image the description concentrates. It is implied that her hands, one of which bears an engagement ring, fumbles at the stones, while her softness, warmth and eyes are emphasised to form a contrast with the stones: her brief loveliness with their enduring, solid coldness. Stone is similarly contrasted with female mortality in the late prose work *Ill Seen Ill Said*, where the grieving old woman at the centre of the piece repeatedly makes her harried way to the white stones that proliferate in the landscape and are identified by Beckett as having a memorial function:

> White stones more plentiful every year. As well say every instant. In a fair way if they persist to bury all. First zone rather more extensive than at first sight ill seen and every year rather more. Of striking effect in the light of the moon these millions of little sepulchres. (*GIV*, 458)

To reach the stones, the old woman first crosses 'the flagstone before her door that by dint by dint her little weight has grooved' (*GIV*, 455). Given the focus of the piece on her agitated movement to and from these powerful stones, we understand that the flagstone has yielded to the passing tread of feet towards the tomb. Thomas Hardy was also drawn by the evocative power of a 'footworn step', which he claimed meant 'more to him than scenery'.[12] The flagstone in Beckett's text, the 'Calm slab worn and polished by agelong comings and goings', is doubly poignant because it is a threshold, and thus represents a movement from the life within the dwelling to the stones, and death, outside (*GIV*, 458).

In his 1937 poem 'Dieppe', Beckett makes use of stone in a manner which is repeated often in his later work, identifying 'the dead shingle' with a dissipating, ebbing energy that has succumbed to the greater

---

[12] Quoted in Philip Larkin, *Letters to Monica*, ed. Anthony Thwaite (London: Faber and Faber, 2010), p. 61.

eroding force of the sea (*GIV*, 37). The first lines of the 1948 poem 'je suis ce cours de sable qui glisse', which he translated as 'my way is in the sand flowing', further distil this image of evanescent, transient material, the matter lost when stone becomes something far more delicate: 'my way is in the sand flowing / between the shingle and the dune' (*GIV*, 39). The deterioration that takes place to make shingle of stone, and sand of shingle, is often described by Beckett in a register alert to the cruelty of this process. Molloy says of the sea that 'Much of my life has ebbed away before this shivering expanse, to the sound of the waves in storm and calm, and the claws of the surf', and this image of 'clawing' at pebbles features in several later texts (*GII*, 63).

The radio play *Embers* is set on a shingle beach. Intimately identified with the stones on which he rests, Henry can neither leave the sea nor cope with his dread of its destructive potential. At one point, he tries to drown out the sound that signifies the erosion of the shingle: the 'suck' of the waves.

> HENRY [*wildly*] Thuds, I want thuds! Like this! [*He fumbles in the shingle, catches up two big stones and starts dashing them together.*] Stone! [*Clash.*] Stone! [*Clash.* '*Stone!*' *and clash amplified, cut off. Pause. He throws one stone away. Sound of its fall.*] That's life! [*He throws the other stone away. Sound of its fall.*] Not this … [*pause*] … sucking! (*GIII*, 206)

Embers privileges Henry's intemperate reaction to the steady, implacable erosion of the beach by the sea by relying upon his frantic descriptions of the sounds of the water, instead of building the presence of the sea using a recorded soundscape of waves, or alternatively, by giving weight to Ada's more conventional interpretation of the 'lovely peaceful gentle soothing sound' of the sea (*GIII*, 206). Through this focus on Henry's appalled and fascinated reaction to the disintegrating threshold between land and water, the play conveys a distinctly horrified interpretation of the impermanence and deterioration inherent in nature.

In the opening lines of his 1948 poem, 'In Praise of Limestone', W.H. Auden refers to the corrosion of stone by water, characterising the seemingly impervious stone that is nevertheless susceptible to deterioration with a touching, almost human vulnerability: 'If it form the one landscape that we the inconstant ones / Are consistently homesick for, this is chiefly / Because it dissolves in water.'[13] Auden's poetic exploration of the disintegration of limestone is comparable to Beckett's dramatic and sonic

---

[13] W.H. Auden, 'In Praise of Limestone', in *Selected Poems*, p. 184.

evocation of shingle. Where Auden's image of stone yielding to water leads to a vision of life after death, however, Beckett draws upon the dissolution of stone by water to very different effect. In one of the final images of *Eh Joe*, Beckett describes the girl's dying moments 'clawing at the shingle', clearing a space in the pebbles and water so she can be at one with the shingle, scooping 'a little cup for her face in the stones' and slipping away with her face in this cup (*GIII*, 396). Like the central characters of *The End* and *Malone Dies*, she goes out with the tide. As elsewhere in Beckett, shingle is shown in *Eh Joe* to be a material fated to yield to the greater force of water, to crumble and deteriorate, which, in Beckett's formulation, makes it much like man.[14]

Throughout *That Time*, stone is used to mark the inexorable passage of time, and to aid the preservation of memory. The three voices that create the monologue of *That Time* are identified as A, B and C. Each voice speaks of some centrally important stone: A obsessively recalls Foley's Folly, the ruin in which he spent hours as a child in contented solitude 'on a stone among the nettles with your picture-book' while his anxious family searched for him, an image that is balanced by his recollection of a later stone on which he sat: a doorstep in the 'pale sun' on which he slept waiting for the night ferry[15] (*GIII*, 419, 421). C keeps returning to the marble slabs in the portrait gallery, public library or post office on which he found rest: 'slipped in when no one was looking and through the rooms shivering and dripping till you found a seat marble slab and sat down to rest and dry off and on to hell out of there' (*GIII*, 418). The sole recurring memory where a stone is shared with another character is B's. The image evokes the benches shared with various degrees of enthusiasm by Beckett's fictional characters, as he recalls the 'long low stone like millstone' on which he sat with a woman in the sun (*GIII*, 418).

That Time ends with a room full of dust, a final image that distils the pattern of Beckett's use of stone elsewhere: introduced as a material element of great longevity, its decay illustrates the impermanence and commitment to oblivion of all things:

> not a sound only the old breath and the leaves turning and then suddenly this dust whole place suddenly full of dust when you opened your eyes from floor to ceiling nothing only dust and not a sound only what

---

[14] This particular use of stone in Beckett's writing recalls the creation of cairns at the edge of tides by the contemporary British land sculptor Andy Goldsworthy.

[15] Beckett's biographers have identified this folly as Barrington's Tower near Foxrock where Beckett played and hid as a boy. See *DF*, 601; *LM*, 28.

was it it said come and gone was that it something like that come and gone come and gone no one come and gone in no time gone in no time. (*GIII*, 424)

This passage recalls the eighteenth-century French philosopher and writer Denis Diderot's argument for the poetic appeal of ruins:

> 'You don't know,' he said, 'why ruins give so much pleasure. I will tell you ... Everything dissolves, everything perishes, everything passes, only time goes on ... How old the world is. I walk between two eternities ... What is my existence in comparison with this crumbling stone?'[16]

Knowlson concludes his anecdote about Beckett's attentive care for stones as a child by noting that in 'Beckett's later work, there is an obsession with decay and with petrification, with stone and with bone' (*DF*, 29). This obsession, I suggest, is because stone has an important memorial function in Beckett's work. The mourning custom of placing stones on graves as a mark of respect was a likely influence on the association of stones with graveyards and dead bodies in Beckett's writing. This is a custom that appears in several cultures.[17] Robert MacFarlane has described how 'certain coffin paths in the west of Ireland have recessed resting stones, in the alcoves of which each mourner would place a pebble'.[18] The narrator of W.G. Sebald's *The Emigrants* visits a grave, 'before I left I placed a stone on the grave, according to custom'.[19] Similarly, in *The Jewish Way in Death and Mourning*, Maurice Lamm has described the use of visitation stones to mark a grave:

> The rabbi may suggest placing a pebble on the monument upon leaving. This custom probably serves as a reminder of the family's presence. Also, it may hark back to Biblical days when the monument was a heap of stones.

---

[16] Denis Diderot, quoted in Rose Macauley, *Pleasure of Ruins* (London: Weidenfeld and Nicolson, 1953), p. 23.

[17] I am concerned here with small stones and pebbles, so I have excluded consideration of dolmens, rune stones and other monumental stone structures. For such studies, see Timo Muhonen, 'A Hard Matter: Stones in Finnish–Karelian Folk Belief', *Things in Culture, Culture in Things*, ed. Anu Kannike and Patrick Laviolette (Tartu: University of Tartu Press, 2013), pp. 114–38; Roger Sansi-Roca, 'The Hidden Life of Stones: Historicity, Materiality and the Value of Candomblé Objects in Bahia', *JMC*, 10.2 (2005), 139–56; Rodney Harrison, 'Stone Tools', *The Oxford Handbook of Material Culture Studies*, ed. Mary C. Beaudry and Dan Hicks (Oxford: Oxford University Press, 2010), pp. 521–42. For a contemporary investigation of stone as a pilgrimage offering, see Emanuele Crialese's 2006 film *Nuovomondo*, set at the start of the twentieth century, where a Sicilian father and son climb to the top of a mountain with stones in their mouths that they add to a pile of similar offerings before an old wooden cross to seek divine approval for their emigration to the New World.

[18] Robert MacFarlane, *The Old Ways: A Journey on Foot* (London: Hamish Hamilton, 2012), pp. 14–15.

[19] W.G. Sebald, *The Emigrants*, p. 225.

Often, the elements, or roving vandals, dispersed them, and so visitors placed additional stones to assure that the grave was marked.[20]

The 'zone of stones' in *Ill Seen Ill Said* recalls the 'abode of stones' to which Lucky referred with increasingly hysterical frequency in his speech more than thirty years earlier in *Waiting for Godot*; both are suggestive of graveyards. Frank Ormsby makes use of a similar topos in 'Among the Dead', his poem commemorating the soldiers of the Second World War who fell in France: 'Memorials in Breton granite, Vaurian stone, / Pyrenean marble, / and a pavement of beach pebbles.'[21]

In 1933, Charles Prentice of Chatto & Windus asked Beckett for a final story to conclude *More Pricks than Kicks*. Beckett submitted 'Echo's Bones', which was roundly rejected by Prentice and not published until 2014. The story opens with Belacqua returned from the dead, and concludes with him sitting on the headstone of his grave and watching as his grave is robbed. He helps to open the coffin, which is discovered to contain nothing but stones.[22] Given the Ovidian title of this story, used again for Beckett's first poetry collection published in 1935, *Echo's Bones and Other Precipitates*, it is evident that Beckett was interested in the stories of people becoming animals or things, and was particularly fond of the story of the nymph Echo who, unloved, becomes an empty voice, her bones turned to stone. *The Grove Companion* suggests that this myth exerts a powerfully inspirational force on Beckett's later works: 'The ghostly, disembodied, externalised voices of Beckett's late fiction and drama, arguably his most profound literary creations, derive initially if not primarily from the myth of Echo and Narcissus' (*GC*, ix). In Ovid's tales, metamorphosis to stone signals the abrupt end to the story.[23] This is not the case in

---

[20] Maurice Lamm, *The Jewish Way in Death and Mourning* (New York: Jonathan David, 1999), p. 192.
[21] Frank Ormsby, 'Among the Dead', in *A Northern Spring* (London: Secker and Warburg, 1986), p. 35.
[22] See *Samuel Beckett's Echo's Bones*, ed. Mark Nixon (New York: Grove Press, 2014), and Mark Nixon, 'Belacque Revididus: Beckett's Short Story "Echo's Bones"', *Limit(e) Beckett* 1 (2010), 92–101, p. 94. It is possible Beckett's decision to have Belacqua's coffin empty of his body and filled instead with stones may echo the legend of Parnell's coffin recounted in the 'Hades' episode of *Ulysses*.
[23] There are many accounts of transformations to stone in Ovid's *Metamorphoses*. See Mercury's transformation of Battus to stone for betraying him or Aglauros changed to marble, both in Book II. In Book IV, Ino's attendants are turned to stone, Atlas is transformed into a mountain, coral is changed from plant to rock and Perseus recounts how he slew Medusa. In Book V, Phineus and his followers are turned to stone and the wolf attacking Peleus's flocks is changed to stone. Ovid, *Metamorphoses*, trans. Mary M. Innes (London: Penguin, 1955), pp. 68–69, 72, 108–9, 111, 114, 114–15, 121–22 and 256–57.

Beckett's work however, where several characters are fixed in sculptural poses, as though they were made of stone.

The first such figure is Watt. He moves 'no more, as far as they could see, than if he had been of stone, and if he spoke he spoke so low that they did not hear him'. The effect on other characters is dramatic: 'Mr Hackett did not know when he had been more intrigued' (*GI*, 180). In *Stirrings Still*, Beckett's last prose work, the central figure regrets not having 'a stone on which to sit like Walther and cross his legs', and makes do by adopting the next best attitude, which was to 'stop dead and stand stock still'[24] (*GIV*, 491). *Embers* also features a character frozen into a sitting position. Ada describes calling to Henry's house and discovering his family in great distress because he has gone missing. She leaves and passes his father on the road: 'He was sitting on a rock looking out to sea. I never forgot his posture. And yet it was a common one. You used to have it sometimes. Perhaps just the stillness, as if he had been turned to stone. I could never make it out' (*GIII*, 208). The scene with the lovers on the millstone in *That Time* shares this quality of extraordinary stillness. In the description of 'all still no sign of life not a soul abroad no sound', there is a suggestion that they sit together at either end of the stone for so long that the wheat turns yellow before them, 'all still just the leaves and ears and you too still on the stone in a daze' (*GIII*, 418). A number of other figures in Beckett's late theatre also sit as though turned to stone. The plays *Ghost Trio* (1975), *... but the clouds ...* (1976), *Ohio Impromptu* (1981) and *Nacht und Träume* (1982) all feature largely immobile central figures, a provocative artistic decision for stage or television theatre.

---

[24] This echoes the self-portrait by the twelfth-century poet Walther von der Vogelweide. In 'I sat upon a stone', Walther's poetic persona sits as though frozen to stone: 'I sat on a stone, and crossed my legs. I put my elbow on them and nestled my chin and cheek in my hand. Thus I probingly considered how one should live on this earth, but could not give myself any advice.' Dirk van Hulle has noted this explicit reference by Beckett to the German poem, and has suggested that in *Stirrings Still* Beckett echoes the philosophical musings of Walther's character. As this precise pose also features in a number of other works that have quite a different register, however, I believe it to be more likely that the physical posture is what mattered to Beckett. See Dirk van Hulle, *The Making of Samuel Beckett's Stirrings Still / Soubresauts and Comment dire / What is the Word* (Antwerp: University Press Antwerp, 2011), p. 90. Giuseppina Restivo argues that in *Endgame* Beckett also draws on Walther's poem. See 'Melencolias and Scientific Ironies in *Endgame*: Beckett, Walther, Dürer, Musil', in *Samuel Beckett Today/Aujourd'hui: Endlessness in the Year 2000*, ed. Angela Moorjani and Carola Veit (Amsterdam and New York: Rodopi, 2001), pp. 103–13. Consider also the entry on Schopenhauer in *Samuel Beckett's Library*: 'Ethics – in the general sense of Walther von der Vogelweide's famous poem about the poet sitting on a stone and wondering how one should live on this earth – was one of Beckett's major interests whenever he engaged in reading philosophy.' See van Hulle and Nixon, *Samuel Beckett's Library*, p. 147.

Perhaps the most thorough process of petrification is described in *Ill Seen Ill Said*: 'Stones increasingly abound', as the living elements of the landscape, grass and lambs alike, succumb to the zone of stones. The old woman of the story is similarly overcome by the material of stone. She is described as maintaining a statue-like posture, whether sitting 'Rigid upright' on her 'old deal spindlebacked' chair in the 'deepening gloom' of her kitchen, or 'Rigid with face and hands against the window pane, standing and staring out for long periods at the chalkstones that shine under the moon' (*GIV*, 451, 452). She is particularly drawn to the central standing stone, a 'rounded rectangular block three times as high as wide. Four'. Having described how the old woman halts when she reaches this standing stone, and stands before it 'as if of stone' herself', the narrator wonders 'Does she envy it?' (*GIV*, 453). The old woman's imperfect mimicry of stone prompts this mention of envy. Toward the end of *Ill Seen Ill Said*, the narrator observes that the old woman is barely living, 'alive as she alone knows how neither more nor less. Less! Compared to true stone', a formulation which suggests that only the perfectly inanimate matter of stone can be truly still and at peace (*GIV*, 467).

This final use of stone is quite distinct from the pebble-like stones that are manipulated by characters to comfort themselves or attack others. As I hope to have shown, Beckett's fascination with the lapidary extends throughout his oeuvre, but takes on a particular quality in the sculptural figures of his later, elegiac works. In contrast with the works of Ovid, the metamorphosis of Beckett's characters takes place discreetly. Beckett's later characters turn to stone so slowly that it is difficult to observe the change as it happens. First, their environments become stone, as in prose works from the 1960s including *All Strange Away*, *Imagination Dead Imagine*, *Ping* and *Lessness*; then the movement of Beckett's characters slows down until they become cold and unchanging. It is a loss of vitality they have long yearned for and simultaneously dreaded.[25] By turning some characters to stone, Beckett grants them a release from the tortuous compulsions to keep going and to keep telling stories. Lacking the spite, determination, great bitter humour and agitation of his earlier, far more engrossing creations, Beckett's final characters take on the rigidity and stillness of stone, and serve as monuments to a more robust vitality and characterisation

---

[25] One such expression of desire to be transformed to a more inert material occurs in *The Unnamable*: 'I'm tired of being matter, matter, pawed and pummelled endlessly in vain. Or give me up and leave me lying in a heap, in such a heap that none would ever be found again to try and fashion it' (*GII*, 341).

that have now vanished in his work. By replacing their vulnerable flesh and desperate need to keep moving and storytelling with the steadfastness of stone, Beckett grants these last characters a quality of peace unthinkable in his earlier works. In a final act of salvage, then, Beckett saves his long-suffering characters from the burden of participation in his imaginary worlds and returns them to a mineral state. These petrified last characters stand in as relics of the creative energy that animated Beckett's earlier writing. This energy was responsible for the great flourishes of colour and description in his work, as it was for the cruel inventive compulsion that forced his suffering characters into existence.

Stone is a natural material, unlike the other objects under study in this book. There is a single, compelling reason why stone persists in Beckett's work long after he has discarded the other miscellaneous rubbish: human-made objects are physical evidence of life. I believe that this is why Beckett thins them from his later and last works, in a bid to unmoor his literary inventions, to avoid the further creation and continuation of life. The ascetic sparseness of Beckett's later works can be better understood if it is seen as the final phase in his career, and an effort to return to silence and stillness the teeming mass he seems to have regretted bringing into being. Beckett was childless, and although he loved animals, never kept a pet (*LM*, 21). These decisions convey his sensitivity to the ethical implications of calling another creature into an existence he characterised as one dominated by suffering. His reluctance to do so in life is matched by his acute sense of responsibility to the products of his imagination.

Having been released from the barracks, Molloy wonders if he will ever see the sergeant again: 'For to contrive a being, a place, I nearly said an hour, but I would not hurt anyone's feelings, and then to use them no more, that would be, how shall I say, I don't know' (*GII*, 23). This comment conveys Beckett's singular response to the ethics of authorial creativity. Studies of the ethical aspects of Beckett's writing have hitherto taken their cue from established philosophical models.[26] Such readings tend to ignore the imaginative logic that informs

---

[26] In 'Beckett and Ethics', Shane Weller surveys ethical responses to Beckett's work, 'from existentialism to post-structuralism to the mathematical ontology of Alain Badiou'. Weller acknowledges that Beckett 'exhibits a preoccupation with the relation between art and ethics throughout his writing life', but does not explore what this relation might be or how the process of creativity might demand an ethical response from the artist. Instead, Weller concludes that the warring compulsions to continue and to stop in Beckett comprise the *anethical*, which Weller describes as 'complex ethics', in which 'neither negation nor affirmation can be accomplished, and in which it is no longer possible to determine any action – or indeed any inaction – as either ethical or unethical.' See Weller, 'Beckett and Ethics', in *A Companion to Samuel Beckett*, pp. 118–29, 118, 122, 128. Weller

and shapes creative practice, and have not therefore examined how Beckett's work constitutes a distinct examination and manifestation of the ethics by which acts of literary creation proceed. Literature, particularly the novel, is naturally orientated towards the past. Beckett takes this latent tendency and spends a lifetime constructing an imaginative space in which to gather the last traces of the Europe that came to an end in the mid-twentieth century. Italo Calvino praised the effect of this quality in Beckett's writing: 'Samuel Beckett has obtained the most extraordinary results by reducing visual and linguistic elements to a minimum, as if in a world after the end of the world.'[27] Given Beckett's identification of his creative compulsion with the needless and pointless suffering of his characters; given, too, his account of how the process of composition became steadily more difficult for him, it seems anomalous that he would continue to write, even until the last days of his life.[28]

In a phrase that seems to comment directly upon Beckett's creative drive, Larkin argued that 'the impulse to preserve lies at the bottom of all art'.[29] I have described Beckett's writing as an art of salvage because I believe that attentiveness to his poor materials reveals the aesthetic and ethic that sustains his creative practice. Salvage refers to waste material that has been saved from shipwreck or fire or otherwise snatched from the jaws of annihilation. The objects rescued by Beckett have been worn out by use. They are ruins and leftovers, but Beckett recasts them and explores the creative potential of such well-worn things in the correspondingly well-worn hands of characters that have themselves been ruined by neglect and marginalisation. Beckett's work is charged with a refusal of the miraculous, of transformation or transcendence of the grim aspects of life and death, yet his writing is animated by an urge to recover and hold onto ephemeral, intangible and evanescent cultural forces and personal memories, even as it winds itself down in his final works to approach the stillness and silence of stone. Beckett's art of salvage stages an encounter with the extinction facing us all, while tenderly hoarding those fleeting moments and odds and ends of which life and art is made.

---

extends this point in his own book-length study of Beckett's complex ethics, *Beckett, Literature and the Ethics of Alterity* (Basingstoke: Palgrave Macmillan, 2006). See also the collection of essays gathered in *Beckett and Ethics*, ed. Russell Smith (London: Continuum, 2008).

[27] Italo Calvino, *Six Memos for the Next Millennium*, trans. Patrick Creagh (London: Jonathan Cape, 1992), p. 95.

[28] Cronin has a large number of entries in the index to *LM* under 'SB – literary life – creative impasses'. Each entry draws on letters in which Beckett expresses the degree to which writing is a struggle for him. See *LM*, 441, 445, 453, 458, 462–63, 475–76, 488–89, 562–63, 485.

[29] Philip Larkin, *Required Writing: Miscellaneous Pieces 1955–1982* (London: Faber, 1983), 'Statement', p. 79.

Bibliography

Primary Sources

Beckett, Samuel, *Disjecta: Miscellaneous Writings and a Dramatic Fragment*, ed. Ruby Cohn (London: Calder, 1983).
Dream of Fair to Middling Women (New York: Arcade, 1992).
Eleutheria, trans. Michael Brodsky (New York: Foxrock, 1995).
Poems 1930–1989 (London: Calder, 2002).
Samuel Beckett: The Grove Centenary Edition, 4 vols, ed. Paul Auster (New York: Grove Press, 2006).
The Letters of Samuel Beckett, 4 vols, ed. George Craig, Martha Dow Fehsenfeld, Dan Gunn and Lois More Overbeck (Cambridge: Cambridge University Press, 2009, 2011, 2014, 2016).

Secondary Sources

Abbott, H. Porter, *Beckett Writing Beckett: The Author in the Autograph* (New York: Cornell University Press, 1996).
Ackerley, C.J. and S.E. Gontarski, *The Grove Companion to Samuel Beckett: A Reader's Guide to His Works, Life, and Thought* (New York: Grove, 2004).
Adorno, Theodor, 'Trying to Understand Endgame', trans. Michael T. Jones, *New German Critique*, 26 (Spring–Summer 1982), 119–50.
Anderson, Mark M., *Kafka's Clothes: Ornament and Aestheticism in the Habsburg Fin de Siècle* (Oxford: Clarendon Press, 1994).
Appadurai, Arjun, ed., *The Social Life of Things: Commodities in Cultural Perspective* (Cambridge: Cambridge University Press, 1986).
Aronson, Sidney H., 'The Sociology of the Bicycle', *Social Forces*, 30.3 (March 1952), 305–12.
Atik, Anne, *How It Was: A Memoir of Samuel Beckett* (Berkeley: Shoemaker and Hoard, 2005).
Auden, W.H., *Selected Poems*, ed. Edward Mendelson (London: Faber and Faber, 1979).
Badiou, Alain, *On Beckett*, ed. Nina Power and Alberto Toscano (Manchester: Clinamen, 2003).
Bair, Deirdre, *Samuel Beckett: A Biography* (London: Vintage, 1990).

Baldwin, Thomas, *The Material Object in the Work of Marcel Proust* (Bern, Oxford: Peter Lang, 2005).
Banville, John, 'Waiting for the Last Word', *The Observer*, 31 December 1989.
  'Samuel Beckett Dies in Paris Aged 83', *Irish Times*, 25 December 1989.
Barfield, Steven, Philip Tew and Matthew Feldman, ed., *Beckett and Death* (London: Continuum, 2009).
Barthes, Roland, *Camera Lucida: Reflections on Photography*, trans. Richard Howard (London: Vintage, 1993).
  Mourning Diary, annotated Nathalie Léger, trans. Richard Howard (London: Notting Hill Editions, 2011).
Beja, Morris, S.E. Gontarski and Pierre Astier, ed., *Samuel Beckett: Humanistic Perspectives* (Columbus: Ohio State University Press, 1983).
Bennett, Alan, *Plays Two* (London: Faber and Faber, 1998).
Bennett, Jane, *Vibrant Matter: A Political Ecology of Things* (Durham: Duke University Press, 2010).
Bernold, André, *Beckett's Friendship: 1979–1989*, trans. Max McGuinness (Dublin: Lilliput Press, 2015).
Bersani, Leo and Ulysse Dutoit, *Arts of Impoverishment: Beckett, Rothko, Resnais* (Cambridge, MA, and London: Harvard University Press, 1993).
Birkett, Jennifer and Kate Ince, ed., *Samuel Beckett* (London: Longman, 2000).
Bishop, Elizabeth, *Complete Poems* (London: Chatto and Windus, 2004).
Bizub, Edward, 'Beckett's Boots: The Crux of Meaning', *Samuel Beckett Today/Aujourd'hui*, 25 (2013), 267–79.
Blackwell, Mark, gen. ed., *British It-Narratives, 1750–1830*, 4 vols., vol. ed. Mark Blackwell, Liz Bellamy, Christina Lupton and Heather Keenleyside (London: Pickering and Chatto, 2012).
Borges, Jorge Luis, *Collected Fictions*, trans. Andrew Hurley (London: Penguin, 1998).
Boxall, Peter, 'The Existence I Ascribe: Memory, Invention and Autobiography in Beckett's Fiction', *The Yearbook of English Studies*, 30 (2000), 137–52.
  '"There's No Lack of Void": Waste and Abundance in Beckett and Delillo', *SubStance*, 37.2 (2008), 56–70.
  Since Beckett: Contemporary Writing in the Wake of Modernism (London: Continuum, 2009).
Brater, Enoch, *Ten Ways of Thinking about Samuel Beckett: The Falsetto of Reason* (London: Methuen Drama, 2011).
  'The Seated Figure on Beckett's Stage', in *A Companion to Samuel Beckett*, ed. S.E. Gontarski (Oxford: Wiley-Blackwell, 2010), pp. 346–57.
  'Beckett's Dramatic Forms, Considered and Reconsidered', lecture presented at the Samuel Beckett Summer School, Trinity College Dublin, 18 July 2012.
Brown, Bill, *A Sense of Things: The Object Matter of American Literature* (Chicago: University of Chicago Press, 2003).
  'Thing Theory', *Critical Inquiry*, 28.1 (Autumn 2001), 1–22.
Bryden, Mary, *Women in Samuel Beckett's Prose and Drama: Her Own Other* (Basingstoke: Macmillan, 1993).

'Beckett, Böll, and Clowns', in *Borderless Beckett – Beckett sans frontières 2006*, ed. Minako Okamuro, Naoya Mori, Bruno Clément, Sjef Houppermans, Angela Moorjani and Anthony Uhlmann (Amsterdam: Rodopi, 2008), pp. 157–72.

'Clowning with Beckett', in *A Companion to Samuel Beckett*, ed. S.E. Gontarski (Oxford: Wiley-Blackwell, 2010), pp. 358–71.

Burman, Barbara and Carole Turbin, ed., *Material Strategies: Dress and Gender in Historical Perspective* (Oxford: Blackwell, 2003).

Burström, Nanouschka M., 'Things in the Eye of the Beholder: A Humanistic Perspective on Archaeological Object Biographies', *Norwegian Archaeological Review*, 47.1 (2014), 65–82

Calvino, Italo, *Six Memos for the Next Millenium*, trans. Patrick Creagh (London: Jonathan Cape, 1992).

Canetti, Elias, *Crowds and Power*, trans. Carol Stewart (London: Penguin, 1981).

The Human Province, trans. Joachim Neugroschel (London: André Deutsch, 1985).

Carrière, Julien, 'Beckett's *Happy Days* and Dante's *Inferno*, Canto 10', *Samuel Beckett Today/Aujourd'hui*, 25 (2013), 197–209.

Caselli, Daniela, Steven Connor and Laura Salisbury, ed., *Other Becketts* (Tallahassee: JOBS Books, 2002).

Beckett's Dantes: Intertextuality in the Fiction and Criticism (Manchester: Manchester University Press, 2005).

Casey, Edward, *Remembering: A Phenomenological Study*, 2nd edn (Bloomington, IN: Indiana University Press, 2000).

Chabert, Pierre, 'The Body in Beckett's Theatre', *JOBS*, 8 (1982), 23–28.

Chesterton, G.K., *Tremendous Trifles* (New York: Dover, 2007).

Cohn, Ruby, *Samuel Beckett: The Comic Gamut* (New Brunswick, NJ: Rutgers University Press, 1962).

ed., *Disjecta: Miscellaneous Writings and a Dramatic Fragment* (New York: Grove, 1984).

Conley, Tom, 'Crutches', *Chicago Review*, 33.2 (1982), 84–92.

Connor, Steven, *Beckett, Modernism and the Material Imagination* (Cambridge: Cambridge University Press, 2014).

Paraphernalia: The Curious Lives of Magical Things (London: Profile Books, 2011).

'Thinking Things', *Essays at Cultural Phenomenology* (2009), www.stevenconnor.com/thinkingthings/thinkingthings.pdf [accessed 2 April 2012].

'Beckett's Atmospheres', in *Beckett after Beckett*, ed. Anthony Uhlmann and S.E. Gontarski (Gainesville, FL: University Press of Florida, 2006).

Cordingley, Anthony, 'Beckett's Ignorance: Miracles/Memory, Pascal/Proust', *Journal of Modern Literature*, 33.4 (June 2010), 129–52.

Coulmas, Florian, *The Blackwell Encyclopaedia of Writing Systems* (Oxford: Blackwell, 1996).

Craig, George, *Writing Beckett's Letters: The Cahiers Series*, 16 (Paris: Sylph, 2011).

Critchley, Simon, *Very Little … Almost Nothing: Death, Philosophy, Literature* (London: Routledge, 1997).

'Who Speaks in the Work of Samuel Beckett?', *Yale French Studies*, 93 (1998), 114–30.

Cronin, Anthony, *Samuel Beckett: The Last Modernist* (London: Flamingo, 1997).
Cummings, Neil, ed., *Reading Things* (London: Chance Books, 1993).
Dannehl, Karin, 'Object Biographies: from Production to Consumption', in *History and Material Culture*, ed. Karen Harvey (London: Routledge, 2009), pp. 123–38.
Davies, Paul, *The Ideal Real: Beckett's Fiction and Imagination* (Rutherford, NJ: Fairleigh Dickinson University Press, 1994).
Davis, Lennard J., ed., *The Disability Studies Reader*, 3rd edn (New York: Routledge, 2010).
De Certeau, Michel, *The Practice of Everyday Life*, trans. Steven Rendall (Berkeley, Los Angeles, London: University of California Press, 1988).
Defoe, Daniel, *Robinson Crusoe*, ed. Angus Ross (London: Penguin, 1999).
Dekker, Thomas, *The Shoemakers' Holiday*, ed. Jonathan Gil Harris (London: Methuen, 2008).
Derrida, Jacques, *The Gift of Death and Literature in Secret*, trans. David Wills (Chicago: University of Chicago Press, 2008).
  The Truth in Painting, trans. Geoffrey Bennington and Ian MacLeod (Chicago: University of Chicago Press, 1987).
Dickens, Charles, *David Copperfield* (London: Penguin, 2004).
  Dombey and Son, ed. Peter Fairclough (London: Penguin, 1985).
  Great Expectations, ed. Angus Calder (London: Penguin, 1985).
  Little Dorrit (London: Arrow, 2008).
Douny, Laurence and Susanna Harris, ed., *Wrapping and Unwrapping Material Culture: Archaeological and Anthropological Perspectives* (Walnut Creek, CA: Left Coast Press, 2014).
Dovlatov, Sergei, *The Suitcase*, trans. Antonina W. Bouis, ed. Katherine Dovlatov (London: Alma Classics, 2013).
Dukes, Gerry, 'The *Godot* Phenomenon', in *Samuel Beckett 100 Years: Centenary Essays*, ed. Christopher Murray (Dublin: New Island, 2006), pp. 23–33.
Dunlevy, Mairead, *Dress in Ireland* (London: Batsford, 1989).
Edelman, Gerald M., *Second Nature: Brain Science and Human Knowledge* (New Haven: Yale University Press, 2006).
Edwards, Michael, 'Beckett's French', *Translation and Literature*, 1 (1992), 68–83.
Esslin, Martin, 'The Theatre of the Absurd', *The Tulane Drama Review*, 4 (May 1960), 3–15.
Favorini, Attilio, *Memory in Play: From Aeschylus to Sam Shephard* (New York: Palgrave Macmillan, 2008).
Fischer-Seidel, Therese, '"The Ineluctable Modality of the Visible": Perception and Genre in Samuel Beckett's Later Drama', *Contemporary Literature*, 35.1 (Spring 1994), 66–82.
Fitzpatrick, Jim, *The Bicycle in Wartime: An Illustrated History* (Sterling, VA: Brassey's, 1998).
Flaubert, Gustave, *Bouvard and Pécuchet*, trans. Mark Polizzotti (Champaign, IL: Dalkey Archive Press, 2005).

Fletcher, John, 'Samuel Beckett and the Philosophers', *Comparative Literature*, 17.1 (Winter 1965), 43–56.

'Malone "Giving Birth to into Death"', in *Twentieth Century Interpretations of Molloy, Malone Dies, The Unnamable*, ed. J.D. O'Hara (Upper Saddle River, NJ: Prentice Hall, 1955), pp. 48–60.

Foschini, Lorenza, *Proust's Overcoat: The True Story of One Man's Passion for All Things Proust*, trans. Eric Karpeles (London: Portobello, 2011).

Gassner, John and Edward Quinn, ed., *The Reader's Encyclopedia of World Drama* (New York: Dover, 2002).

Gauzi, Francois. 'Vincent van Gogh (1886–87)', in *Van Gogh in Perspective*, ed. Bogomila Welsh-Ovcharov (New Jersey: Prentice-Hall, 1974), pp. 33–34.

Gee, Sophie, *Making Waste: Leftovers and the Eighteenth-Century Imagination* (Princeton: Princeton University Press, 2010).

Gessner, Niklaus, *Die Unzulänglichkeit der Sprache: eine Untersuchung über Formzufall und Beziehunglosigkeit bei Samuel Beckett* (Zurich: Junis Verlag, 1957).

Gibson, Andrew, *Reading Narrative Discourse: Studies in the Novel from Cervantes to Beckett* (London: Macmillan, 1990).

Glanville, Jo, '"Godot is here": How Samuel Beckett and Vaclav Havel Changed History', *The Guardian*, 15 September 2009.

Glass, Peyton, 'Beckett: Axial Man', *Educational Theatre Journal*, 29.3 (October 1977), 362–73.

Glendinning, Simon, *On Being with Others: Heidegger, Derrida, Wittgenstein* (London: Routledge & Kegan Paul, 1998).

Gontarski, S.E., ed., *A Companion to Samuel Beckett* (Oxford: Wiley-Blackwell, 2010).

The Theatrical Notebooks of Samuel Beckett, Vol. IV, The Shorter Plays (London: Faber and Faber, 1999).

The Intent of Undoing in Samuel Beckett's Dramatic Texts (Bloomington, IN: Indiana University Press, 1985).

Beckett's Happy Days: A Manuscript Study (Ohio: Ohio State University Libraries, 1977).

Gontarski, S.E., and James Knowlson, ed., *The Theatrical Notebooks of Samuel Beckett, Vol. II, Endgame* (London: Faber and Faber, 1992).

Gordon, Lois, *The World of Samuel Beckett: 1906–1946* (New Haven: Yale University Press, 1996).

Gramsci, Antonio, *Letters from Prison*, trans. Lynne Lawner (New York: Harper, 1973).

Graver, Lawrence and Raymond Federman, ed., *Samuel Beckett: The Critical Heritage* (London: Routledge and Kegan Paul, 1979).

Grene, Nicholas, *Home on the Stage: Domestic Spaces in Modern Drama* (Cambridge: Cambridge University Press, 2014).

Grotowski, Jerzy, T.K. Wiewiorowski and Kelly Morris, 'Towards the Poor Theatre', *The Tulane Drama Review*, 11.3 (Spring 1967), 60–65.

Gunn, Dan, 'La bicyclette irlandaise: Flann O'Brien et Samuel Beckett', *L'Errance. Tropismes No. 5* (1991), 143–71.

Harrison, Rodney, 'Stone Tools', *The Oxford Handbook of Material Culture Studies*, ed. Mary C. Beaudry and Dan Hicks (Oxford: Oxford University Press, 2010), pp. 521–42.

Hartley, L.P., *The Go-Between* (London: Penguin, 1958).

Hawkins, Gay and Stephen Muecke, ed. *Culture and Waste: The Creation and Destruction of Value* (Lanham: Rowman & Littlefield, 2003).

Heaney, Seamus, *Human Chain* (London: Faber and Faber, 2010).

Heidegger, Martin, *Being and Time: A Translation of Sein Und Zeit*, trans. Joan Stambaugh (New York: State University of New York Press, 1996).

'The Thing,' in *Poetry, Language, Thought*, trans. Albert Hofstadter (New York: Harper & Row, 1971).

The Fundamental Concepts of Metaphysics: World, Finitude, Solitude, trans. William McNeill and Nicholas Walker (Bloomington: Indiana University Press, 1995).

Hennessy, Mark, 'The Hat that Never Went Away – It Just Took Long Vacations', *Irish Times*, 14 October 2010, p. 14.

Herlihy, David V., *Bicycle: The History* (New Haven and London: Yale University Press, 2004).

Hesla, David, *The Shape of Chaos: An Interpretation of the Art of Samuel Beckett* (Oxford: Oxford University Press, 1971).

Hill, Leslie, ' "Fuck life": *Rockaby*, Sex, and the Body', in *Beckett On and On …* (London: Associated University Presses, 1996), pp. 19–26.

Hill, Raymond Thompson, 'The Enueg', *PMLA*, 27.2 (1912), 265–96.

Hoffman, Frederick J., *Samuel Beckett: The Language of Self* (New York: Southern Illinois University Press, 1964).

Hofmann, Michael, ed. and trans., *Joseph Roth: A Life in Letters* (London: Granta, 2013).

Holly, Michael Ann, 'Mourning and Method', *The Art Bulletin*, 84 (December 2002), 660–69.

Holtorf, Cornelius, 'Notes on the Life History of a Pot Sherd', *JMC* (March 2002), 7.1, 49–71.

Horovitz, Israel, 'A Remembrance of Samuel Beckett', *Paris Review*, 142, (Spring 1997), 189–93.

Horrigan, Michele, *The Root of the Matter* (Limerick: Askeaton Contemporary Arts, 2014).

Howard, Alan J., 'The Roots of Beckett's Aesthetic: Mathematical Allusions in "Watt"', *Papers On Language And Literature*, 30.4 (1994), 346–52.

Hutchinson, John, *Seanie Barron: Sticks* (Dublin: Douglas Hyde Gallery, 2015).

Inoue, Reiko, 'The Mound of Sand in *Happy Days*: Tomb to Womb', *The Harp*, 14 (1999), 60–69.

Jansen, Leo, Hans Luijten and Nienke Bakker, ed., *Vincent van Gogh: The Letters* (Amsterdam and The Hague: Van Gogh Museum & Huygens ING, 2009).

Johnson, Nevill, *The Other Side of Six: An Autobiography* (Dublin: The Academy Press, 1983).

Jones, Mary, *The Other Ireland: Changing Times 1870–1920* (Dublin: Macmillan, 2011).

Josipovici, Gabriel, *What Ever Happened to Modernism?* (New Haven, CT, and London: Yale University Press, 2011).
Kafka, Franz, *The Complete Short Stories of Franz Kafka*, ed. Nahum N. Glatzer (London: Vintage, 2005).
  Metamorphosis, trans. and ed. S. Corngold (New York: Norton, 1996).
  The Diaries of Franz Kafka 1910–1923, ed. Max Brod (Minerva, 1992).
Kamenetz, Herman, 'A Brief History of the Wheelchair', *Journal of the History of Medicine and Allied Sciences*, 24.2 (April 1969), 205–10.
Keating, Sara, 'Happy Days Actress Is Up to Her Neck in It', *Irish Times*, November 8, 2010.
Keatinge, Benjamin, '"The Hammers of the Stone-Cutters": Samuel Beckett's Stone Imagery', *Irish University Review*, 37.2 (Autumn–Winter 2007), 322–39.
Kennedy, Andrew, *Samuel Beckett* (Cambridge: Cambridge University Press, 1989).
Kennedy, Seán, ed., *Beckett and Ireland* (Cambridge: Cambridge University Press, 2010).
Kennedy, Seán, and Katherine Weiss, ed., *Samuel Beckett: History, Memory, Archive* (New York: Palgrave Macmillan, 2009).
Kenner, Hugh, *Samuel Beckett: A Critical Study* (London: Calder, 1962).
Kiberd, Declan, *The Irish Writer and the World* (Cambridge: Cambridge University Press, 2005).
Kiely, Robert, 'Samuel Beckett Harping: No Place to Go, No Place to Go', *Harvard Review*, 5 (Fall 1993), 76–94.
Knechtel, John, ed. *Trash* (Cambridge, MA: MIT Press, 2006).
Knowlson, James, *Damned to Fame: The Life of Samuel Beckett* (London: Bloomsbury, 1997).
  ed., *Happy Days: The Production Notebook of Samuel Beckett* (London: Faber and Faber, 1985).
  'A Writer's Homes – A Writer's Life', in *A Companion to Samuel Beckett*, ed. S.E. Gontarski (Oxford: Wiley-Blackwell, 2010).
  'Beckett's "Bits of Pipe"', in *Samuel Beckett: Humanistic Perspectives*, ed. Morris Beja, S.E. Gontarski and Pierre Astier (Columbus, OH: Ohio State University Press, 1983).
Knowlson, James, and John Haynes, *Images of Beckett* (Cambridge: Cambridge University Press, 2003).
Knowlson, James, and Elizabeth Knowlson, ed., *Beckett Remembering/Remembering Beckett: Uncollected Interviews with Samuel Beckett and Memories of Those Who Knew Him* (London: Bloomsbury, 2007).
Kopytoff, Igor, 'The Cultural Biography of Things: Commoditization as Process', in *The Social Life of Things: Commodities in Cultural Perspective*, ed. Arjun Appadurai (Cambridge: Cambridge University Press, 1986), pp. 64–91.
Kott, Jan, 'A Note on Beckett's Realism', trans. Boleslaw Taborski, *The Tulane Drama Review*, 10.3 (Spring 1966), 156–59.

Küchler, Susanne and Daniel Miller, *Clothing as Material Culture* (Oxford, New York: Berg, 2005).
Lamm, Maurice, *The Jewish Way in Death and Mourning* (New York: Jonathan David, 1999).
LaMotta, Vincent and Michael Schiffer, 'Behavioural Archaeology:. Toward a New Synthesis', in *Archaeological Theory Today*, ed. Ian Hodder (Cambridge: Polity, 2001), pp. 14–64.
Larkin, Philip, *Collected Poems*, ed. Anthony Thwaite (Victoria: Marvell and Faber, 2003)
  Letters to Monica, ed. Anthony Thwaite (London: Faber and Faber, 2010).
  Required Writing: Miscellaneous Pieces 1955–1982 (London: Faber and Faber, 1983).
Latour, Bruno, *Science in Action. How to Follow Scientists and Engineers through Society* (Milton Keynes: Open University Press, 1987).
  'The Berlin Key or How to Do Words with Things', in *Matter, Materiality and Modern Culture*, ed. P.M. Graves-Brown (London: Routledge, 2000), pp. 10–21.
  Reassembling the Social: An Introduction to Actor-Network-Theory (Oxford: Oxford University Press, 2005).
Lawley, Paul, 'Samuel Beckett's Relations', *JOBS*, 6.2 (Spring 1997), 10–13.
  '"The Rapture of Vertigo": Beckett's Turning-Point', *The Modern Language Review*, 95.1 (January 2000), 28–40.
Lawrence, D.H., *Lady Chatterley's Lover* (London: Penguin, 2006).
Levi, Primo, *Moments of Reprieve*, trans. Ruth Feldman (London: Penguin, 2002).
Lukács, György, *The Meaning of Contemporary Realism*, trans. John and Necke Mander (London: Merlin, 1963).
Lurie, Alison, *The Language of Clothes* (Feltham: Hamlyn, 1983).
Macauley, Rose, *Pleasure of Ruins* (London: Weidenfeld and Nicolson, 1953).
MacFarlane, Robert, *The Old Ways: A Journey on Foot* (London: Hamish Hamilton, 2012).
Majmudar, Amit, 'George Steiner, Last of the Europeans', *Kenyon Review*, 34.4 (Fall 2012), 178–87.
Matton, Frank, 'Beckett's Trilogy and the Limits of Autobiography', in *Beckett On and On …*, ed. Lois Oppenheim and Marius Buning (London: Associated University Presses, 1996), pp. 69–82.
Maude, Ulrika, *Beckett, Technology and the Body* (Cambridge: Cambridge University Press, 2009).
  '"whole body like gone": Beckett and Technology', *JOBS*, 16:1&2 (2007), 150–60.
Mays, J.C.C., 'Young Beckett's Irish Roots', *Irish University Review*, 14.1 (Spring 1984), 18–33.
  'Samuel Beckett (1907–89)' [sic], in *Field Day Anthology of Irish Writing*, 3 (Derry: Field Day Publications, 1991), p. 237.
McCoy, Jack, 'The Ulster Coat', *Irish Arts Review (1984–1987)*, 2.4 (Winter, 1985), 18–23.

McDonald, Rónán, 'The Ghost at the Feast: Beckett and Irish Studies', in *Beckett and Ireland*, ed. Seán Kennedy (Cambridge: Cambridge University Press, 2010), pp. 16–30.
The Cambridge Introduction to Beckett (Cambridge: Cambridge University Press: 2006).
McGahern, John, *Creatures of the Earth: New and Selected Stories* (London: Faber, 2006).
McMullan, Anna, *Theatre on Trial: Samuel Beckett's Later Drama* (London: Routledge, 1993).
Menzies, Janet, 'Beckett's Bicycles', *JOBS*, 6 (Autumn 1980), 97–105.
Mercier, Vivian, 'A Pyrrhonian Eclogue,' *The Hudson Review*, 7 (Winter 1955), 620–24.
Beckett/Beckett (New York: Oxford University Press, 1977).
'The Uneventful Event', *Irish Times*, 18 February 1956.
Miller, Daniel, *Material Culture and Mass Consumption* (Oxford: Basil Blackwell, 1987).
Material Cultures: Why Some Things Matter (Chicago: University of Chicago Press, 1998).
Mitchell, David T. and Sharon L. Snyder, *Narrative Prosthesis: Disability and the Dependencies of Discourse* (Ann Arbor, MI: University of Michigan Press, 2000).
Mitchell, Glenn, *The Laurel and Hardy Encyclopaedia* (London: Batsford, 1995).
Monasta, Attilio, 'Antonio Gramsci (1891–1937)', *Prospects: The Quarterly Review of Comparative Education*, 23.3–4 (1993), 597–612.
Mooney, Sinéad, 'Beckett in French and English', in *A Companion to Samuel Beckett*, ed. S.E. Gontarski (Oxford: Wiley-Blackwell, 2010), pp. 196–208.
Moorjani, Angela, and Carola Veit, ed., *Samuel Beckett Today / Aujourd'hui: Endlessness in the Year 2000* (Amsterdam and New York: Rodopi, 2001).
Morrison, Kristin, *Canters and Chronicles: The Use of Narrative in the Plays of Samuel Beckett and Harold Pinter* (Chicago and London: University of Chicago Press, 1983).
Muhonen, Timo, 'A Hard Matter: Stones in Finnish–Karelian Folk Belief', *Things in Culture, Culture in Things*, ed. Anu Kannike and Patrick Laviolette (Tartu: University of Tartu Press, 2013), pp. 114–38.
Mundhenk, Michael, 'Samuel Beckett: The Dialectics of Hope and Despair', *College Literature*, 8.3, Samuel Beckett (Fall 1981), 227–48.
Murray, Patrick, 'Samuel Beckett and Tradition', *Studies: An Irish Quarterly Review*, 58.230 (Summer, 1969), 166–78.
Neubauer, John, 'Bakhtin versus Lukács: Inscriptions of Homelessness in Theories of the Novel', *Poetics Today*, 17.4 (Winter 1996), 531–46.
Nixon, Mark, ed., *Samuel Beckett's Echo's Bones* (New York: Grove Press, 2014).
'Belacque Revididus: Beckett's Short Story "Echo's Bones"', *Limit(e) Beckett*, 1 (2010), 92–101.

' "Writing Myself into the Ground": Textual Existence and Death in Beckett', in *Beckett and Death*, ed. Simon Barfield, Philip Tew and Matthew Feldman (London: Continuum, 2009), pp. 22–30.

Nora, Pierre, 'Between Memory and History: Les Lieux de Mémoire,' *Representations*, No. 26, Special Issue: Memory and Counter-Memory (Spring 1989), 7–24.

Nugent-Folan, Georgina, 'Ill buttoned': Comparing the Representation of Objects in Samuel Beckett's *Ill Seen Ill Said* and Gertrude Stein's *Tender Buttons*', *JOBS*, 22.1 (2013): 54–82.

O'Brien, Eoin, *The Beckett Country: Samuel Beckett's Ireland* (Dublin: Black Cat Press, 1986).

'Zone of Stones: Samuel Beckett's Dublin', *Journal of the Irish Colleges of Physicians and Surgeons*, 16.2 (April 1987), 69–77.

O'Brien, Eoin and Dickon Hall, 'Nevill Johnson's Dublin', *Irish Arts Review*, 19 (Winter 2002), 68–75.

O'Brien, Flann, *The Third Policeman* (London: Folio, 2006).

O'Dowd, Anne, *Common Clothes and Clothing 1860–1930* (Dublin: National Museum of Ireland, 1990).

O'Hara, J.D., ed., *Twentieth Century Interpretations of Molloy, Malone Dies, The Unnamable* (Upper Saddle River, NJ: Prentice Hall, 1955).

Okamuro, Minako, Naoya Mori, Bruno Clément, Sjef Houppermans, Angela Moorjani and Anthony Uhlmann, ed., *Borderless Beckett – Beckett sans frontières 2006* (Amsterdam: Rodopi, 2008).

O'Leary, Joseph S., 'Beckett and Radio', *Journal of Irish Studies*, 23 (2008), 3–11.

Olson, Liesl, *Modernism and the Ordinary* (Oxford: Oxford University Press, 2009).

Orlando, Francesco, *Obsolete Objects in the Literary Imagination: Ruins, Relics, Rarities, Rubbish, Uninhabited Places, and Hidden Treasures*, trans. Gabriel Pihas, Daniel Seidel and Alessandra Grego (London: Yale University Press, 2006).

Ormsby, Frank, *A Northern Spring* (London: Secker and Warburg, 1986).

O'Toole, Fintan, 'Oblomov in Dublin', *New York Review of Books*, 56.13, 13 August 2009.

'The Fantastic Flann O'Brien', *Irish Times*, 1 October 2011.

Ovid, *Metamorphoses*, trans. Mary M. Innes (London: Penguin, 1955).

Pascal, Blaise, *Pascal's Pensées*, trans. W.F. Trotter (New York: E.P. Dutton, 1958).

Payne, Blanche, Geitel Winakor and Jane Farrell-Beck, *The History of Costume: From Ancient Mesopotamia through the Twentieth Century*, 2nd edn (New York: Harper Collins, 1992).

Perec, Georges, *Thoughts of Sorts*, trans. David Bellos (London: Notting Hill Editions, 2011).

Perloff, Marjorie, ' "In Love with Hiding": Samuel Beckett's War', *The Iowa Review*, 35 (Spring 2005), 76–103.

Pfister, Manfred, *A History of English Laughter: Laughter from Beowulf to Beckett and Beyond* (Amsterdam: Rodopi, 2002).

Piette, Adam, *Remembering and the Sound of Words: Mallarmé, Proust, Joyce, Beckett* (Oxford: Clarendon Press, 1996).
Price, Alexander, 'Beckett's Bedrooms: On Dirty Things and Thing Theory', *JOBS*, 23.2 (2014), 155–77.
Quayson, Ato, *Aesthetic Nervousness: Disability and the Crisis of Representation* (New York: Columbia University Press, 2007).
Quinn, Margaret, *Objects in the Theatre of Samuel Beckett: Their Function and Significance as Components of his Theatrical Language*, McMaster University, 1975.
Reid, Alec, 'Samuel Beckett: The Reluctant Prizeman', *Politico*, 1 November 1969, pp. 1–5.
Restivo, Giuseppina, 'Melencolias and Scientific Ironies in *Endgame*: Beckett, Walther, Dürer, Musil', in *Samuel Beckett Today / Aujourd'hui: Endlessness in the Year 2000*, ed. Angela Moorjani and Carola Veit (Amsterdam and New York: Rodopi, 2001), pp. 103–13.
Ricks, Christopher, *Beckett's Dying Words: The Clarendon Lectures, 1990* (Oxford: Clarendon Press, 1993).
Robertson, Ritchie, *Kafka: A Very Short Introduction* (Oxford: Oxford University Press, 2004).
Robinson, Fred Miller, *The Man in the Bowler Hat: His History and Iconography* (London: The University of North Carolina Press, 1993).
Robinson, Richard, 'An Umbrella, a Pair of Boots, and a 'Spacious Nothing': McGahern and Beckett', *Irish University Review*, 44.2 (2014): 323–40.
Sala, George, *Gaslight and Daylight* (London: Chapman and Hall, 1859).
Sansi-Roca, Roger, 'The Hidden Life of Stones: Historicity, Materiality and the Value of Candomblé Objects in Bahia', *JMC*, 10.2 (2005), 139–56.
Scammell, Michael, 'In Pursuit of Solzhenitsyn', *The Wilson Quarterly (1976–)*, 10.3 (Summer 1986), 144–57.
Schiffer, Michael, 'Archaeological Context and Systemic Context', *American Antiquity* 37 (1972), 156–65.
Schoeffler, O.E. and William Gale, *Esquire's Encyclopaedia of Twentieth Century Men's Fashions* (New York: McGraw-Hill, 1973).
Sebald, W.G., *A Place in the Country*, trans. Jo Catling (London: Hamish Hamilton, 2013).
    The Emigrants, trans. Michael Hulse (London: Vintage, 2002).
Sebald, W.G., and Jan Peter Tripp, *Unrecounted: 33 Texts and 33 Etchings*, trans. Michael Hamburger (London: Penguin, 2005).
Shanks, Michael, David Platt, and William L. Rathje, 'The Perfume of Garbage: Modernity and the Archaeological', *Modernism/Modernity* 11. 1 (2004), 61–83.
Sinclair, Iain, 'The Raging Peloton', *LRB*, 33.2 (20 January 2011), 3–8.
Smith, Russell, ed., *Beckett and Ethics* (London: Continuum, 2009).
Sofer, Andrew, *The Stage Life of Props* (Ann Arbor, MI: University of Michigan Press, 2003).

Solzhenitsyn, Aleksandr, *One Day in the Life of Ivan Denisovich*, trans. H.T. Willets (London: Vintage, 2003).
Sterne, Laurence, *The Life and Opinions of Tristram Shandy, Gentleman*, ed. Ian Campbell Ross (Oxford: Oxford University Press, 2009).
Stewart, Paul, *Sex and Aesthetics in Beckett's Work* (New York: Palgrave Macmillan, 2011).
Stokley, James, 'Cross Glitters Overhead', *The Science News-Letter*, 42 (August 1942), 138–39.
Strathern, Marilyn, *The Gender of the Gift* (Berkeley, CA: University of California Press, 1988).
Swanson, Victoria, 'Confining, Incapacitating, and Partitioning the Body: Carcerality and Surveillance in Samuel Beckett's *Endgame, Happy Days*, and *Play*', *Miranda*, 4 (June 2011), 5–28.
Taylor, Lou, *Mourning Dress: A Costume and Social History* (London: Allen and Unwin, 1983).
Thomas, Julian, *Time, Culture and Identity: An Interpretive Archaeology* (London and New York: Routledge, 1996).
Thompson, Michael, *Rubbish Theory: The Creation and Destruction of Value* (Oxford University Press, Oxford, 1979).
Tilley, Christopher, *An Ethnography of the Neolithic: Early Prehistoric Societies in Southern Scandinavia* (Cambridge: Cambridge University Press, 1996).
Tóibín, Colm, 'Book of the Week', *The Guardian*, 21 August 2010.
Trigg, Dylan, *The Aesthetics of Decay: Nothingness, Nostalgia, and the Absence of Reason* (New York: Peter Lang, 2006).
Tworek, Agnieszka, '*Endgame* Incarcerated: Prison Structures in Beckett's Play', *JOBS*, 16.2 (2007), 247–58.
Van Hulle, Dirk, *The Making of Samuel Beckett's Stirrings Still / Soubresauts and Comment Dire / What is the Word* (Antwerp: University Press Antwerp, 2011).
Van Hulle, Dirk, and Mark Nixon, *Samuel Beckett's Library* (Cambridge: Cambridge University Press, 2013).
Viney, William, *Waste: A Philosophy of Things* (London: Bloomsbury, 2014).
Von Morstein, Petra, 'Magritte: Artistic and Conceptual Representation', *The Journal of Aesthetics and Art Criticism*, 41 (Summer 1983), 369–74.
Washizuka, Naho, 'Pity and Objects: Samuel Beckett's "Dante and the Lobster"', *Journal of Irish Studies*, 24 (2009), 75–83.
Watson, Janell, *Literature and Material Culture from Balzac to Proust: The Collection and Consumption of Curiosities* (Cambridge: Cambridge University Press), 1999.
Watts, William, *A Memoir* (Dublin: The Lilliput Press, 2008).
Weiner, Annette B. and Jane Schneider, ed., *Cloth and Human Experience* (Washington: Smithsonian Books, 1989).
Weller, Shane, *Beckett, Literature and the Ethics of Alterity* (Basingstoke: Palgrave Macmillan, 2006).
  'Beckett and Ethics', in *A Companion to Samuel Beckett*, ed. Gontarski (Wiley-Blackwell, 2010), pp. 118–29.

Wellershoff, Dieter, 'Toujours moins, presque rien: essai sur Beckett,' *Cahier de L'Herne*, trans. R. Denturck (Paris: Cahiers de L'Herne, 1976), pp. 169–82.
West, Rebecca, *Black Lamb and Grey Falcon* (London: Canongate, 2006).
Wilmer, S.E., ed., *Beckett in Dublin* (Dublin: Lilliput Press, 1992).
Wodehouse, P.G., *Ring for Jeeves* (London: Random House, 2009).
— *The Jeeves Omnibus*, 3 vols (London: Hutchinson, 1991).
Wood, James, 'Rite of Corruption', *LRB*, 32.20 (21 October 2010), 13–14.
— 'Addicted to Unpredictability', *LRB*, 20.23 (26 November 1998), 16–19.
Woodward, Kathleen, 'Transitional Objects and the Isolate: Samuel Beckett's "Malone Dies"', *Contemporary Literature*, 26.2 (Summer 1985), 140–54.
Wulf, Catharina, *The Imperative of Narration: Beckett, Bernhard, Schopenhauer, Lacan* (Brighton: Sussex Academic Press, 1997).
Yeats, W.B., *The Major Works*, ed. Edward Larrissy (Oxford: Oxford University Press, 1997).
— *Explorations* (London: Macmillan, 1989).

Films

Crialese, Emanuele, dir., *Nuovomondo* (Rai Cinema, 2006).
O'Mórdha, Seán, dir., *As The Story Was Told* (BBC, 1996).

Index

Ackerley, C.J., ix, 15, 27, 121, 124
Abbott, Porter H., 16, 102, 103
Adorno, Theodor W., 62
alarm clocks, 196
Appadurai, Arjun, 9n19
Arnold, Bruce, 210
art of salvage, i, 3, 206, 207, 220, *See also* salvage
Atik, Anne, 46, 171
Auden, W.H., 122, 213, 214
Austen, Jane, 20

Bacon, Francis, 136
bags, 2, 11, 17, 36, 89, 132, 162, 167–178, 180–182, 184, 191, 196, 200, 203–205
    handbag, 2, 175
    Lucky's bags (*Waiting for Godot*), 177, 178
    medicine bag, 174, 175
    money-bags, 36
    Moran's bags (*Molloy*), 132
    nightbag in *That Time*, 89
    sack, 28, 157, 160, 174
    Winnie's bag (*Happy Days*), 17, 167–178, 180–182, 184, 191, 196, 200, 203–205
Bair, Deirdre, 78, 94, 95
Banville, John, 19, 20, 63
Barron, Seanie, vi, 150–152
Barthes, Roland, 68, 91
Beckett, William (Bill), 73–78, 83–85, 100, *See also* father
Beckett, Frank, 32, 33, 79
Beckett, May, vi, 31, 35, 72, 77, 78, 90–104, *See also* mother
Beckett, Samuel
    A Piece of Monologue, 60, 104, 105
    Act Without Words II, 28
    All Strange Away, 83, 88, 106, 118, 192, 218
    All That Fall, 29
    Breath, vi, 4, 5, 153

    ... but the clouds ..., 89, 96n39, 217
    Cascando, 83, 88, 150, 209n7
    Come and Go, 60, 96n39, 98, 99
    Company, 76, 77, 83–85, 89, 104, 110
    'Dieppe', 212
    Dream of Fair to Middling Women, 51, 73, 74, 110, 125, 129
    'Echo's Bones', 216
    Echo's Bones and Other Precipitates, 115, 127, 216
    Eh Joe, 96n39, 111, 156, 202, 203n63, 211, 214
    Eleutheria, 36
    Embers, 52, 59, 78n16, 174, 175, 213, 217
    Endgame, 29, 59, 73, 103, 110, 121, 125, 135, 136, 139, 140, 143, 155, 169, 187, 191, 217n24
    'Enueg I', 92n34, 127, 145
    'Enueg II', 92n34
    Film, 81, 97, 98, 104, 108, 121, 126, 128n27, 134, 135
    First Love, 35, 77, 92n34
    Fizzles 1 106, 203n63
    Fizzles 3: Afar a Bird 83, 88, 150
    Footfalls, 15, 60, 73, 96n39, 102, 105, 111, 203n63
    From an Abandoned Work, 76, 84, 88, 89, 92n34, 111, 115, 132, 150, 156
    Ghost Trio, 96n39, 111, 217
    'Gnome', 46
    Happy Days, 17, 18, 71, 96, 97, 102, 144, 162, 166, 167, 169–172, 174–179, 181, 184–188, 190–192, 196–198, 200–205
    How It Is, 29, 49, 52, 87, 92, 97, 98, 109, 149, 159, 174
    Ill Seen Ill Said, 5, 14n33, 60, 61, 83, 89, 102, 212, 216, 218
    Krapp's Last Tape, 52, 74, 101, 103, 109, 187, 193, 202
    'Malacoda', 34, 39, 92n34

235

Beckett, Samuel (*cont.*)
  Malone Dies, 2, 3, 17, 50, 57, 84, 87, 93, 97, 106, 108, 110, 145, 154n44, 155, 160, 162, 165, 169, 170, 172, 179, 181, 186, 188, 192, 194, 200–205, 207, 208n5, 209, 214
  Mercier and Camier, 52, 81, 83, 121, 133, 150, 156, 157, 174, 209
  Molloy, 4–6, 18, 28, 29, 35, 40, 43, 46, 49, 80, 83, 87, 88, 91–94, 103–105, 107, 108, 113, 117, 123–125, 128n27, 131–133, 145–149, 151, 153, 154, 156, 158, 166, 173, 183, 207, 210, 211, 213, 219
  More Pricks than Kicks, 53, 186n29, 216
  Murphy, 34, 36, 45, 107, 108, 135, 137, 138, 141, 142, 166, 186n29
  'my way is in the sand flowing', 213
  Nacht und Träume, 154n44, 217
  Not I, 17n42, 96n39, 167, 203n63
  Ohio Impromptu, 81, 83, 217
  'One Evening', 81, 102
  Proust, 14, 28, 67, 74
  Quad, 59
  Rockaby, 99–102, 105, 107–109, 143
  'Sanies I', 127
  'Sanies II', 92n34
  'Serena I', 186n29
  'Serena III', 115, 128
  Stirrings Still, 79, 83, 89, 90, 115, 217
  Texts for Nothing 8 28, 55
  Texts for Nothing 9 57
  Texts for Nothing 12 133, 134
  Texts for Nothing 13 198
  That Time, 17n42, 60, 86, 89, 132, 190, 214, 217
  The Calmative, 86, 126, 174, 175, 209
  The End, 35, 36, 86, 92n34, 106, 110, 174, 175, 211, 214
  The Expelled, 34, 35, 77, 106, 157, 209
  The Lost Ones, 192
  The Unnamable, 5, 18, 75, 93, 132, 146, 148, 149, 153, 202, 211, 218n25
  'thither', 92n34
  Waiting for Godot, 27, 29, 40–42, 44–46, 48, 49n56, 53, 61, 86, 105, 117, 118, 177, 178, 187, 202, 216
  Watt, 15, 16n39, 46, 50, 51, 74, 79, 83, 84, 87, 90, 92, 93, 103, 104, 112, 113, 118, 130, 131, 150, 202, 211, 217
  Worstward Ho, 60, 79, 85, 89
Beckett on Film project, 4, 191n36
beds, 16, 57, 69, 70, 78, 83n27, 91, 103, 104, 106, 107, 112, 139, 142, 143, 154, 155, 164, 166, 167, 174, 183
  bed-bound characters, 57, 104, 106, 139, 142, 143, 154, 155, 164, 166, 167, 174, 183
  maternal beds, 16, 69, 70, 91, 103, 104, 107, 112
  sick-bed, 78
  writing in bed, 83n27
bedrooms, 14, 69, 91, 103, 104, 106
  maternal bedroom, 69, 91, 103, 104
bells, 124, 126, 162, 182, 185, 189, 196–199
  bicycle bells, 124, 126, 182
  bell in *Happy Days*, 162, 185, 189, 196, 197, 198
Belmont, Georges, 31, 32
Bennett, Alan, 113
Bennett, Jane, 10
Bernhard, Thomas, 105
bicycles, 12, 15, 17, 29, 115–117, 118n9, 119n13, 120–137, 143–146, 153, 158, 159, 182
  abandonment of, 132–135, 146
  affection for, 123–126, 132
  'Cartesian Centaur', 119n13, 126, 127
  cycling impediments, 29, 117, 130–132, 146
  effects on narrative, 121, 123, 127, 128, 135, 137, 145
  bicycle wheels in *Endgame*, 125, 126, 136
  elegiac bicycles, 134, 135
  erotic bicycles, 129, 130, 158, 159
  escape from romance, 126, 128, 158
  hobby-horse, 122, 123
  nostalgia for, 120–122
birth, 57, 76, 104–107, 111–114, *See also* pre-natal memories
  comparison with authorial invention, 113, 114
Bishop, Elizabeth, 192, 196
Blackwell, Mark, 7n13, 20
Blin, Roger, 141
boots, 14–16, 22, 23, 25, 27, 28, 47–62, 64, 65, 67, 157, 182, 196
  mismatched and ill-fitting boots, 50–52
  old boots and death, 58–61
  old boots as still lifes, 52–58
  old boots and the twentieth-century, 61–67
Borges, Jorge Luis, 70
bowler hats, 15, 16, 22, 25–28, 31–34, 36, 37, 39–48, 64, 65, 67, 208n6
  bourgeois bowlers, 27–40
  comic bowlers, 41–43
  thinking caps, 43–47
Boxall, Peter, 6n11, 16n39
Brater, Enoch, 140, 141, 175, 178
Brown, Bill, 10n20
Bruce, Brenda, 185
Bryden, Mary, 45, 52, 111
Burman, Barbara, 171
Büttner, Gottfried, 208

Calder, John, 31
Calvino, Italo, 220
Canetti, Elias, 22, 204, 205
Casey, Edward, 10, 69
Chabert, Pierre, 117

Index

Chaplin, Charlie, 41, 42
Chesterton, G.K., 172, 173
childhood, 31, 79, 84, 102, 208
Cixous, Hélène, 111
Cohn, Ruby, 42n41, 64n78
Connor, Steven, vii, 1n2, 3, 10, 14, 17n42, 30n15, 117, 118, 177, 178, 208n5, 211n10, 223
Cooldrinagh, 31, 32, 72, 91, 95, 100, 102–104
Craig, George, 24n6, 62, 179
creative practice, 2n4, 5n9, 6, 57, 202, 220
Critchley, Simon, 58n68, 163n1
Cronin, Anthony, 6, 21, 32, 51n58, 60, 62, 63, 78, 83–85, 91, 94, 95, 100, 104, 187n31, 220n28
crutches, 11, 17, 28, 29, 45, 115–117, 118n9, 119n13, 120, 127, 131, 137, 140, 144–150, 155, 158, 159, 182
    assistance to lame characters, 17, 140, 145, 149, 155
    effects on narrative, 17, 127, 158, 159
    grim perseverance with, 144, 146, 148, 149
    paired with sticks, 145
    pleasurable motion of, 116, 137, 145–147, 149, 155, 158
    in series between bicycles and wheelchairs, 116, 124, 145, 150
    used while cycling, 29, 117, 123, 131, 145, 146
    wielded as weapons, 132, 144, 147, 148, 158, 159
Cummings, Neil, 12n29

Dante, Alighieri, 2, 125n21, 192
defecation, 113
Defoe, Daniel, 186, 191–193, 199
Derrida, Jacques, 3n5, 54n62, 113
Dechevaux-Dumesnil, Suzanne, 2, 61, 62, 141
Dickens, Charles, 51, 107, 138, 140, 144
    A Christmas Carol, 144
    David Copperfield, 138
    Dombey and Son, 51
    Great Expectations, 140
    Little Dorrit, 107
Diderot, Denis, 215
Dike, Catherine, 156
dolls, 8, 43, 142, 143
    characters as doll-like playthings, 142, 143
    doll-like logic to dress of Beckett's characters, 8, 43
Dovlatov, Sergei, 22, 23, 67
Dunlevy, Mairéad, 82, 83n25

Edelman, Gerald, 69, 70
ethics of literary invention, 18, 58n68, 158, 159, 161, 206, 217n24, 219, 219n26, 220
excavatory art, 67
exile, 16, 22–25, 61, 195

father, 32, 34, 36, 39, 43, 60, 68–79, 81, 82, 84–86, 89, 92–94, 100, 103, 111–113, 120, 150, 157, 215n17, 217
Favorini, Attilio, 74n11
Fehsenfeld, Martha, ix, 1n2, 176, 177, 198n52
Fitzpatrick, Jim, 134n32
Flaubert, Gustave, 39–41, 46, 48
Foschini, Lorenza, 83n27, 94n35
Foxrock, 29, 31, 72, 86, 94, 95, 97, 214n15
fugitive writing, 16, 24, 67

Gee, Sophie, 8
Glendinning, Simon, 3
Gontarski, S.E., ix, 1n2, 15, 16, 27, 121, 124, 184, 196, 197
Gramsci, Antonio, 186, 193, 194, 196, 200, 201
greatcoats, 11, 12, 15, 16, 27, 43, 60, 68, 69, 72–76, 79–90, 109, 111, 132, 150
    Bill Beckett's greatcoat, 72–76, 79, 81–86, 150
    discarded greatcoat, 88, 89, 132
    elegiac greatcoats, 88–90
    ludic greatcoats, 87–90
    Macmann's greatcoat (*Malone Dies*), 87
    Molloy's greatcoat (*Molloy*), 87, 88
    ulster greatcoat, 82, 83
    Watt's greatcoat (*Watt*), 84, 87
    wrapping materials, 69, 86, 109, 111
Grene, Nicholas, vii, 103
Gunn, Dan, 66, 119n13, 127n25

Hamburger, Michael, 70
Hamsun, Knut, 210
Hardy, Oliver, 41, 42, 80, *See also* Laurel, Stan
Hardy, Thomas, 212
Hartley, L.P., 123–125
Havel, Václav, 187
Hawkins, Gay, 8
Heaney, Seamus, 81, 82
Heidegger, Martin, 3n5, 10, 207, 208
heimat, 22
heirlooms, 11, 16, 17, 69–72, 75, 86, 90, 94n35
    maternal heirlooms, 72, 75, 90
    paternal heirlooms, 11, 72, 75, 82, 86, 150
Hennessy, Mark, 26
Herlihy, David, 122, 123
Hofmann, Michael, 112
Horovitz, Israel, 18, 19
Hutchinson, John, 149

inventory, 9, 165, 179–185, 200, 203, 204

Johnson, Nevill, 33–35, 45, 208n6
Josipovici, Gabriel, 25
Joyce, James, 25, 32, 51, 63, 65, 74, 77, 179
    'Ecce Puer', 77

238　　　　　　　　　　　Index

Kafka, Franz, 20, 113, 159
　'In the Penal Colony', 159
　The Metamorphosis, 20
Kennedy, Andrew, 30
Kennedy, Seán, 1n2, 17n42, 27n13
Kenner, Hugh, 42n41, 45, 119n13, 126, 127, 143, 186n29, 210n10
Kertész, André, 79n18
Kiely, Robert, 24, 25n7, 186n29
Knowlson, James, ix, 1n1, 2, 51, 56n65, 62, 68, 71, 73, 77, 78, 79n17, 84, 91, 93, 95, 96, 100, 103, 104, 112, 128, 176, 186, 187, 198n52, 208, 215
Kott, Jan, 186n28, 197

ladies' hats, 94–99
　characters in *Come and Go*, 98, 99
　Lady Pedal's hat (*Watt*), 97, 98
　Maddy Rooney's hat (*All That Fall*), 97
　May Beckett's hats, 94, 95, 98
　Winnie's hat (*Happy Days*), 97
Lamm, Maurice, 215
Larkin, Philip, 71, 212n12, 220
last modernist, 6, 21, 63
Latour, Bruno, 9n19, 11
Laurel, Stan, 41, 42, 80, *See also* Hardy, Oliver
Lawrence, D.H., 138
Levi, Primo, 200
Linehan, Rosaleen, vi, 176, 177
Linnaeus, Carl, 207, 208
literary prosthetics, 17, 115, 116, 118n9, 119, 120, 135, 144, 158–161, *See also* props
Lukács, György, 24, 25
lumber-room, 20, 21
Lurie, Alison, 39, 95, 97

McCoy, Jack, 83
McDonald, Rónán, 30, 31
MacFarlane, Robert, 215
McGahern, John, 14, 107
MacGreevy, Thomas, 24, 24n6, *See also* McGreevy, Thomas
McGreevy, Thomas, 24n6, 33, 65n79, 78, 79, 92, 93, 100, 113, 129, *See also* MacGreevy, Thomas
McMillan, Dougald, 1n2
McMullan, Anna, 17n42
Magritte, René, vi, 37–39, 41
material imagination, i, iii, 1n2, 10, 21, 30n15, 118, 208n5, 211n10
Maude, Ulrika, 117, 118, 127
Mays, J.C.C., 15, 209n7
memory, 16, 17, 63, 68–71, 74, 75, 78, 79, 89–92, 100, 109, 113, 169, 171, 178, 181, 203, 206, 214

Beckett's personal memories, 16, 19, 69, 70, 78, 79, 206
mediated through the body and place, 69, 70
in *Proust*, 74, 75
sites of memory, 17, 17n41, 68, 69, 71
Winnie's memories (*Happy Days*), 169, 171, 178, 181
Menzies, Janet, 127n25
Mercier, Vivian, 40, 42n41, 43, 52, 97, 117
Miller, Daniel, 7
Minihan, John, 2
miscellaneous rubbish, v, 1, 4–6, 8, 10, 12, 153, 207, 211, 219
Mitchell, David T., 116
Mitchell, Glenn, 42n39
Mitchell, Pamela, 79
Mooney, Sinéad, 30n15, 65
mother, 4, 24, 30, 32, 34, 60, 68–73, 75, 76, 78, 90–94, 97, 98, 100, 102–106, 108–114, 124, 143, 147n40
Muecke, Stephen, 8

Neumann, Frederick, 121, 122
Nixon, Mark, 58n68, 74, 113, 216n22, 217n24

objects, 1–7, 9–24, 26, 28, 37, 43, 48, 49, 53–56, 59, 62, 64, 65, 69, 71, 72, 75, 88–91, 94, 115, 116, 118n9, 119, 120, 127, 132, 133, 135, 137, 145, 151, 153, 154, 159, 161–176, 179–186, 191–193, 195, 201, 202, 203n63, 204, 205, 207–209, 211, 219, 220
　abandoned, 12, 53–55, 133, 173, 205
　agency of, 9–11
　Beckett's imaginative attachment to, 1, 2, 71, 72, 201n62
　characters' affection for, 2, 6, 12, 13, 15, 145, 151, 153, 154, 172–174, 179, 180, 193, 209
　discarded, 9, 20, 54, 191, 205, 219
　it-narratives, 7
　ludic, 18, 88, 89, 132, 135, 137
　methodology of this book, 3, 4, 6, 10–12, 16–19, 21, 169, 170
　storytelling objects, 162–170, 206
　worn-out objects, 12, 13, 15, 16, 20, 53, 72, 206
O'Brien, Eoin, 15, 23n5, 34n24, 84n28, 86, 96
O'Brien, Flann, 78, 85, 106, 125, 127n25, 129, 130, 148
O'Dowd, Anne, 82
Olson, Liesl, 14
O'Mórdha, Seán, 56, 57n66
Orlando, Francesco, 12, 13, 200n58
Ormsby, Frank, 216
O'Toole, Fintan, 106, 129, 130, 148
Ovid, 216, 218

Index

Page, Sheila, 68, 84n28, 96
Pascal, Blaise, 115
Perec, Georges, 20n46, 180
Perloff, Marjorie, 36, 61
phenomenology, 10, 117, 118, 171, 172
Piette, Adam, 74n11
pockets, 2, 7, 9, 11, 17, 81–83, 87, 132, 145, 157, 170–175, 180, 183, 200, 202, 203, 205, 209–211
   greatcoat, 81–83, 87, 88
   in *Malone Dies*, 2, 17, 145, 170–174, 180, 183, 203
   in *Mercier and Camier*, 157
   in *Molloy*, 132, 173, 210, 211
   pocket-held objects, 7, 9, 88, 170–173, 180, 205, 209
policemen, 29, 124, 131, 146, 157, 211
pre-natal memories, 112
prison literature, 185–188, 200, 201
props, 3, 11, 17, 19, 23, 27, 40, 41, 69, 87, 99, 116, 119, 120, 144n39, 145, 148–150, 155, 156, 175, 178n18, 184, 191, 196, *See also* literary prosthetics
   comic props, 27, 40, 41
   imaginary prop-box, 3, 19, 23, 178n18
   narrative props, 11, 17, 116, 120, 145, 148
   outmoded props, 19
   stage properties, 99, 119, 136, 175
Proust, Marcel, 14, 28, 63, 74, 75, 83n27, 94n35
Pynchon, Thomas, 20

Quayson, Ato, 116, 117

relics, 13, 15, 16, 22, 23, 47–50, 55, 64, 65, 67, 192, 196, 219
   humble relics, 48–50, 55
   of 'old decency', 47
   of a vanished world, 16, 22, 23, 67

Ricks, Christopher, 58, 59
Robertson, Ritchie, 20n47
Robinson, Fred Miller, 26, 27, 36, 37, 39, 41–45, 47
rocking chairs, 16, 69, 70, 72, 90, 91, 107–109, 110n57, 111, 137, 143
   and death, 107–109, 143
   soothing qualities of, 108, 109, 110n57
Roth, Joseph, 112
Rushdie, Salman, 162

Saki (H.H. Munro), 20
salvage, i, iii, v, 3, 9, 13, 16–18, 64, 67, 70, 72, 161, 178, 179, 186, 196, 202, 206, 207, 209, 219, 220, *See also* art of salvage

Sebald, W.G., 6, 70n6, 215
Shenker, Israel, 23n5, 63, 90n32
Sinclair, Iain, 130
Sinclair, Peggy, 73, 74
Snyder, Sharon L., 116
Sofer, Andrew, 119
Solzhenitsyn, Aleksandr, 186, 195–197, 199, 200
Steiner, George, 63, 64
Sterne, Laurence, 123, 153, 179
Stewart, Paul, 58n68, 113, 114
sticks, 3, 4, 11, 17, 18, 35, 115, 116, 118n9, 119, 120, 140, 143, 145, 149–151, 153–160, 166, 167, 182, 194–196, 205, 211
   assistance to lame characters, 116, 120, 145, 150, 151, 153, 158
   comparison with authorial pencil, 159, 160, 166
   effects on narrative, 120, 150, 166
   gaff, 145, 155
   goad, 145, 160, 167
   sex aids, 151, 153, 154, 159
   tally stick, 196
   used as punt-pole, 143, 154, 155
   wielded as weapons, 35, 151, 154, 156–158, 160, 166
stones, 2, 60, 88, 96n38, 132, 173, 174, 207–220
   Beckett's tenderness towards, 208
   characters' affection for, 2, 173, 174, 209
   characters turned to stone, 217–219
   coda to Beckett's material canon, 208, 209, 220
   on graves, 60, 215, 216
   projectiles, 211
   ruins, 215
   sucking stones, 2, 88, 132, 173, 209–211
   'zone of stones', 60, 96n38, 216, 218

Taylor, Lou, 100, 101
Thompson, Michael, 8
Tóibín, Colm, 81
treasure, v, 3, 17, 18, 72, 90, 170, 171, 174, 176, 179, 181, 196, 201n62, 202–205
Trigg, Dylan, 8n14
Trinity College Dublin, 13n32, 32, 46, 64, 76–78, 129

Ussy-sur-Marne, 1n1, 55, 56, 66

Van Gogh, Vincent, vi, 54–57
Van Hulle, Dirk, 74, 217n24
Viney, William, 8, 207

Walser, Robert, 6, 40
waste, 1, 4, 6n11, 8, 31, 195, 207, 220
wheelchairs, 17, 107, 116, 120, 135–144, 154, 159
   ad hoc, 135
   despotic characters in wheelchairs, 135, 136, 139
   immobility prompting fantasies of floating, 144, 154
   motion of, 116, 136–138, 140
   poor relation of bicycle, 136, 144
   in series between bicycles and beds, 143
   throne-like, 107, 136, 139–141
widow's weeds, 12, 16, 68–70, 90, 99–103, 114

maternal figures of mourning, 99, 102, 103, 114
   May Beckett's, 90, 100, 102, 103
   Victorian mourning practices, 100–102
Wodehouse, P.G., 39, 41, 44n44
womb, 71, 105, 106, 111, 112, 191n36
Wood, James, 188, 201, 210

Yeats, W.B., 5n9, 18, 19, 30, 63, 155, 156
   'Sailing to Byzantium', 18, 19
   The Cat and the Moon, 155, 156
Yeats, Jack B., 64

CPSIA information can be obtained
at www.ICGtesting.com
Printed in the USA
LVHW080412250220
648027LV00011BA/147